# He Reo Tuku Iho

# HE REO TUKU IHO

## Tangata whenua and te reo Māori

Awanui Te Huia

TE HERENGA WAKA
UNIVERSITY PRESS

Te Herenga Waka University Press
Victoria University of Wellington
PO Box 600 Wellington
teherengawakapress.co.nz

ISBN 9781776920174

Published with the generous support of a grant from Ngā Pae o te Māramatanga

Printed by YourBooks, Wellington

*Max Life Aranui*

*Forever in our hearts*

# Contents

# List of Tables

# List of Figures

# Foreword

Tēnei te whakaaraara i a mahira. Huakina mai te tatau o tēnei whare kia kite ai koe i ngā taonga whakahirahira.

For the descendants of the people in whom the Māori language originates, for those who are poised to embark on the challenge of learning Māori or maintaining it as a spoken language, this book is a welcome addition for the individual and the whānau. For the researcher, the educator, the linguist and the politician, and anyone involved in restoring te reo Māori as a language with vibrance and energy here in Aotearoa – or any of the above interested in reclaiming and rejuvenating Indigenous languages under pressure to survive around the world – there are learnings to be taken to refine strategies for acquisition, implementation and sustainability across communities. Nau mai te karu, whakatau mai.

Anā te whao. Nōu te ringa hei hanga i te ora ki tōu reo.

You have the tools at your disposal.

The author has been a learner of te reo Māori and then, after graduating, a lecturer and researcher in Māori language acquisition and revitalisation. Along the way she has been a young mother and partner and incorporated that learner, teacher and researcher experience into her own whānau. What this provides is an astute feel for the barriers and enablers across multiple settings as lived experiences which, with the support of her recent research, have unfolded into the advice and the suggestions, the cautions and realities, all shared here. Her writing can help tangata whenua to navigate the complexities of learning Māori, maintaining it, and seeing the practical and logical steps of achieving one's language goals. In the words of Mason Durie, referenced by Awanui, 'Diverse needs require diverse solutions.' And no, it isn't easy, as testified by the contributors to her research. The trauma, the language disruption, the availability and access to resource and access the emotion; the anxiety, the connectivity and tests of identity; the racism and the effects of colonisation and so on, all exist. But *yes*, as challenges they can be overcome, or at least, with the suggestions Awanui proposes, approached in ways that make the journey easier. Nau mai te rongoā.

Whiria he kaha mōu, ko koe anō taua whiri, ko koe tonu tōu kaha: The solution lies with you.

One area of particular interest to me in this book sits with the individual, and relates to interpersonal relationships. Amid its simplicity, an element of dare and bravery is pivotal to effecting the personal changes that will determine the success of Māori language learning and maintenance endeavours for the individual and the whānau. To ensure language goals are indeed met, there is no room for 'chance'; the adage of leaving it in the hands of some higher order simply will not cut it. There is an inherent need to make conscious decisions about relationships between the learner and the community they require to support them. Changes in societal behaviour towards the Māori language are also necessary. And while this may appear to distance Māori from the whanaungatanga aspect Māori people value, it can also be seen as a way of further enhancing relationships among people with a common goal. Nau mai te kaha.

Mānuka takoto, amohia ake: Challenge laid, challenge accepted.

Awanui appeals to all New Zealanders and the important role that non-Māori can play in re-establishing Māori as a natural language in our country. She then issues a strong challenge to Māori to interact with the language. To be exposed to it and expose it to others. Awanui shows how we can all support the growth of the Māori language; we, as individuals, as whānau and as communities.

E te reo Māori, kia toa koe hei iti kotahi harakoa mō te iwi, mō te motu.

Oh, Māori language – let your survival resonate as a small but extremely significant achievement from which the people across this land might draw happiness.

*Emeritus Professor Poia Rewi*
*September 2022*

# Introduction

Over the past few years, te reo Māori has seen a resurgence of energy in public domains. Numbers of students enrolling in Māori language courses have increased considerably. Some organisations and media have integrated te reo into their profiles. We are beginning to see an increase in te reo on public signage. And many books are now available to help people learn basic te reo. But sustaining language-learning practices requires a collective vision.

This book focuses on the lived experiences of tangata whenua who have a whakapapa connection to te reo. It shares their experiences of learning or beginning to learn their ancestral language. There are many ways in which tangata whenua connect with te reo Māori, given the ways in which te reo Māori has been directly impacted by colonisation. The specific relationship that tangata whenua have with te reo is different from the relationships of those with no whakapapa connection. Language learners who have made shifts to reclaim te reo Māori as their mother tongue – whether it was last spoken by their mother, grandmother, great-grandmother, great-great-grandmother or beyond – engage in acts of personal and collective transformation, which are shared throughout this book.

For Māori language learners in particular, te reo Māori needs to be approached as a language for practical use, relevant to our daily lives in a range of contexts.

The decision that tangata whenua make, and have made in the past, to learn and use our language is tied to movements of reclamation. Reclaiming our cultural knowledge involves the reclamation of our heritage language. Like the reclamation of cultural knowledge, language reclamation is a slow-burning process. It is connected to a wide set of social, political, environmental and economic conditions, including the return of stolen tangata whenua lands, an end to white supremacy and racism, and the equitable distribution of economic resources. These are just some of the conditions that would contribute significantly to Indigenous language revitalisation, and second language-learning dialogues sometimes neglect these critical factors. Because an end to racism and colonialism requires drastic action over an extended period, language revitalisation takes time and resources.

As an Indigenous language learner, teacher and researcher, one of the challenges I have observed when exploring second language literature is the focus on the individual learner. Many books about learning te reo teach us basic sentence structures and phrases that can be incorporated into our homes and workplaces, but few help us to create the right conditions for our language-learning quest to be fruitful; few provide us with the tools for system change. Our approaches need to take into context our history, our personal and collective narratives around te reo, and the social and political contexts that help or inhibit language growth. Given the right conditions, it is possible to return our heritage language to our own minds, hearts and mouths, and those of our future generations.

This book shares the experiences of tangata whenua who have attempted to learn te reo Māori, as well as those who are highly fluent speakers of te reo, to normalise some of the challenges we are facing. This book also offers questions to wānanga individually and collectively about how we can integrate our language back into our daily lives. By processing the challenges we may experience during the language-learning journey, we are better able to consider our responses to interactions or events that might affect our decision to learn and use te reo Māori.

In 2019, my team and I conducted a national research project, Manawa Ū ki te Reo Māori, that explored motivations for and barriers to Māori language acquisition and use. The technical report, *Manawa Ū ki te Reo Māori: A study of language motivations to enhance the use and acquisition of te reo Māori* (Te Huia, Ahu, Muller and Fox, 2019), can be found on the Te Mātāwai website, tematawai.maori.nz. We surveyed pre-learners, learners and speakers of te reo Māori and conducted bilingual interviews with 57 Māori, who have whakapapa connections with 54 iwi. The findings of Manawa Ū ki te Reo Māori are presented throughout this book. It is my hope that readers connect with the experiences of those who participated, and that this book as a whole encourages readers to explore their own histories, identities and thought processes that assist in the expedition towards decolonisation and language reclamation.

The title of this book, *He Reo Tuku Iho*, indicates its focus on the intergenerational relationships that we have as individuals with a whakapapa connection to te reo Māori. The aroha connection that we all have with our tūpuna, our living relations, and those yet to come are all tied together in our collective desire to ensure that te reo Māori thrives, now and in the future.

# Locating the author

As a Māori woman who is an academic, it is important for me not to assume to separate my *self* from my *work*. Teaching and researching te reo Māori at Te Herenga Waka—Victoria University of Wellington has become the focus of my occupation; however, what came first was my aroha for te reo. My aroha for te reo Māori initially came from our grandfather and the connection that I have with him. Koro Jack was a native speaker of te reo Māori. In the years I knew him, he would watch Te Karere religiously (prior to the establishment of Māori Television) as his only reo Māori connection on most days.

Our koro was a tamaiti whāngai of Raureti Te Huia, who was an authority on our cultural history. Koro Raureti (along with others, including Te Puea) also contributed significantly to the film *Rewi's Last Stand* with sound (produced in 1940, following the 1925 version, which was a silent film (Cooper, 2018)). One of the points of interest with this film was that the cast included direct decendants of those who fought at the Battle of Ōrākau. These included both Māori and colonial settlers, which was something that Rudall Hayward, the film maker, also requested Te Puea's help in achieving. Koro Raureti played the role of Rewi Maniapoto in the film. I remember watching the film as an adult and seeing our koro Jack as a young boy.

19

I have mixed feelings thinking about that film. On one hand, it is filled with treasured images of our tūpuna, such as our great koro Raureti, my own koro Jack, who was born in 1924 and who passed away in 1998, and other relations who played the roles of our tūpuna who fought at Ōrākau, some of whom were in living memory of those acting in the film. However, the film is troubling in some respects, including the ways in which our people are portrayed and the focus on a peculiar relationship between Bob, a colonial settler who personifies a 'white saviour', and Ariana, a 'pretty half-caste girl' (Cooper, 2018, 76) who has an unusual and guarded relationship with Ngāti Maniapoto, her mother's people. The final version of the film was cut by half for a British post-World War II audience, and the footage that was cut was lost (Cooper, 2018).

I mention *Rewi's Last Stand* because the battle of Ōrākau is part of the historical narrative of our whānau, our hapū of Ngāti Paretekawa, and the many other hapū and iwi who came to support our people in this historical war of resistance against colonial domination. It is part of how I make sense of who I am in relation to the world. Language loss and reclamation is deeply personal. The political position that Manga, as Rewi Maniapoto was affectionately called, and all of our tūpuna held within our tribal region of Waikato Maniapoto gives their descendants a point of reference for resisting the seemingly irresistible forces of colonisation. Furthermore, the colonial greed and dehumanisation of our people that led to the battle depicted in that film is one reason why I am forced to be in a position where I am learning the language of my tūpuna as a second language. Dispossession of Indigenous lands, natural resources, and parts of our identity through violent methods all contribute to the subjugation of Indigenous languages by colonial languages. We must continue to fight against language extinction.

Sitting with koro watching Te Karere was practically my only exposure to reo Māori in the home growing up (besides the tapes of Hirini Melbourne that Mum used to play). As a Māori woman born in the 1980s, I have seen the revitalisation of te reo Māori growing up around us. Due to my own historical narrative, it was not until I was in my early 20s that I was fortunate to meet whānau from our nanny's (Ngāti Rongo, Ngāi Tūhoe) side of the whānau, where te reo Māori was still very much normalised amongst her whānau. The relationships that I developed as an adult with her side of the whānau became hugely influential in my desire to learn more about the language and culture of our tūpuna. Our journey with te reo Māori is a political one. As Indigenous language learners, we know that our relationship with te reo Māori is not just 'nice to have'. Our acquisition and use of te reo Māori is laden with values and meaning, which makes the process of learning and speaking te reo unlike that of any other second language.

The aroha that I feel towards my language is connected to the aroha that I feel towards my tūpuna and my whānau in its wider senses – as well as my immediate whānau, including my husband and our tamariki, I include their tamariki for generations to come. For these reasons, I choose to explore how my thoughts inform my choices, and how my emotions enable me to be useful and helpful to my language and those I interact with.

Part of the choice to grow our whānau in a society where te reo Māori is normalised stems from an understanding that, as parents, our use of te reo Māori with our tamariki is not enough to sustain our children's desire to use te reo long-term. Language revitalisation takes the efforts of the community to be successful (Hunia, 2016; Muller, 2016). With this in mind, our whānau recently moved to Ōtaki, on the lands of the hapū, Ngāti Pare, in a town where a child can learn from kōhanga reo and kura kaupapa/whare kura and attend Te Wānanga o Raukawa – all within walking distance. Since moving to Ōtaki, for the first time in my life I have had Māori-speaking neighbours, I've been able to use te reo at the supermarket with the checkout attendant and buy a coffee from Hori's café using te reo, paying in koha, and I can walk down the street and hear people speaking te reo Māori. The unique qualities of Ōtaki include the sustained efforts that have been made to revitalise te reo Māori (Winiata, 2014). We are grateful to live here knowing the many hard years that it has taken those who are from here and who have invested in te reo Māori revitalisation goals to grow this Māori-speaking community, which takes consistent commitment.

I am conscious that my writing of this book comes from a position of privilege. I refer to some of these privileges in terms of the absence of hate directed towards me for occupying certain identity positions. These privileges afford me the ability to live without fear that I will be violently targeted due to my occupation of such positions. Other identities afford me access to places of cultural significance and the ability to forge and maintain relationships, which are not a given for all Māori. Some privileges of which I am aware include economic privilege, class privilege, and heteronormative ways of being (including being cisgender, i.e. born female and identifying as a woman, and being married to a cisgender Māori man). I also conform to some standards of beauty as viewed from the lens of white supremacy (including medium-brown skin tone, and facial features that indicate that I am of Māori and Pākehā heritage, with a 'normal' body mass index). I have fertility privilege, being a mother of two children; I am able-bodied; I do not suffer from debilitating mental illnesses; I do not have dependants who have abnormal health conditions; and I benefit from having an 'achieved' cultural identity that incorporates being an active speaker of te reo and having meaningful relationships with whānau and marae. It is important to note such a position at the beginning of a book like this, because these privileges give me a certain outlook on the world, which inevitably shapes the ways in which I make sense of my environment and my research.

These privileges do not mean that I have not experienced suffering, hardship or emotional challenges. Instead, I note them to suggest that someone with different circumstances might reach conclusions different from my own. The reason for locating myself within this research is to avoid the misguided assumption that the process of information-sharing is neutral and uninfluenced by the environments in which we live.

My academic training is in psychology and te reo Māori; therefore, the way that I present information about experiences of te reo Māori is likely to be influenced by the disciplines that have shaped my understandings. My personal experiences also impact my writing, as I have spent over ten years teaching te reo Māori in a university and even longer learning about te reo.

Similar to the observations made by Adrienne Maree Brown (2019), it is worth noting that the language I use in this book is the language available to me at the time of writing. If the ways in which we discuss decolonisation, identity and tangata whenua shift in the future, my language and thinking may also shift. This book does not dispute the varied experiences and relationships that Māori have with language generally; it aims to share some ways in which some tangata whenua portray their experiences of learning or actively using te reo Māori.

It is my hope that those reading this book will find it meaningful. A range of views from Māori language learners are shared here; I hope that readers will draw from these voices some ideas, questions, and maybe even solutions that help them to make sense of their own language-learning journey.

# 1. Methods and methodology

The methods and methodology that inform the thinking and research for this book are outlined in this chapter. This chapter also includes information about participants in the research project Manawa Ū ki te Reo Māori, including gender, ethnicity, age, place of residence and language proficiency.

Kaupapa Māori is the methodology that informs the findings presented in this book. Due to the work of generations of Māori thinkers, we have theories and a literacy that allow us, as tangata whenua, to embed our lived experiences within research contexts under the mantle of Kaupapa Māori methodology. Led by myself, with a team of Māori researchers including Tai Ahu (also my husband), Dr. Maureen Muller, and Ririwai Fox, we also had a substantial team of research assistants, including Alana Haenga O'Brien, Kahu Haimona, Ataria Sharman, Venise Clarke, Te Tāruna Parangi, and finally Melissa Fiu, from Rotuma (an island of Fiji), who provided administrative support. This research was conducted in ways that prioritise the mana and rangatiratanga of those who shared their views with us. The Kaupapa Māori methodology asks that we consider how our research contributes directly to improving our communities' experiences as Māori.

In the qualitative elements of this research, 57 Māori learning their reo tūpuna (ancestral language) shared stories and experiences about themselves and other Māori who had attempted to learn te reo. In some of these stories, learners became fluent speakers. In other stories, learners voiced feelings of exclusion and rejection. The sharing of pūrākau, or 'story work', encourages people to make sense of their realities (Archibald, 2008). Story work complements our overarching Kaupapa Māori methodology – a methodology that allows individuals to be the authority, holding mana rangatira over their own narratives.

The types of sharing that occurred for Manawa Ū ki te Reo Māori allowed me and my fellow researchers the opportunity to hear voices that are not often brought to the forefront. An interviewee could share their emotions about their reo learning experiences, including anxiety, shame, guilt, frustration, elation, satisfaction, love, accomplishment, reconnection, reclamation, disconnection, enlightenment, belonging-ness – and many other responses. The learning experiences of Māori ancestral language learners were intertwined with historical trauma. Therefore, historical trauma theory helped us to understand the language-learning experiences of our people within the wider context of colonisation. As Pihama, Cameron and Te Nana (2019) explain: 'Both Kaupapa Māori and historical trauma theory call on a collective approach to healing collective trauma and its impacts' (20). Both theories helped us to interpret Māori language learners' stories and relay our interpretations to a Māori language learner audience.

After I had a kōrero with a focus group in Te Papaioea (Palmerston North), a couple of interviewees began to speak more informally. One woman said, 'I'm surprised that this research hasn't been done before.' I laughed and said, 'It has. But there are always new things to learn and new voices to hear from.' The process of colonisation is not in a state of rest. Therefore, as Indigenous peoples who are committed to retaining our language, we remain alert and dynamic in our responses. The overarching goal of this research is to highlight new perspectives, as well as old ones that continue to shape our realities. By engaging with our participants under the mantle of Kaupapa Māori methodology, we were able to consider our experiences as Māori in a way that takes our ways of being as normative. We continue to maintain rangatiratanga over our lived experiences, which is explicated within Kaupapa Māori theory.

As Māori, our experiences are diverse. The realities that are normal to one person do not always translate seamlessly to others. I do not assume to know how all Māori might feel as ancestral language learners, nor how individuals may respond to their unique language histories and current realities. However, this book offers perspectives that have been shared with me directly or with my colleagues, Dr Maureen Muller, Tai Ahu and Ririwai Fox, through the lived experiences of Māori who have attempted or are in the process of attempting to regain and reclaim te reo Māori.

A note on the terms 'proficiency' and 'fluency'. Here, proficiency tends to refer to *te tika o te reo*, while fluency is perhaps best described as *te rere o te reo* – borrowing from the Panekiretanga (the Institute of Māori language Excellence) mantra 'Ko te reo kia tika, ko te reo kia rere, ko te reo kia Māori'. A person who is proficient in te reo can understand grammatical structures, they know when it's appropriate to use kīwaha or colloquial sayings, and they are likely to have a wide vocabulary. Their knowledge of language features may be extensive, but this doesn't necessarily mean that they would consider themselves fluent. Those with proficiency may still struggle to put sentences together on the spot, finding it difficult to produce language under pressure. By contrast, a person who is fluent may be able to speak te reo Māori without stammering or pausing in search for an appropriate phrasing. However, even a fluent individual may not have achieved 'te tika' or 'te Māori' o te reo. Therefore, individuals can be both fluent and proficient, or they can be either.

Proficiency and fluency perhaps are not adequate terms for the third aspect, *ko te Māori o te reo*. This requires extensive knowledge of both te reo Māori and its cultural context. Second language learners who have proficiency, fluency, and Māoriness of thought will likely understand how to phrase their language in a way that is communicated and received by Māori-speaking audiences, which often requires an ability to read audiences, including when to incorporate humour or witticisms. Reaching this point is the goal for many aspiring speakers, and there are considerable challenges along the way.

## Core values underpinning reo Māori learning

In understanding the experiences we share as Māori ancestral language learners, we drew upon four values (Fig. 1). Aroha, rangatiratanga, mana and tūhono shaped the way we might interpret the information that participants shared.

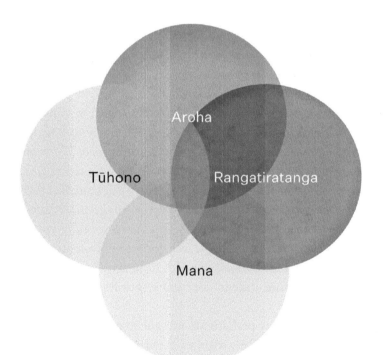

Fig. 1. Core values underpinning reo Māori learner experiences

*Aroha*: In its purest sense of unconditional compassion for the self and for others, aroha enables individuals to engage in language learning with flexibility and dynamism. Aroha at the centre allows for a greater range of social interactions where te reo Māori is the means of communication, opening possibilities for language use and revitalisation. Aroha in combination with other language goal-directed actions, including those that challenge learners, promotes rather than inhibits language use.

*Rangatiratanga*: In the context of te reo Māori revitalisation, rangatiratanga acknowledges that we are in the process of cultural and linguistic reclamation in response to colonial oppression. As ancestral language learners, we have the authority to learn and use our language in dynamic ways across myriad contexts as our birthright. Rangatiratanga encourages us to take ownership of our thought processes, self-beliefs and ability to achieve language proficiency. We can see value in our heritage language, and we shift towards a self-determined reo Māori future. Rangatiratanga encourages us to reclaim te reo as our own, rather than perceiving ourselves as manuwhiri to te reo.

*Tūhono*: Tūhono encompasses the understanding that te reo is connected with ourselves, our culture, our tūpuna, atua and whenua. Tūhono enables a sense of grounding and centring. It contributes to our understanding of ourselves in relationship to those we are a part of and inherently connected to through established whakapapa lines. Tūhono can help to alleviate some of the stressors associated with identity reclamation that may arise during processes of ancestral language learning. Within tūhono, te reo Māori allows us to connect with kaupapa (including events and concepts) that might have seemed distant or inaccessible prior to language acquisition.

*Mana*: As a central means for achieving understanding relative to mātauranga Māori, te reo Māori continues to be tightly interwoven with concepts of personal and collective mana. Personal and collective mana can be impacted when we are in situations where the language is used across a range of functions or occasions. In Manawa Ū ki te Reo Māori, participants indicated feeling that when they were able to uphold their personally set standards for interacting in te reo, this positively contributed to their mana and that of the groups they were a part of. Interpersonal language communications place us in positions where we may feel that our personal or collective mana is either upheld or made vulnerable depending on the context of use.

## Study 1: Quantitative Methods

*Participants and survey design*
A total of 1049 individuals took part in our research for Manawa Ū ki te Reo Māori. Because of the systematic branching of questions (for instance, if a person answered yes or no to a particular question they would be sent along a particular path of questions) and some missing responses, the number of people who answered each set of questions varied. We excluded 69 participant responses because there were too many missing responses. We also excluded a further 267 participants who did not identify as Māori or who did not respond to this question. Therefore, the total number of responses included in this book is 713.

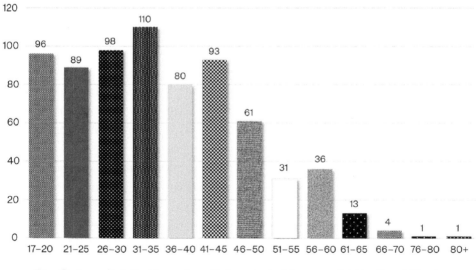

Fig. 2: Age distribution of participants in Manawa ū ki te Reo Māori

This includes 547 female participants, 167 male participants and four participants of self-identified gender, which these participants chose to identify as queer and non-binary. The mean age was 31, with a median age of 35. Individuals younger than 17 were excluded from this study due to ethical constraints.

Of all participants who identified as Māori, 202 identified as both Māori and Pākehā. Participants also identified with ethnicities including Samoan, Cook Islander, Niuean, Chinese, and Indian. A total of 542 participants reported being parents or grandparents.

In terms of regional spread, Te Whanganui-a-Tara had particularly strong representation (200), due to the number of participants who completed the survey at Te Matatini ki te Ao, hosted in Te Whanganui-a-Tara in 2019, and at an introductory language course at Te Herenga Waka—Victoria University of Wellington. People were invited to participate in the Manawa Ū ki te Reo Māori survey through a range of networks. Some completed it via an app created by Te Matatini, while others completed it directly at Te Matatini. Five researchers and assistants (all wāhine Māori) helped to collect responses. One of the benefits of having researchers sit with participants as they completed the survey was that a researcher could read questions aloud to those who preferred, including kaumātua and kuia. Researchers also listened to participants talk about their reo Māori personal histories, which contributed to the qualitative questions in the subsequent study. Outside Te Matatini, the online survey link was shared with pouako from Te Ataarangi, who invited students to complete the survey.

The survey was reviewed by Māori language researchers and quantitative survey design advisors, including Sir Richard Benton, Dr Ruakere Hond, Prof. Chris Sibley, Dr Arama Rata, Mikaia Leach and Jonathan Kilgour, to ensure we were asking questions in a way that would allow us to interpret the answers effectively. Survey topics included:

- contexts in which te reo was used
- exposure and interactions with other speakers
- the role of employment

- community value of te reo Māori
- attitudes toward te reo
- cultural roles and responsibilities
- the experiences of parents and grandparents
- identity-based motivations.

The survey was approved by the Victoria University of Wellington Human Ethics Committee.

*Language proficiency*

Understanding the results of the Manawa Ū ki te Reo Māori survey requires us to look at the proficiency levels of participants. People with different levels of proficiency tend to have different motivations and obstacles to learning or using te reo Māori.

We asked four reo questions regarding spoken reo, reading, writing and understanding. The survey utilised items from the 2001 Survey on the Health of the Māori Language (Statistics New Zealand, 2002), which was also used in the most recent Te Kupenga survey (Statistics New Zealand, 2014), and gave us data to compare our findings with.

Table 1: Self-reported proficiency of participants from Te Kupenga Statistics (TK) and Manawa Ū ki te Reo Māori (MŪ)

| Age range | | Well / very well | | Fairly well | | Not very well | | A few words or phrases | | Total | | % of total | |
|---|---|---|---|---|---|---|---|---|---|---|---|---|---|
| TK | MŪ | TK | MŪ | TK | MŪ | TK | MŪ | TK | MŪ | TK | MŪ | TK | MŪ |
| 15–24 | 17–25 | 8 | 39 | 13 | 22 | 33 | 24 | 46 | 15 | 131k | 185 | 28 | 26 |
| 25–34 | 26–35 | 11 | 41 | 15 | 28 | 33 | 21 | 42 | 10 | 85k | 208 | 18 | 29 |
| 35–44 | 36–45 | 10 | 35 | 11 | 26 | 34 | 27 | 45 | 12 | 88k | 173 | 19 | 24 |
| 45–54 | 46–55 | 8 | 33 | 11 | 25 | 32 | 24 | 49 | 18 | 79k | 92 | 17 | 13 |
| 55+ | 56+ | 17 | 33 | 10 | 40 | 29 | 15 | 45 | 13 | 87k | 55 | 18 | 8 |

These four items were combined, and the average for each participant was taken to gain a mean proficiency score. Items were ordered from 1 to 5, with 1 being 'no more than a few words or phrases'; 2 'not very well'; 3 'fairly well'; 4 'well'; and 5 'very well'.

Participants in Manawa Ū ki te Reo Māori had much higher proficiency across each age range compared with the national averages of Te Kupenga (Table 1). As Te Kupenga is a national study, the number of participants is far greater than for the Manawa Ū study. Also, age ranges differ slightly between the two. These results indicate that participants in Manawa Ū include those likely to have greater access to te reo Māori than participants in Te Kupenga. The results below are also presented in the technical report *Manawa Ū ki te Reo Māori: A Study of Language Motivations to Enhance the Use and Acquisition of te Reo Māori* (Te Huia, Ahu, Muller, & Fox, 2019), available through Te Mātāwai.

Those with both low and high fluency reported differences in te reo use across domains (Fig. 3). Te reo was most frequently heard at the marae and when visiting relatives or friends. According to both groups, te reo was least often used in spaces for sports and religious activities.

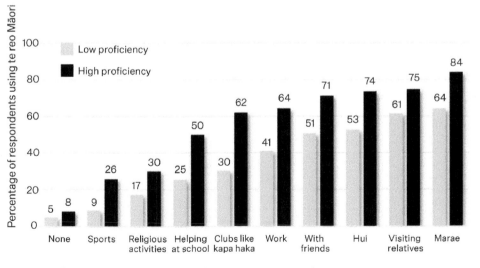

Fig. 3: Frequency of te reo Māori use in everyday activities

## Study 2: Qualitative Methods

The qualitative study was designed to explore some of the narratives held by Māori language users and learners. A total of 38 wāhine and 19 tāne were interviewed. Ages ranged from 18–74, with an average of 39.7 and a median of 38.5 (Fig. 4). Only one participant did not disclose their age. Interviews ranged from 22 minutes to 1 hour, 37 minutes. The mean duration was 47 minutes and 21 seconds.

Interviewees included 57 tangata whenua from nine locations: Te Tai Tokerau, Tāmaki Makaurau, Kirikiriroa, Waipā, Whakatāne, Rotorua, Tauranga, Manawatū, Te Whanganui-a-Tara and Hokitika. Three people were interviewed outside their residential region. Their residential regions were Ōtautahi, Ōtepoti and Manawatū. In the results of the qualitative study, each quotation is labelled with the participant's age and their residential region rather than the place at which they were interviewed. Interviewees belonged to a total of 54 respective iwi. Some belonged to more than one iwi (see Table 2).

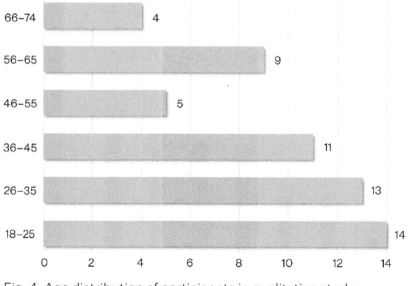

Fig. 4: Age distribution of participants in qualitative study

Participants had the option of being interviewed in either te reo Māori or English. A total of 39 used te reo Māori and English intermittently, with 13 using English solely and 5 using te reo Māori solely.

Interviews were conducted by three members of the research team: Dr Maureen Muller, Tai Ahu and myself. Most of us had a prior relationship with the interviewees. In instances where this was not the case, a group had agreed to participate through someone in our networks who was able to support the research process.

Table 2: Total iwi connections in qualitative study

| Iwi Affiliations | n | Iwi Affiliations | n |
|---|---|---|---|
| Hokianga | 1 | Ngāti Raukawa | 2 |
| Iwi Mōrehu | 2 | Ngāti Raukawa ki te Tonga | 1 |
| Maurea | 1 | Ngāti Ruanui | 1 |
| Muaūpoko | 1 | Ngāti Ruateatea | 1 |
| Ngā Ariki (Ngā Ariki Kaipūtahi) | 1 | Ngāti Tahu | 1 |
| Ngāi Tahu/Kai Tahu | 3 | Ngāti Tamaterā | 3 |
| Ngāi Tai ki Torere | 1 | Ngāti Toa Rangatira | 2 |
| Ngāi Te Rangi | 2 | Ngāti Tukorehe | 1 |
| Ngāi Tūhoe | 8 | Ngāti Tūwharetoa | 6 |
| Ngā Puhi | 9 | Ngāti Wai | 2 |
| Ngā Ruahinerangi | 1 | Ngāti Whakaue | 2 |
| Ngāti Awa | 3 | Ngāti Whaoa | 1 |
| Ngāti Haua | 1 | Ngāti Whare | 1 |
| Ngāti Hineru | 1 | Ngāti Whātua | 1 |
| Ngāti Kahu | 2 | Rangitāne | 2 |
| Ngāti Kahungunu | 6 | Rongomaiwahine | 2 |
| Ngāti Kahungunu ki te Wairoa | 2 | Rongowhakaata | 3 |
| Ngāti Kauwhata | 1 | Taranaki | 3 |
| Ngāti Koata | 1 | Te Aitanga a Māhaki | 1 |
| Ngāti Konohi | 1 | Te Arawa | 6 |
| Ngāti Māhanga | 1 | Te Atiawa | 4 |

| Ngāti Manawa | 4 | Te Atihaunui a Pāpārangi | 2 |
| Ngāti Maniapoto | 7 | Te Aupouri | 5 |
| Ngāti Oneone | 1 | Te Rarawa | 2 |
| Ngāti Porou | 9 | Te Whakatōhea | 2 |
| Ngāti Pikiao | 2 | Te Whānau a Apanui | 1 |
| Ngāti Rangiwewehi | 1 | Waikato/Tainui | 8 |

| Total iwi represented | 54 |
| Total participants | 57 |

Participants had the option of using their given name or a pseudonym. We conducted interviews at marae, workplaces, kura, homes and cafés, depending on what was most convenient and comfortable for participants.

The findings of our research are shown throughout this book. Elements from both the qualitative and quantitative findings are included to help create a cohesive narrative about how individuals with an ancestral connection to te reo Māori acquire and use te reo.

# 2. Practical support for learning te reo

Processes of colonisation have interrupted our intergenerational patterns of language learning. As Indigenous ancestral language learners, we often have no choice but to learn our reo tūpuna outside of our home or natural whānau engagements, beginning the process in unfamiliar places. We are often forced into positions where we must engage with formal methods that emphasise reading and writing. This is problematic, primarily because it takes away our sense of agency and can have the impact of prioritising one type of learner over others. Learning te reo Māori may require us to reclaim our agency over our learning.

In our research for Manawa Ū ki te Reo Māori, we found that learning environments that encouraged manaakitanga and whanaungatanga helped tangata whenua to have positive learning experiences. When the environment was high trust and respectful, learners expressed feeling more able to practise without fear of reprimand for the mistakes they would inevitably make. Learning settings and teaching styles that aligned with their preferences also helped create a positive experience.

In our language learning, we are often required to be interdependent. However, we can also take ownership of our learning through independent study methods. In this chapter, we'll explore ways in which ancestral language learners interact with formal learning environments, some strategies that support them in both independent and interdependent learning, and practical tips for their everyday lives.

## Hoa haere, and choosing a course

One of the challenges that many students reported in the Manawa Ū study was limited time and resources for attending classes. For tangata whenua, anticipated and unanticipated trauma can also arise during the ancestral language learning experience, which adds to the challenges that prospective learners of te reo Māori are asked to cope with. Building a support network of individuals who can help us through some of the tough times may help, so that we have the capacity to unpack some of this trauma.

The concept of 'hoa haere' is put forward by Taina Pohatu (2008), who encourages Māori researchers to work collaboratively to allow for the traversing of kaupapa in a supported way. Pohatu indicates that there is an intergenerational nature to the ways in which particular kaupapa are carried out. The concept of hoa haere was also suggested to me by Māori language academic Matiu Rātima (see Te Huia, 2013). Having a friend who can traverse the language-learning space is important, as friendships allow us to debrief and work through challenges that are specific to language learning, as well as issues that might relate to being Māori and an ancestral language learner.

According to the most recent research, taking a Māori language course/wānanga is the most common way in which learners engage with te reo Māori (Bright, Lawes, Keane, & McKinley, 2018). A large range of courses are available, and it is important to choose one that is suited to your individual learning style. Te Ataarangi is perhaps the most well-known community-centred language class. Their methods of teaching have included 'the rākau method', which works well for many students, particularly kinaesthetic learners.

Wānanga offer a range of study options, as do universities. It is worthwhile spending time researching programmes and talking to previous students about their experiences of a course or study programme. Some courses, particularly those that limit numbers for smaller class sizes, have extensive waiting lists, so it is useful to book in advance. Prior to starting a course or study programme, you can work on specific activities independently.

Any Māori language teacher or long-term language learner will have observed the exponential growth in the availability of online resources. The impact of COVID-19 has created a massive global shift in the use of technology to deliver teaching – te reo Māori included. As recently as 2019, I, along with many other Māori language teachers, had doubts about whether large groups of students would benefit from learning te reo Māori online. Having taught te reo online for three years since 2020, I'm still undecided (or, rather, less optimistic) about how I feel about learning te reo Māori solely online, given the impersonal nature of this mode of learning. In addition to the inevitable COVID-19 fatigue that we are all likely feeling, teaching online seems to have some serious drawbacks, particularly when trying to engage with high numbers of tauira who may be seeking an experience that is more tied to their affirmation as Māori, rather than the transmission of technical information about sentence formation.

At university many courses now offer 'dual delivery', whereby a course is accessible both online and in person. Teaching online has given Māori language teaching staff and students permission to explore the ways in which student engagement with language-learning material can happen without in-person conversation. There are pros and cons. One of the positives I have seen is that students can view recorded material multiple times at home, a familiar space where anxiety is likely to be low. Furthermore, the 'breakout room' function, in platforms like Zoom, allows students to have small-group activities in private spaces.

Currently, Zoom is the most common tool for engaging online. For large groups using the breakout room function, the synergies between group members can be low, and students can opt out of these engagements. However, for those who choose to engage, these rooms allow students to interact with class members they might be unlikely to sit beside in a physical space. By the end of the course, most people have engaged in small-group discussions with vast numbers of students. However, one disadvantage to being placed automatically into a breakout room is that students might not be grouped with those they have a natural affinity towards.

Online courses require students to have a stable internet connection, which is difficult for those based in rural areas or in homes with multiple users of one connection. Technology can also present a barrier for some tauira. If you opt for an online Māori language class, it would be useful to pair it with in-person learning, as the relationships that you develop can be more enduring when face to face.

## Rangatiratanga over learning experience

Over 20 years ago, Richard Benton (1999) submitted a report to the government about actions that would benefit the revitalisation of te reo Māori. Front and centre of his findings was the concept of agency, or rangatiratanga. When we feel that we have rangatiratanga over our learning, we are more likely to feel in charge of the outcomes associated with learning. Therefore, any actions we can take to increase our feelings of rangatiratanga, such as focusing on the elements of learning we have control over, will be of benefit.

Socio-cultural factors will always come into play. Throughout their language-learning experience, many Māori ancestral learners will explore their whānau history of language loss and reclamation. Our rangatiratanga about our identity as Māori affects our feeling of agency to pursue Māori language proficiency or fluency. Our language-related trauma and our various identity positions are only a few of the factors we might be managing prior to even beginning to learn te reo.

Formally learning our reo tūpuna can be highly emotional due to the relationships we have with whānau who are living as well as with tūpuna who have passed on. The injustices that have been inflicted upon us as Indigenous people are often made more salient through the process of ancestral language reclamation. So we need to learn how to become attuned to our thoughts and feelings, and how to work through them. Popular meditation techniques encourage us to observe emotions that arise without becoming overwhelmed by them. Trauma therapists explain that trauma lives in the body (Duran, 2019; Menakem, 2021; van der Kolk, 1996) and that in order to transition to a state of healing, a person who has experienced a trauma (as most have) needs to learn to connect with the emotions that are housed in the body. Menakem (2021) offers practical techniques that can help us work through the physical pain of inherited trauma.

Additionally, Menakem (2021) describes two types of pain. 'Dirty pain' is the pain that results when we are not willing to address the realities that keep us in a state of unconscious pain. This avoidance enables the pain to continue. By comparison, 'clean pain' is the pain of consciously dealing with one's trauma. Clean pain requires us to look at our histories and our learned responses for coping with trauma that has been held in the body. We address some of the root causes of trauma head-on.

For Indigenous language learners, the process of learning te reo Māori often brings up highly emotive questions about identity and self. These emotions are likely to correspond with physical pain. Techniques such as breath work – noticing how the body and breath respond to a thought that has arisen during a language-learning class – may help us to slow down our fight-or-flight responses. When the body experiences stress, the mind diverts energy towards the perceived cause. To have the best chance at acquiring our ancestral language, Māori language learners need to direct energy to the learning activity as opposed to external stressors. As we become aware of our emotional thought processes, we will begin to see the patterns. Once we can understand the patterns, we may be able to acknowledge the thought or feeling without being side-tracked by it.

When we feel overwhelmed by our emotions, our motivation to keep learning te reo Māori can be affected. Over time, the heavy emotions that become associated with language learning may make the activity of learning too painful to contemplate. Keeping in touch with our minds and bodies while intentionally taking part in language learning can help us to unhook the two components.

## Language anxiety: Quantitative findings

Internationally, language research consistently indicates that when learners of a second language are highly anxious, their ability to process new information about the language, and to use the language, decrease (MacIntyre & Gardner, 1994; MacIntyre, 1995). In our research for Manawa Ū ki te Reo Māori, we explored the factors that contributed to language anxiety for Māori language learners. Our results indicated that when teaching style matches a learner's preference, anxiety is lower. This confirms the importance of individuals finding the method of learning that best suits them. Clear course instructions also helped to reduce anxiety. When learners know what to expect from a course, they don't have to guess or assume what might be expected of them.

Some of the pressures that Māori ancestral language learners experience are identity related, and are based on comparisons that they make between themselves and others. As part of our research, we asked Māori ancestral language learners how they felt about learning te reo. Participants were asked to rate their agreement or disagreement with the following statements on a 7-point Likert scale:

- 'If I make a mistake using te reo, I feel like it will affect how "Māori" others will think I am.'
- 'I compare myself to other Māori speakers.'
- 'I feel like I am expected to know te reo Māori because I identify as Māori.'

Those with higher levels of proficiency agreed less with these statements. In comparison, Māori with lower levels of proficiency tended to agree more with the statements. What this might indicate is that learning te reo Māori is a challenging identity space for those who are beginning their learning journey, particularly when they see their achievements (both successes and failures) as being directly tied to their in-group membership claims.

Identity, and the criteria that allow people to claim a particular identity, is also tied to power. People who meet a perceived set of criteria for a given identity are in a more powerful position than those who see a set of criteria as critical for entry but do not meet them. For instance, if I want to have others agree that I'm Māori, and I see my group entry as being tied to my ability to speak te reo, my entry into the group relies on my ability to converse in te reo. Individuals can experience language anxiety when they perceive their language skills as a core component of their Māori identity. By comparison, fluent Māori speakers are less likely to focus on how their language abilities are tied to their Māori identity. Their fluency may allow them to take certain identity positions for granted, as their Māori identity is less often queried by other power holders (including by those who are also fluent).

However, fluent speakers of te reo did report some symptoms of language anxiety. This tells us that learning te reo Māori is not a neutral experience. As ancestral language learners, we are all working through some type of pressure that comes from learning the language that is our ancestral birthright. Language anxiety does seem to subside as fluency increases, but because we have fewer native speakers in our Māori language speaking communities, fewer people are able to undertake culturally specific roles that require fluency, including second language learners. This means that as we gain proficiency, we're likely to be put into situations where we need to speak the language in public. Using our ancestral language as a second language, combined with knowing the correct way to enact a cultural role (such as kaikōrero or kaikaranga) in public, adds to the pressure that some fluent speakers might experience in reo Māori contexts.

Whether our proficiency in te reo is high or low, tangata whenua experience multiple pressures during the process of overcoming colonial oppressions. Individuals sometimes feel that they need to bring certain knowledge and skills to the language classroom prior to engaging in te reo Māori lessons, such as knowledge of whakapapa, politics and history; knowledge of popular Māori music and personnel; some knowledge of tikanga – and the list continues. While these are all encouraged as positive contributions to identity and culture, they are not requirements for entry into the Māori language classroom.

*Mauri tau, mauri rere: Knowing how to calm the body*
In our research for  the Manawa Ū study, part of the stress that tangata whenua reported feeling was the fear of failure or of appearing incompetent in the presence of others. Feeling incompetent in te reo Māori produces a special type of response, given that we know how much value is placed on te reo Māori, and that being a Māori speaker or not can impact on our feelings of belonging to our cultural ingroup.

When our bodies are tense or anxious, we are less able to take in new information, particularly when that information is tied to emotions we might be feeling as ancestral language learners. So the first thing that a learner can focus on is their own body. Learning how we respond to stress, and ways in which we can bring the body into a state of mauri tau, or calmness, is useful in language-learning situations.

Menakem (2021) provides a series of practical exercises for individuals as they work towards understanding their emotional states. What Menakem refers to as 'body work' is based on his training with first responders in highly stressful situations. Some of his exercises focus on noticing sensations and thoughts. He offers readers the opportunity to sit with their trauma or their thoughts of a stressful event for up to a minute, and simply notice how the body responds. Gradually, individuals might extend the length of time that they can sit with their discomfort.

These exercises aim to help individuals regulate their emotions, which involves fully feeling challenging emotions (as opposed to avoiding or suppressing them) without being completely overwhelmed. By repeating 'exposure' to the emotion over time, the emotion loses some of its potency, and eventually allows a person to 'metabolise' their pain. The goal is not to rid a person of uncomfortable emotions altogether, but to acknowledge that challenging emotions exist in our bodies and that how we respond to them affects the decisions we make.

If we consider the challenges that Māori language learners might experience from a Māori perspective, our goal as learners is to have control or rangatiratanga over our bodily experiences during our ancestral language learning. Bringing the body into a state of mauri tau will help to steer us away from states such as mauri rere.

In *He Pātaka Kupu*, the Pātaka dictionary (Te Taura Whiri i te Reo Māori, 2008), 'mauri tau' is described as 'E tau ana te mauri, kāore e wehi ana' (444). The description refers to the presence of a settled mauri, one that is not fearful. Interestingly, the usage example relates to learning: 'Ko te tangata ka mauri tau i te whakamātautau, tērā tonu e puta, ko te tangata ka mauri rere, auare ake'. This translates to English as: 'The person who is mauri tau during an examination will do well, while the person who is in a state of mauri rere will not have a chance'. In comparison, mauri rere is described in *He Pātaka Kupu* as 'E oho ana te mauri, e wehi ana, kāore e mōhio me aha' (444), translating to English as 'The mauri is alert, fearful, and unsure what to do'. The two usage examples for mauri rere describe people responding to a traumatic situation, such as warfare, or the burning of a house with one's child inside. While both examples from the Pātaka dictionary concern extreme experiences, feelings like mauri rere can exist in Māori language learning settings when a person feels powerless.

For learners of te reo, learning to come into a state of mauri tau during stressful situations is always useful. Learning to control our emotional states takes considerable, intentional, regular practice, and our ability to do this can be strengthened over time. While returning to a state of mauri tau during challenging experiences can be learned independently, the practice also has benefits during interdependent learning activities, described later in this chapter.

Most second-language learners will understand the feeling that arises when faced with speaking to someone well versed in te reo. Even individuals who can return to a state of mauri tau can experience feelings of mauri rere when under pressure to perform. In the Manawa Ū study, some participants reported feeling tense and nervous when te reo Māori was the main language of communication, and feeling unsettled or upset in Māori language-speaking spaces. These physiological symptoms are the body's way of communicating that a person is not in a neutral space with neutral stimuli. When the body is in a state of unease, it is more difficult to concentrate on the task at hand. If learners view Māori language-speaking environments as frightening or uncomfortable, they are less able to concentrate on learning or using te reo Māori.

How can we calm ourselves when entering these spaces? Anything that shifts the focus away from the 'self' is helpful. It is useful to think about the four 't's: *tau hā, take, taituarā* and *tuku*.

*Tau hā*: Breath and whakatau mauri. Find a way of calming the mind and body. In preparing for childbirth, some women are trained to breathe in for four counts and out for six. This technique can be used in many stressful situations, including language learning, to help us to whakatau mauri, or centre ourselves. Intentional breathing helps to reduce the amount of cortisol being produced in our bodies. As we practise tuning in to ourselves, we can learn to recognise feelings of discomfort and respond more quickly. Mindfulness helps us to take in our surrounding environment, acknowledge feelings of discomfort, and let those feelings pass rather than suppressing them or becoming overwhelmed by them.

*Take:* Put the take, or kaupapa, first. Why are you in this Māori language-dominant space? When we attend Māori language-speaking gatherings, it is usually intentional. In most environments, te reo is not common enough for people to merely stumble upon such a gathering.

Therefore, if we find ourselves in a reo Māori-speaking space, it's usually because the kaupapa takes precedent. If you experience heightened levels of discomfort once you are in such an environment, returning to the first 't', tau hā, is useful.

*Taituarā:* Find a safe person or safe people. The advice to find a taituarā was given to our group by Prof. Pou Temara while at a Panekiretanga wānanga. It is advice I have applied on many occasions since. It is rare that a person would attend a reo Māori space without a single person whom they know, but if you are alone physically, you will always carry tūpuna with you. As someone who has dealt with debilitating levels of anxiety, feeling that my tūpuna are with me helps time and again. If you know in advance that you are likely to suffer from anxiety in a reo Māori space, it can be helpful to speak in advance with someone who is attending. Let them know that you would appreciate some support, and create a plan to give you a sense of security.

*Tuku:* Release unhelpful emotions and patterns of avoidance. When we are experiencing discomfort, figuring out the cause can be difficult. But it is important to consider where these feelings come from. Ancestral language learning requires us to have aroha for ourselves and others. In this context, aroha refers to a deep, unwavering sense of compassion which is unconditional. Having aroha for ourselves requires that we acknowledge our achievement in attending and participating as best we could at the time with the resources available to us. As part of this, we need to release the feelings that no longer serve us through processes of whakawātea. We might engage with the natural environment or do some type of physical activity to shift tension from the body.

Occasions where I have felt stressed in this way were usually those where a high level of performance was required. For instance, I might be required to play a cultural role, or I feel that my behaviours are being monitored or judged by others whom I hold in high regard. But I have very rarely regretted attending such an event, despite feelings of anxiety and unease beforehand.

## Independent elements of Māori language learning

There are benefits to knowing how to learn both independently and interdependently. When learners engage in both independent and interdependent activities, their language-learning outcomes improve.

One of the most significant barriers to fluency is the lack of a language-speaking community. While a language community is critical, learners can take a number of independent actions to increase their knowledge of te reo Māori. Reclaiming agency will help to reduce anxiety and increase possibilities for positive, long-term Māori language learning outcomes.

Learning with peers or whānau can be empowering when the goals for fluency are shared by the rōpū. Shifting from the classroom setting to 'real life' requires interdependence, and investment in relationships.

Harris (2017) notes some common themes that arose from a second-language learning programme:

a) Communicating in the target language for 'real purpose';
b) Language skills, both receptive and productive skills, including writing, reading, speaking and listening;
c) Language-learning skill and knowledge of language, including the ability to learn the language; and
d) Cultural awareness, including 'familiarity with authentic materials and knowledge of the country, as well as actual contact with native speakers' (18).

Points (a) and (d) are reliant on individuals having contact with a more authentic language community, while points (b) and (c) include components that can be self-directed.

Part of knowing more about the self involves knowing what we enjoy. Making independent language tasks enjoyable and meaningful will likely improve the chances that you will do them. This is not to diminish the complexity of language learning, but to help learners see how independent activities can support it.

In the Manawa Ū study, some individuals chose to learn

independently through 'teach yourself' books, including *Māori Made Easy* by Scotty Morrison, and TV shows streamed online such as *Ako* and *Ōpaki*, presented by Pānia Papa, and *Kōrero Mai*. *Kōrero Mai* and *Ako* both offer downloadable resources.

When we know how to study independently, learning a language (and most things) becomes a lot more achievable. In our research with over 1000 students of te reo Māori, learners indicated a moderate to strong correlation between disorganised learning (not having ideal study practices for learning te reo) and language anxiety ($r$ = .33). While anxious learners have been found to put more time into studying, their efforts don't result in more productive outcomes (MacIntyre & Gardiner, 1994). If we are to reduce language anxiety and improve chances of language-learning success, we need to become organised.

How can we become more organised in our learning? Some guiding principles are:

- Having clear and regular communication between learner and teacher.
- Identifying key learning resources, such as texts, audio files, websites and interactive activities.
- Maintaining a language-learning routine, such as setting a regular time to complete tasks (with at least 20 minutes per activity).
- Expanding vocabulary by focusing on domains of use, whereby learners focus on a topic area and collect the vocabulary around it.
- Breaking down sentence patterns. Understanding how grammar works can be immensely helpful when learning a language.
- Giving time and attention to receptive language skills (reading and listening) and productive language skills (writing and speaking).

Those who formally engage in learning te reo Māori also require good-quality resources that are designed with key objectives in mind. Bright and colleagues (2018), who conducted a review of resources available to Māori language learners, showed that most of the resources available were print publications. Resources were mostly intended for whānau

use and were targeted at beginner and intermediate learners of te reo
Māori. Furthermore, most of the resources were designed for primary-
school-aged children and their parents and caregivers (Bright, Lawes,
Keane & McKinley, 2018, 7).

Clearly, resource development is needed, particularly for adult
learners of te reo Māori and for those with higher levels of proficiency. If
our main language activity is classroom-based, then resources for these
classes need to be of good quality. Individuals who learn te reo Māori
through classes or wānanga should identify the resources offered by
their course coordinator.

*Increasing vocabulary*
The Ministry of Education has a list of the 1000 most frequently used
words in te reo Māori.* Learning these words in a meaningful way will
help learners to begin identifying topics of conversation when they
encounter te reo. Methods of learning vocabulary have been made easier
with online teaching aids like Quizlet and Memrise – the list of apps is
ever growing – that allow users to upload lists from Word documents or
Excel sheets, which can save a lot of time.

A tip for vocabulary learning is to memorise unrelated words at the
same time. If, for instance, you're learning opposite terms at the same
time, it's easy to forget which is which. You might be left in a tricky
situation when you use the word with the opposite meaning from what
you intended. I remember learning 'takaro' (to play) and 'takoto' (to lie
down) in the same word list at high school, and it plagued me for many
years!

Becoming comfortable with using a dictionary is also important.
Regular use of a dictionary helps to extend the language corpus and to
reduce feelings of helplessness. People who use dictionaries regularly are
less likely to need to revert to English because of a lack of knowledge

* See tereomaori.tki.org.nz/Teacher-tools/Te-Whakaipurangi-Rauemi/High-
frequency-word-lists

about a particular word. Below, Heather discusses her relationship with her dictionary.

> **Heather:** Actually it's good just to pick up a dictionary now and then and just flick through the pages and read. 'Oh, oh is that right,' you know? Yeah, or just flick to a page randomly and just start reading – I don't know, five kupu. You might not remember them but you know something's gone in there and you might hear it. Even though you don't know what it means maybe, it's triggering something. (Rotorua, 36–45)

While learning vocabulary can be done independently, it is also good to try learning words with a group. One participant group shared that they learned a strategy from Kura Whakarauora that helped them retain kupu as a whānau.

> **Louise:** Kura Whakarauora, that really helped me. There was a lady in particular who was in the same situation as me and she wanted to learn the reo, she wanted her kids to be brought up in the reo so what she did is make a board, so that's what I've done at home, put heaps of kupu on there, learn those kupu and once we've got all those kupu we switch the board over so we're constantly learning words or having like a word bank. So I can say to the kids, 'He aha tēnei rā, what is the day today' and they can say 'Rāmere, Rāhoroi' . . . so just going to those wānangas and making time. (Tauranga, 35–45)

Scotty and Stacey Morrison's *Māori at Home* (2017) is also useful, particularly for words specific to tasks inside and outside the home.

*Learning sentence patterns*
When you set out the sentence patterns that you are learning, you will start to see the similarities and differences between them. This can also help you to see the categories of words that can be used in

a sentence. An example of how to visualise a basic active sentence is given in Table 3.

Before making a table, we need to know the function of the sentence type. Therefore, this activity will require support from a kaiako and potentially a textbook or other reo Māori resource.

Repeating this exercise with each sentence type creates small incremental steps in our learning. Making a list of sentence patterns that you are familiar with is a good place to start. Once you are familiar with one pattern, mastering the next one becomes more manageable. Repetition is a valuable tool when embedding new sentence patterns in our long-term memory.

*Developing receptive and productive language skills*
Productive language skills refer to speaking and writing; receptive skills refer to reading and listening. It is necessary to allow time for each. Table 4 lists activities that utilise both productive and receptive skills.

Creating a table is one way to show you at a glance where you are focusing your attention and where you might need to spend more time to enhance your overall learning. Being specific with goals, including how much time you spend on an activity, helps you to be clearer about the task ahead. Specific targets also help you to monitor your progress.

Table 3: Active sentences

| Tense aspect mood marker (TAM) | Verb | Subject | Object marker i/ki | Object |
|---|---|---|---|---|
| Kei te | hoko | ahau | i | te pēke. |
| I | tunu | rāua | i | te kai. |
| Kua | whakahokia | te tauira | i | ā rāua pukapuka. |
| I te | hīkoi | ngā tamariki | ki | te kura. |

Table 4: Activities to promote receptive and productive language skills

|  | Reading | Listening | Writing | Speaking |
|---|---|---|---|---|
| Revising vocabulary and sentence patterns on Quizlet / revision cards | ✓ |  |  |  |
| Reading a book aloud | ✓ |  |  | ✓ |
| Writing in a daily journal | ✓ |  | ✓ |  |
| Writing letters (to fictitious or real people) |  |  | ✓ |  |
| Watching reo Māori documentaries, movies, TV, YouTube | ✓ | ✓ |  |  |
| Listening to podcasts, iwi radio stations, waiata |  | ✓ |  |  |
| Singing waiata reo Māori |  |  |  | ✓ |
| Transcribing conversations of Māori speakers | ✓ | ✓ | ✓ |  |
| Memorising a passage of text by a native-speaking author |  |  |  | ✓ |
| Simultaneous translation |  | ✓ |  | ✓ |

*Reading*

Read books at the level at which you are learning. The most recent stocktake of Māori language resources showed that print publications, including books, journals and magazines, are the resource most available to learners (Bright et al., 2018). Within this stocktake, most Māori language revitalisation goals focused on enhancing speaking and writing (productive skills), whereas reading and listening (receptive skills) were a secondary focus. To realise our language revitalisation goals, we need to develop our productive and receptive skills concurrently. This is one reason why initiatives such as Kotahi Rau Pukapuka have been established, with its goal of publishing 100 books in te reo Māori.

A number of books and texts include translations from te reo to English, which is excellent for independent learning. For example:

a) Decide on the passage of te reo that you will try to translate to English.
b) If possible, photocopy the passage so that you can mark up the page.
c) Skim-read each sentence and highlight any words that you do not know.
d) Use the highlighted words to create a vocabulary list. Include all possible translations for the target words in your list so that you have options ready when you read the passage a second time.
e) Read the passage again, including the meanings of the words you have found.
f) Write down your translation.
g) Check your translation against that given by the author.

Some translators take creative freedom to ensure that the underlying meaning of the original text is conveyed. Finding a piece of text that is appropriate to your proficiency level is important, because attempting to translate a text that includes too many unknown language features and unfamiliar vocabulary may be off-putting.

Understandably, for adult learners, it can be frustrating to read material that is aimed at young children. However, reading helps to solidify language patterns. If adult learners have children in their household, they might read to them. Sounding out the words can help with pronunciation and familiarisation with new vocabulary, and children benefit from having books read to them.

Be intentional in your learning. As mentioned in the guide above, keep a pen and a notebook available when working through new texts. Briefly scroll through a page and search for unfamiliar words, noting them down. Try not to go from a book to your phone to look up a word. (Inevitably, you will become distracted and end up knowing a lot more about how to cook chicken tagine or some other piece of non-essential information than the translation.) Instead, make a list of words to look up in one sitting.

*Listening*

A number of options are available for listening to te reo, including the wide variety of reo Māori music, podcasts and interviews with Māori speakers from Ngā Taonga Sound & Vision. YouTube is a good source of interviews with older native speakers, and iwi radio stations provide learning about iwi-specific dialects. If you are enrolled in a course, ask for recommended resources for your particular stage. Waiata Māori are increasingly available; these are enjoyable and useful in intentional study.

Many beginner-level audio resources aim to help listeners grasp the sounds of words. These are sometimes overly enunciated, in a way that does not occur in ordinary speech. Therefore, it is helpful to listen to how native speakers use the language when they are speaking naturally. If needed, use an app to slow down recordings so that you can hear the speaker more slowly.

**Anahera:** I think that as soon as I began to learn te reo, what I found was that there are lots of environments online where you can hook into reading and what have you. Accessing the learning resource centre where they got lots of books was really helpful. [. . .] Taringa is a really great podcast because when they do Mahuru Māori, it's entirely in te reo and I listened to it when it came out the first year they did it [. . .] I couldn't understand almost anything. (Te Whanganui-a-Tara, 45–55)

*Writing*

One of the benefits of writing in te reo Māori is that, later in our learning journey, we can look back on our writing and measure our progress. Before we learned to declutter, my husband and I kept our undergraduate essays in te reo Māori. We were both highly embarrassed by our clumsy grammatical errors. Even though we are both still learning te reo and will continue to be learners for our earthbound lives, it was great to see the types of errors that we made – it showed that our understanding has improved over time through intentional practice. I have since discarded these bits of writing, as I no longer need them to validate myself as a learner. However, at the time, it was refreshing and strangely comforting to see just how far I had come in 20 years, and that things can get better.

Writing a journal or diary is an excellent way to improve written reo Māori skills. You are free to write whatever you choose without feeling like your work will be critiqued. Keeping a journal also helps you to use te reo Māori in a way that is relevant to your life. Journal writing is usually 'free writing', meaning that you write continuously without worrying about form or grammar. You become engaged in a sense of flow. If you don't have the correct vocabulary to complete a sentence, don't stop writing; instead, write out the sentence in full, including non-Māori words where needed, and go back over your entry later, looking up the vocabulary that needs translating into te reo.

Keeping a 'kupu hou' book is a good idea, as all of the new words are listed in one place. Alternatively, write your kupu hou list at the back of your journal.

Letter-writing is another great way to practise writing te reo Māori, and people are often happy to receive a handwritten letter as opposed to a text message or email. Send letters to friends in class, or send whānau who kōrero Māori letters with a return-stamped envelope.

Teach-yourself books also provide opportunities for writing. Many of these resources require learners to check their written answers against those given at the end of the section or book.

*Speaking*

Activities that encourage learners to speak te reo are not usually independent learning tasks. However, we can speak aloud to ourselves in the car, while watching TV, and anywhere else we are comfortable. A highly proficient second-language speaker whom I interviewed for my PhD research enjoyed translating *Coronation Street* while watching it. As a television drama, it included lots of clearly spoken interpersonal dialogues, some of which were altercations. This person found it enjoyable to think about ways that such dialogues could happen in te reo Māori. They have become an incredibly competent speaker of te reo and a Māori language advocate.

My friends and I like to play a game in the car where we simultaneously translate songs. The older songs in which the lyrics are not sung too quickly are the most fun – and it's easier to translate songs that we know off by heart in English, because we get a head start with the translation.

Māori language grammar academic Dr Winifred Bauer encourages students to learn by heart passages of Māori text from native speakers by reciting the passages aloud. It is useful to understand what is being expressed so that the student can recite the passage with the correct intonation and rhythm.

Learning waiata by heart is another way of learning expressions, and is likely to be more manageable than memorising passages of text. Having completed Māori language courses alongside kaihaka (kapa haka performers), it was clear that they were able to draw from a deep knowledge of waiata when composing impromptu karanga.

### Dependence and interdependence in language learning

Many language learning tasks can be done independently, but gaining proficiency also requires dependence, or in some cases interdependence. Developing meaningful relationships is part of this, and our relationships are crucial in achieving fluency. Relationships with fellow learners, teachers and mentors are explored in this section.

Our Manawa Ū ki te Reo Māori findings highlighted the importance of a good fit between student and teacher. We asked reo Māori learners to indicate whether their teachers, peers and family were encouraging of their learning. Most encouraging were teachers, followed by peers, and finally family members. Furthermore, there was a positive correlation between having an encouraging teacher and not experiencing disorganised learning. From this we might assert that teachers have an impact on the perceived difficulty of language learning.

Our interviews with tangata whenua language learners supported the idea that teachers with ngākau whakaiti/ngākau mahaki had positive relationships with students. The value of ngākau whakaiti was particularly necessary for younger teachers with kaumātua and kuia in their classes.

Teachers are instrumental in creating language norms in their relationships with students. They often hold more power in the relationship, as they are in charge of creating an environment and establishing the interpersonal communication norms in the classroom. Their relationships with students allow them to initiate reo Māori conversations, reinforcing te reo Māori as a normative language. When learners were engaged in tikanga-related learning, particularly when learning elements that were considered tapu, or related to wairua, intentional and culturally appropriate teaching practices were necessary. Teachers who made efforts to provide a culturally safe environment, particularly when teaching karanga or whāikōrero, were praised.

Reo Māori students were very complimentary towards teachers who adapted to each learning situation. These teachers were able to read the room, work with people's energy levels, and interpret the emotional needs of their students. Students understood that being able to teach te reo Māori is a specific skill that is not afforded all speakers of te reo Māori. In other words, not all teachers are created equally; we cannot assume that because a person is fluent in te reo Māori they will be able to teach it well.

Kaiako who were interviewed in the Manawa Ū study indicated that teaching was immensely fulfilling. The following dialogue between two kaiako emphasises this point.

> **Andrea:** I think we underestimate a lot in regards to the learning that you receive when you teach, especially with te reo Māori because that is 'ako', it's not just about learning, it's a two-way thing. Students teach me something new all the time, I'm constantly surprised.
>
> **Tai:** It's that wairua thing you know, you're getting that ako but you're getting all the other things, like the wairua of the mahi come across you and you get that, you feel it in your ngākau and your whatumanawa, in your hinengaro, just everything becomes immersed in, and every time you have a class it just gets brighter and brighter in terms of your wairua, your tuakiri gets fed, your body gets fed, it's just an amazing thing [. . .] if you're with a kaiako that has so many different learning strategies and methods and knows all those different theories and things like that and they can mix it up. It's a wonderful learning and you have to go through it to be a kaiako. You've gotta go and learn all those different learning theories, Māori ones, invitational, collaborative, and all that. You just put all that into the learning and mix it all up and you have to know who your tauira are and the different learning styles they have and try to be flexible with your work and be able to change it when you need to. If they're not getting it one way, they'll get it this way perhaps. (Waikato, 56–65)

When teachers were asked why they became teachers, reciprocity or utu was a common reason. Second-language learners were often grateful for the opportunity to learn te reo Māori by formal means, and becoming a teacher was a way to pass on the gift of te reo Māori.

*Building peer-relationships among speakers of varying ability*
Giving feedback is a sensitive task for ancestral language learners, as our community attaches so much to being correct in our language delivery. As previously noted, a saying from Panekiretanga encompasses three concepts: 'Ko te reo kia tika, ko te reo kia rere, ko te reo kia Māori.' ('Language that is correct, language that is fluid, and language that is inherently Māori.') In an interview outside of this study, renowned Māori language advocate Pānia Papa suggested that there is an intentionality behind the ordering within the whakataukī, whereby the correctness of language is thought to come before fluidity or Māoriness of thought (Te Huia, 2013). Gloyne (2014) adds to these assertions: 'Ko te ako i te reo, ko te kōrero i te reo. Ko te kōrero i te reo, ko te whakaora i te reo. Ko te whakaora i te reo he mahi whakaheke werawera, ao noa, pō noa – he pae tawahiti rau' (307). Effectively, Gloyne highlights the fact that learning te reo is tied to a wider set of obligations that are perhaps realised once we have mastered the basics.

Beginners are likely to focus on the first two components, correctness and fluidity, while the final component, Māoriness of thought, comes later. Learners are likely to reach the final stage by paying close attention to the ways in which our people have interpreted and analysed their material and spiritual worlds.

Our relationships with those who give us language-related feedback will influence how we perceive that feedback, and how likely we are to take it on and make positive changes.

Individuals who join language classes can find a sense of security in numbers. Having similar interests and abilities as others may make learning more comfortable, particularly for those who have not formally engaged in language learning before. Wikitōria highlights this point:

**Wikitōria:** There was a couple of other [colleagues] that joined up at the same time as me. We just thrived on each other. But in saying that, it still, yeah, that confidence level, it seemed to get in the way. (Te Papaioea, 55–59)

Relationships between speakers and non-speakers of te reo Māori can feel uneasy in language-speaking situations. Wally Penetito (2011) writes that, in our Māori society, 'The first way to define what it means to be Māori is to identify those who know their Māoritanga. Statistically, they make up a distinct minority within Māoridom and this is their power' (39). Fewer than 20% of Māori kōrero Māori. Let us consider the experiences of both groups.

In Penetito's assertion, those who know their Māoritanga have power. He is not suggesting that this power is specifically connected to te reo Māori, but we can see that Māori who know te reo Māori tend to be more highly represented amongst those who can identify their marae, actively visit their marae, and know their pepeha (Statistics New Zealand, 2013, 2018), all of which contribute to identity claims-making processes (McIntosh, 2005). The 2013 Te Kupenga study indicated that 'Māori who spoke te reo Māori very well or well had been to their marae at some time in their life', with 73% of this group having visited their marae in the last 12 months. In comparison, 45% those who indicated knowing only a few words or phrases in te reo had visited their marae. The subsequent Te Kupenga study, in 2018, signposted that 'using te reo in daily life themselves' was of little or no importance to 48.8% of participants. These statistics show a distinct set of challenges that are operating within our culture. On one hand, almost half of Māori who participated in the Te Kupenga study (2018) indicated that te reo is not of daily importance, but on the other hand, we understand the symbolic value, the power and responsibility, that go with being able to speak te reo Māori. These are power-related challenges that we are facing within ourselves. They need to be worked through in wānanga, where viewpoints can be shared safely.

Māori language speakers can face immense pressure to uphold the cultural performance elements that both speakers and non-speakers expect of them. Since there are fewer reo Māori speakers, they are usually highly sought after for Māori culture-related tasks. Because of this heavy 'service load', they may view the task of language learning in more utilitarian terms. For instance, learning te reo may be seen more as an act of contribution to the language-related challenges we're facing.

If we consider the comparison of climate change to Māori language decline, those who are closest to the issues of the climate crisis and rising sea levels (such as those from Te Moana-nui-a-Kiwa) may be more aware of the impending crisis that we are facing globally. Some speakers of te reo Māori are likely to be closer to the issues of language decline and therefore more acutely aware of the challenges that we face in keeping te reo Māori alive and thriving.

Some speakers may want to encourage others to learn te reo Māori in order to help them cope with the language and cultural revitalisation pressures. While we acknowledge that Māori speakers hold power in Māori cultural contexts, they are also doing a lot of heavy lifting to ensure that cultural and linguistic erasure does not occur and that cultural maintenance is upheld.

The challenges that exist for highly proficient speakers and learners have their roots in the colonial conditions in which we are situated. Issues of identity and belongingness, language loss, language revitalisation, and the right to vocalise discomfort all contribute to the complexity of the relationships between Māori who speak te reo and Māori who do not. However, the challenge for us as language learners and people who are invested in language revitalisation is to learn to rely on one another. The future of our language depends on us. We are all part of the potential solution.

The relationships between those with low proficiency and those with high proficiency are interwoven. Learners are in somewhat of a bind, as they are reliant on feedback from those with greater proficiency to help them progress. However, shame is often attached to linguistic mistakes, blocking the benefits of receiving corrections. Whakamā is a reason why very few adult reo Māori language learners are likely to feel comfortable being corrected. In their long-answer responses for our Manawa Ū study, many individuals who were not confident speakers of te reo Māori referred to being corrected in an off-putting manner as a central barrier to their motivation to continue learning te reo.

For grammatical feedback to be useful, a few things are necessary: (a) a high-trust relationship between learner and proficient speaker, (b) appropriate timing of feedback, and (c) intentionality.

When a relationship is founded on trust and respect, both parties are aware that corrections are given without malice or to assert dominance. The timing of feedback relies on the proficient speaker being aware of language-learning processes and mindful in their interactions. Learners need opportunities to use their language fluidly, which includes making errors, and proficient speakers need to time their 'teaching moment' appropriately so as not to inhibit learners from using the language. Intentionality relates to the dual nature of the relationship. While (b) requires the proficient speaker to be self-aware, (c) asks the learner to be intentional and humble in their learning. I am aware that this last statement may sound patronising; however, what I mean is that if a learner is asking for support, it is indeed necessary to be open to corrections from those who want to provide that support.

> **Sarsha:** I'll get there because I'm just too shy to say anything and I don't like to say it if I think it's wrong because I know it's wrong. I do actually know when it's wrong so I'm thinking, 'Well, I understand that – ooh, that didn't sound right' but so I don't wanna say it myself even when they say, oh, 'Kāore he hē, kāore he tika, kōrero,' but if you keep kōrero hē, it's gonna stay like that and I don't wanna be that you know [. . .] I just wanna be tika. So that's probably why I don't say it unless I know how to say it. [. . .] What I do know I will say. What I don't know I won't bother. (Rotorua, 65–69)

As Indigenous people who are attempting to keep te reo Māori alive and thriving, we are working with the tools and resources available to us. Thinking about the concepts of interdependence, of utu, the giving and receiving of knowledge, we can consider what this means for us as ancestral language learners. Learners with low proficiency attempting to improve their reo may feel inept when they are developing relationships with fluent speakers. However, if we understand that learning guided by utu takes place over the long term, we may feel less pressure to demonstrate our value or ability to reciprocate in the present moment.

> **Rangitāne:** In the past when [challenging or shameful] things like that have happened, I've really retreated. Internally and in the moment as well, I think lately I've tried to really strategise my way through that and acknowledge it. You know, ask them to speak a little bit slower or maybe, you know, hope, fingers crossed, that they'll speak a little in simple terms that I'll understand but, yeah. In the past it used to be an emotional, embodied thing, but not so much that now. I'm a little bit, I've had time to look at why I'm responding in that way, and, you know, I've got a better way of thinking about it these days.
> (Kirikiriroa, 40–44)

*Communicating in te reo Māori for 'real purpose'*

Thinking about using te reo Māori for 'real purpose' requires us to consider what our language speaker community might look like. For many new adult learners of te reo Māori, the most accessible language community will be in the classroom. Some learners can rely on whānau who are reo Māori speaking, but in our research we found this was not the reality for many people. Therefore, adult learners are often in search of like-minded reo Māori speakers. Opportunities to engage in wānanga-style learning through programmes like Kura Reo, Kura Whakarauora and other local wānanga offer a unique experience, as learners with similar goals come together from different regions. Hui reo Māori also offer opportunities to hear te reo Māori spoken for an extended period, which is an unusual experience for most adult second language learners.

One of the benefits of attending wānanga reo is the range of language advancements that people of varying proficiency can gain. It is vital that already proficient speakers can progress towards native-like fluency through direct instruction from native speakers. While many people are learning the basics of te reo Māori, fewer can express themselves in a diverse range of scenarios. The more often that we need to code-switch to English to express ourselves, the more likely it is that English will become the dominant language in a conversation.

In our research for Manawa Ū, those who had access to hui reo Māori used these spaces mainly to listen to te reo Māori rather than speak te reo. Some learners expressed that when they tried to use te reo in hui Māori, either the response in Māori was not pitched at their level, or individuals responded in English. Both response types had the effect of limiting te reo Māori use in real-life situations. Therefore, outside of formal learning contexts, learners tended to practise mainly with people who were also learners or who they knew would respond at a level that matched their proficiency.

Experiences that push our levels of comfort through to experiences of total immersion can create shifts in language production, or te reo kia rere. We found that, apart from the study participants who had trained at Te Ataarangi, participants who gained the most benefit from total immersion wānanga were those at an intermediate level. Their basic understanding of te reo Māori allows these students to understand what is happening in conversations, which helps them to feel less stress and anxiety in those settings. Total immersion wānanga simulate 'real life', in that the conversations are not dominated by teacher-led instruction.

As Marlana noted, having at least some ability to communicate in te reo Māori was valuable.

**Marlana:** I would love to be in a rumaki kind of environment, immersion, reo Māori immersion environment all the time. I wouldn't

understand half of what is going on, um, oh, I'd get an idea pretty
quick. I think I can pick up fast [. . .] I can understand things okay.
But my confidence is not there, and my ability to reply is limited in
te reo. I probably default, not probably, I do default to answering and
responding in English, in Pākehā. Um, yeah, so, my ability to converse
I would say is limited and I think that is largely because of confidence.
(Kirikiriroa, 40–44)

We face notable challenges when we are not yet able to produce
sentences in te reo Māori, and when we are not yet confident. However,
making wānanga reo attendance a goal to work towards can help us to
progress from in-class learning through to 'real life' language use.

### Mentor–mentee relationships

Mentorship is perhaps a more valuable requirement for learners of te reo
Māori than for learners of other second languages, due to fewer chance
interactions that can help us grow our language abilities. Those who are
especially committed to learning te reo Māori to near native fluency
need specific guidance from those who are able to communicate in te reo
across contexts and at great depths. A basic scoping of second-language
learners who have reached high levels of proficiency demonstrates that
these speakers have, at some point in their learning journey, come to
the attention of those with the skills to mentor. There is a time pressure
associated with learning te reo Māori for those with high levels of
proficiency, given that most of our native speakers are closer to the end
of their lives.

However, mentorship is not available to all learners. Usually it is
an exceptional circumstance: not all students will experience or have
access to it. To increase their chances of being mentored, a learner needs
to be willing to invest a great deal in their own abilities as well as in
developing a strong relationship with the person whose knowledge and
time are being sought.

When considering the viability of a mentor–mentee relationship, the 'power distance' between the two individuals is likely to be a factor. Power distance is defined by Hofstede (2011) as 'the extent to which the less powerful members of organisations and institutions (like the family) accept and expect that power is distributed unequally' (9). Cultural groups who are more relationally connected in orientation tend to agree with general statements like 'Older people are both respected and feared' (9). When the power distance is too great, the mentee may feel whakamā in the presence of the mentor, so the outcome is likely to be less fruitful for both parties.

Mentorship requires reciprocity. Both people need to see the value that each brings to the relationship. The personal and group attributes of each person can help to reduce the power distance between mentor and mentee. At a group level, whakapapa relationships can affect the likelihood that a person will be mentored, due to personal or collective pre-existing relationships. At an individual level, when both people feel that they are coming into the relationship not as equals but as qualified givers and worthy receivers of knowledge, positive outcomes are likely.

The support of a mentor is likely to be highly valuable for a learner at any stage of proficiency. At the introductory to intermediate stages of learning, those who are not able to rely on whānau for direct Māori language instruction can seek out a mentor outside the whānau. This might be a tutor or formal teacher, or someone considered a tuakana – someone who is slightly more advanced but still a learner themselves.

The time that a mentor gives to a mentee will vary. Students can create stronger relationships with their instructors in small classes than in large classes. In the courses that I teach, for example, a single 100-level class can include more than 200 students, which is at least double the size of classes in 2010. Irrespective of class size, for beginner-level students, requesting time from your instructor is a good step. Gaining a mentor at introductory to intermediate levels is achievable.

Mentees with high proficiency may find it challenging to gain a mentor, based on the availability of native speakers or individuals who specialise in esoteric language features. Those who do find a native speaker to mentor them are likely to have demonstrated to their mentors their personal commitment to te reo Māori and their willingness to be mentored. Someone who exhibits a ngākau whakaiti – humility and commitment to grow – is likely to be a preferred mentee.

In his doctoral thesis, Matiu Rātima includes Te Rita Papesch's Māori language-learning journey as a case study, which was subsequently published as a co-authored journal article (Rātima & Papesch, 2013). Rātima describes Papesch affectionately:

> Her disposition is direct but kind. She speaks her mind, but not without consideration for others. [. . .] Many of her former students have gone on to become te reo teachers and highly proficient Māori speakers themselves. (387)

Through her numerous teaching roles, Papesch has contributed the knowledge she received back to the Māori language-speaking community. Her Māori language-learning journey is noteworthy because, despite beginning to learn te reo as a 27-year-old, she 'had a vision of her entire whānau as a Māori-speaking whānau' (383) – a goal she has actualised.

The mentoring that Papesch received from highly esteemed tohunga, including Professor Tīmoti Kāretu, the late Professor Te Wharehuia Milroy, the late Sir Robert Te Kotahi Mahuta and the late John Rangihau, contributed to her cultural and linguistic development. Rātima writes that there were two key elements to her support by these tohunga: whakapapa and utu. Papesch's openness to criticism was also important, making her a preferred candidate for mentorship.

Papesch describes how she learned under John Rangihau, a tohunga of cultural knowledge that was situated within his iwi of Ngāi Tūhoe. He was especially generous in his gifting of time and specific knowledge to Papesch, which helped her to improve her practice in the art of haka. Papesch had achieved national status for her role as kaitātaki wahine of her kapa haka at the time of her tutelage by Rangihau, yet she was still open to learning and improving her skills. At the time she was seeking mentorship, she was perhaps limited in her ability to give back to Rangihau directly. It is likely that they both understood that, in time, she would reciprocate.

## Summary

In this chapter we have explored some of the techniques and resources that learners of te reo Māori have found useful in their efforts to improve their proficiency. The role of rangatiratanga is crucial. Learners can engage in many activities, both independent and interdependent, to improve their language abilities. The more time we spend learning, the stronger our ability to recall words and sentences becomes.

Learning te reo Māori requires a lot of emotional support. Developing relationships with the people who support our progress is important at all levels of proficiency. I acknowledge that systematic challenges can prevent tangata whenua from accessing their language. This chapter is not intended to focus feelings of blame or guilt on tangata whenua who have tried to learn te reo but have not been supported to overcome the trauma that prevents them from encoding and retrieving their ancestral words. Rather, I encourage tangata whenua to think about language-learning strategies they have not yet tried, as they may lead to a different outcome.

Understanding how to keep our bodies in a state of mauri tau during our learning will help us to take in new information, particularly when this information is emotionally charged. Our emotional state has an impact on our bodies, and our bodies influence our capacity to learn. Being aware of environmental factors that help to keep us in mauri tau, and knowing our learning preferences and styles will help our processing of te reo. Critical awareness is also important, particularly when we are trying to distinguish between a challenging, uncomfortable learning situation that we just need to push through and a learning situation that is not well-suited to us.

Teachers, peers and whānau can be immensely helpful in creating and maintaining Māori language norms. Being clear about our goals is also important. Above all, language learning is a lifelong process. Being prepared for the long game will help us to sustain the motivation to keep learning and keep reaching for higher levels of proficiency.

*Questions to wānanga*

1. What are some independent learning activities that you have enjoyed? Are there other independent activities that you will try? Select some that you feel will be useful for you.

2. Have you tried to understand how your body responds when you think about a stressful life event? What activities might help to bring your body into a state of mauri tau when you experience a challenging thought or learning situation?

3. What makes you feel in control of your learning?

4. What makes learning enjoyable for you?

5. Have you enrolled in a language course before? If so, what was enjoyable about it? What aspects of the teacher–learner relationship did you enjoy? How were you encouraged to get together with peers?

6. How much time are you able to put aside regularly to focus on developing a language skill, including reading, writing, listening and/or speaking?

7. What rewards will you offer yourself if you meet your learning goals?

# 3. Benefits of ancestral language learning

The benefits of ancestral language learning are now well recognised globally. Te reo is a means of communicating with those who are living users of our reo tūpuna; it also provides us, as tangata whenua, with glimpses into the lives of our ancestors, showing us how they interpreted the world. For those who come to learn our ancestral language outside of the home, learning te reo Māori provides a platform to explore identity and personal whānau histories that are intertwined with our language.

When we begin the long journey of learning our reo tūpuna, we need hope, inspiration, and stories to aspire to. In this chapter, we will hear from Māori language learners who have begun the process of reclaiming their reo tūpuna. We will hear why they started their journey and how they persisted. This chapter also focuses on the unique ways in which te reo Māori connects us, as tangata whenua, to the beauty of our whakapapa relationships.

Te reo allows us to communicate, but it also gives us tools to connect more deeply. This is one of the gifts that it gives to us as its people. In our research for Te Manawa Ū ki te Reo Māori, we found that tūhonohono, the ability to connect, was a central motivation for

Māori language learners. A sense of connection was also why learners persisted when struggling. Unlike learning a first language, the process of learning a second language, particularly one with a heritage connection, is intentional.

The ability of te reo to connect and ground us ā-wairua was just one reason why Māori wanted to learn te reo. Some other reasons that participants shared were:

- the ability of te reo to express cultural meaning in ways not available in English;
- the inherent beauty of te reo;
- gaining a view into the worlds of our tūpuna;
- understanding mātauranga Māori through the lens of te reo Māori;
- healing of transgenerational trauma;
- reclamation of Māori identity;
- self-reclamation, or a collective sense of self.

Identity exploration in Māori language-learning contexts can also lead to conversations about language loss within whānau. For many Māori, the personal impacts of colonisation on whānau are brought to the forefront during their learning. This can be incredibly difficult to overcome, which is one reason Māori might make multiple attempts to reach intermediate or advanced proficiency in te reo. Māori language learning affords us opportunities to unpack traumas that have been enacted upon us through intentionally harmful colonial processes.

In Pākehā-dominant spaces, Māori experiences of discrimination and racism can be relentless. Māori can find reprieve in environments that are supportive of Māori language and culture; the relationships that tangata whenua develop with te reo itself can also provide solace.

*Expressing cultural meaning not available in English*
Learning te reo Māori gives us access to ways of knowing that are aligned with the culture of tangata whenua. It shows us a uniquely Māori way of viewing the world, including the interconnections

between our physical and spiritual worlds. This point was made by one of our research participants.

**Tihou:** I think, it's just in the way that, so when I think about reo, I see it as a way that the world was seen in a very holistic type of way. (Hokitika, 30–34)

Māori who had reached a high level of proficiency also indicated that they enjoyed the ways in which te reo helped them to release emotions. Both receptive and productive Māori language activities helped them to find a state of mauri tau during times of distress. Having the words to articulate emotions helped, but hearing the language, particularly through waiata or karakia, allowed individuals to connect more deeply with their emotional states.

**Ana H.:** Āe, you know tata tonu tō māua wehetanga atu, māua ko tōku ex me kī [laughing], i au e rongo ana, whakarongo ana ki te waiata rā, kāre au i paku aha ki ngā kupu. I rongo ā-wairuatia, nā reira i tangi pai au i taua wā. Kāre au i te mārama he aha te take, oh kei te pōuri noa iho, engari tētahi rā i whakaaro me noho ki te whakarongo ki ngā kupu. Nā tēnā i rongo, āe, nō reira e hono ki ngā wairua. Ko tēnā ko te reo Māori.

———

**Ana H.:** Yes, just after we broke up, my ex and I, when I heard or listened to that song, I wasn't really paying attention to the words. I felt a wairua connection, which at that time, made me cry deeply. I am not sure why, I was sad for sure, but one day, I decided that I should pay attention to the words of the song. From that action, I felt it, yeah, I felt a wairua connection. That's the power of te reo. (Taitokerau, 50–54)

In this instance, Ana H. describes how hearing waiata helped to alleviate her feelings of intense sadness during a relationship separation. The ability to hear her ancestral language in combination with music helped her to grieve.

Often, first language speakers of te reo Māori, or highly competent speakers, preferred to use te reo to communicate their emotions during times of distress. Speakers of te reo also discussed how arguments could be less direct or verbally aggressive in te reo than in English. Te reo allowed them to discuss the true, underlying issues during times of conflict, without escalating a disagreement by using certain phrases or swear words that are used in English but not te reo Māori.

> **Kōtuku:** I feel like if I am ever angry at someone, I will speak in te reo Māori to them. It's the only way I can get all my feelings out. If I speak in English, it's just like nothing, but if I'm speaking in Māori if I am sad, angry or happy, it is always in te reo Māori. That is the only way. And when I'm like, i te wā, e pōuri ana, I will most probably speak Māori and that is when it is more healing for me.
>
> **Ana H.:** The way it is, the meaning behind the kupu and everything, yeah.
>
> **Kōtuku:** Everything just comes out.
>
> **Ana H.:** Even with anger, when I'm angry or when I was, like, having an argument with someone, speaking in te reo Māori is nice because it kind of defuses some the words that aren't actually necessary, like that are just hateful words, you just get the wairua of them, the essence of the kōrero not those [unkind words] that just make it awful.
>
> **Kōtuku:** Yeah, that is so true.
>
> **Ana H.:** We don't really have swear words, doesn't that just go to show how beautiful our language is, [laughter] like, you know?
>
> (Te Papaioea, 20–24)

There are many ways in which te reo Māori allows Māori to express emotion, and fluency gives us freedom to express ourselves within culturally guided parameters. Its beauty is in its unique ability to hold our world views.

## The inherent beauty of te reo Māori

The kōrero that was shared across our kaikōrero indicated that the beauty of te reo Māori underpinned a desire to learn and speak it. Learners who perceived te reo Māori as beautiful in and of itself were encouraged to learn more vocabulary, phrasing, kīwaha and whakataukī. Hearing te reo spoken aloud was important for those at all stages of proficiency; it helped them to register its beauty and power. Even if learners were not sure what was being said, they were able to appreciate the sounds, rhythm and intonation as distinct from English and other languages. Those with higher levels of proficiency, who also appreciated the beauty of te reo, were encouraged to extend their language skills based on a desire to sound more native.

> **Tihou:** When I think about the beauty, I think it's learning about a way to see the world. For me, that's what I love about it. It is not necessarily about kaikōrero or something in particular, all of them are beautiful to me. Even just like normal te reo, te reo ōpaki. Pai ki au aua momo kīwaha me ērā. It's on all levels, so it's more about the different way of seeing the world [. . .] you have to really try hard to see the world that way in English, I think.

When asked whether the motivation to learn and speak te reo Māori was due to the struggles associated with te reo Māori revitalisation or to the intrinsic beauty of te reo, Tihou responded:

> **Tihou:** I would say probably the bigger driver for me that sustains me more is the beauty than the fight. I think the fight is more, *I have to do this* as opposed to *I want to do this*. (Hokitika, 30–34)

This demonstrates that two forces are at play for Māori language learners. One is based on the pressures of learning an Indigenous language that has few speakers, and the other is based on the enjoyment of learning. In addition to the inherent beauty of te reo

Māori, individuals spoke about being able to convey meaning more accurately in te reo, particularly in situations of cultural significance, such as when expressing grief or gratitude.

> **Te Reimana:** I feel like te reo is more powerful than English. Or it has more, it's just got a [. . .] more meaningful message when you mihi back in te reo rather than just saying thanks in English. [. . .] It carries a different sort of weight in the kōrero that you speak. (Ōtepoti, 20–24)

Wanting to pay appropriate respects in a reo Māori-dominant context was a motivation for some individuals to learn, particularly pre-learners and those at introductory levels. In a way, although performative tasks such as conducting mihi did not happen regularly in daily life, these events still stood out to learners and stayed in their minds as a motivation for the future.

Supporting the points Te Reimana makes, Tā Hirini Moko Mead (1997) writes:

> Apart from a difference in style [from Pākehā gatherings], a different range of skills is required at Māori gatherings. Oratory is a field where there is a certain amount of competitiveness in the dramatic performance or in the ability of the orator to turn a neat phrase. The highly skilled orator is admired and loved because he adds quality to the event. Likewise, people who can sing waiata with beauty and artistry add depth to the occasion, thus contributing to the ecstasy which some people experience at a hui. (90)

Irrespective of language ability, Māori who attend hui Māori are likely to feel the 'ecstasy' associated with skilled oratory, which may contribute to a desire to participate more fully by learning te reo.

Below, Te Rangihau makes a few points not previously covered in this book, which include the role of the divine.

**Te Rangihau:** He uaua te ako i te reo mehemea kāore te tauira i te tino hiahia ki te ako. Engari ki te manako ā-wairua te tangata ki te reo, kāore e roa ka mau. Hei tauira, i au e taitamariki ana kāore ahau i tino whakaaro nui ki tō tātou reo [. . .]. Engari ka pakeke haere ahau ka oho ake taku wairua ki nga tini āhuatanga rerekē o te ao. Kātahi ka tīmata taku whakaaro nui ki tō tātou reo hei oranga mōku. Mai i terā wā ki nāianei kei te puta tonu ngā tini manaakitanga ki runga i ahau me taku whānau. Pēnei i taku mahi mō taku iwi o Hineuru. Ko tō tātou reo kei te kawe i ahau. I mua hoki, i mahi ahau mō Te Karere me Wakahuia, ko tō tātou reo anō te tikanga. [. . .] Nā te Atua tēnei manaakitanga nui i ūhia ki runga i a tātou hei oranga.

———

**Te Rangihau:** It's difficult to learn if the student doesn't really want to learn. But if a person has a spiritual yearning for the language, it will be a more direct process to proficiency. For instance, as a child, I didn't really give much thought to te reo. However, as time progressed, my wairua was awakened to the different attributes of the world. I then started to focus on te reo as a part of my own wellness. From that point till now, my whānau and I have received multiple blessings. For instance, the work that I do with my iwi Ngāti Hineuru. My language helps support me [in this role]. Prior to that role, I worked for Te Karere and Wakahuia, again, te reo was the reason. It's a gift from God for our wellbeing. (Ahuriri, 55–59)

Te Rangihau indicates that a person needs to want to speak te reo Māori, and that there are ways to transition from having few aspirations as a language speaker to making te reo a prominent feature of one's life. Te Rangihau includes his relationship with God as a means of interpreting why we should appreciate te reo.

Individuals also spoke about the connection between language and ways of knowing our surroundings. Learning te reo Māori opened conversations about cultural norms and tikanga that are specific to Māori ways of being and knowing.

**Adam:** [Learning te reo Māori] was probably just to find out a bit more about myself. To speak another language. I think in New Zealand, lots of, I mean, you know, it opens your eyes up to a lot of different things. It's not just being able to say 'hi' and 'bye' in another language. There's the whole, you know with te reo Māori, you have tikanga, kawa, all the different principles that come with it. I think it opens your mind to a lot of possibilities. (Te Whanganui-a-Tara, 26–30)

A deeper understanding of te reo helped speakers to understand cultural practices. Some learners were able to explore and better appreciate the underlying principles of such practices.

**Rerewha:** I think knowing te reo Māori and understanding the context of a Māori worldview to an in-depth level, for me, makes me understand why we do what we do and also helps to kind of motivate, in terms of doing all those things like manaakitanga, and understanding that it is way beyond the simple things like, if you are a translator too, hospitality. (Ahuriri, 20–24)

For fluent speakers, te reo Māori was fully integrated into most elements of daily life. Many individuals made the point that te reo Māori is the 'waka' or medium by which other cultural ways of knowing can be fully understood.

**Tai:** Reo Māori, it's not just reo Māori, it's not just the language but it's like the waka that carries the mātauranga of te ao Māori, everything from whakapapa to [. . .] anything you can think of in ao Māori is on this waka and this waka is te reo and we're all connected to it and it is part of our oranga and our wellbeing and I would say if you're really passionate about te reo you are connected. If you walked into my office and I'm sure I'm not the only one, everything in there is like [. . .] in every nook and cranny is something to do with te reo not just books but pieces of paper, photos it's just all over the place and I would not be happy if I didn't have that you know. The reo is what has given me so much in my life that it's a part of me. (Waikato, 56–60)

Due to the processes of colonisation, our ability to wānanga together has been diminished. Learners of te reo tended to spend time learning through wānanga about tikanga and their underlying principles. Te reo speakers in this study affirmed that learning te reo Māori demystified cultural practices.

> **Kristina:** The reo is the waka, it's like the thing that you know. You can sing the waiata and you can do the haka and you can go to the things and do the pōwhiri and it's all foggy and you don't understand what's going on and you just go, 'Huh?' But then when you have the reo and everything is like super clear and you know why. It gives so much clarity about [. . .] not just the situation, but about like who you are as a person. (Waikato, 26–30)

Uncovering cultural practices and histories also gave Māori the space to contemplate the connections between their lives, language and culture, which helped some individuals to gain clarity around their identity.

### Connecting and grounding in te reo

One idea that often arose during discussions was that te reo Māori filled a part that had been 'missing'. The term 'missing' is in quotation marks because it is clear that many Māori who are non-Māori-speaking are not living in a constant or even partial state of deficit, or of feeling that they are lacking due to not being proficient in te reo Māori. However, some Māori who were interviewed were clear that they felt a sense of 'missingness'. As they began learning te reo Māori, they were encouraged to learn about other parts of themselves and their whakapapa, including living whānau and histories. In Māori values-centred spaces, the collective self is often prioritised, so learners were given the opportunity to contemplate their identity, sense of belonging, and connectedness in Māori language-learning environments.

**Ana H.**: Āe, pērā i [tōku tuakana], i rongo au i te umm, e ngaro ana tētahi mea i roto i ahau, nō reira koirā te take i tīmata ki te ako i te reo, ahakoa i te kura waenga, pakupaku noa iho te reo i ako mātou, me kī, ko ngā waiata, koinā noa iho.

———

**Ana H.**: Yes, similar to my older sister, I felt um, something was missing within me, so that was the reason why I started learning, despite at intermediate, we had very little exposure, for instance, there were merely a few songs. (Taitokerau, 50–54)

In addition to Ana H.'s point, Whaitiri considers why she and other tangata whenua might be drawn to learning te reo.

**Whaitiri:** You will always feel like there's something missing, I feel like that's how Indigenous people are, we just need to be connected to something. [. . .] Maybe, as Indigenous people or as Māori, we need that physical homing [. . .] we need to be grounded somewhere, and so when we are like, not grounded as Māori . . . You might just want to [have] that sense of belonging and maybe that would be a drive for someone who would want to learn their language, I guess. Just because that is all a part of it. (Waikato, 20–24)

The words 'homing' and 'grounded' are notable when thinking about the context of this interview with Whaitiri. It took place at our marae at Mangatoatoa in Kihikihi, during a wānanga where we travelled to various places of tribal significance. Like other iwi, our people suffered from the impacts of land confiscations. When tangata whenua are made landless, the need to find something that connects us back to our home is intensified, which perhaps contributes to the yearning for connection that some reo Māori learners feel.

*Transgenerational trauma and Māori language acquisition*

Within Māori language-learning settings, there is room to reimagine narratives in ways that uphold the strengths of our people and our histories. Part of the colonial process of dispossession is to define and redefine history to suit a European narrative, as the late Moana Jackson (2020) writes:

> Although in the simplest sense colonisation is the violent denial of the right of Indigenous peoples to continue governing themselves in their own lands, the colonisers have told stories that redefine its causes and costs. The fact that colonisation necessarily involved the brutal taking of Indigenous peoples' lands and lives has also been reframed and justified in stories that range from pseudo-scientific and legal rationalisations to blatantly racist presumptions. (133–134)

The Waitangi Tribunal reports provide numerous examples of trauma due to state-imposed violence. At the core of the cultural identity of a people is language, and pressures to assimilate Māori into a Pākehā-dominant society have been at the base of Māori language loss. New Zealand's colonial government aimed to strip Māori of our cultural uniqueness as tangata whenua. At a global level, imperialist forces have understood the devastation that language loss has on Indigenous peoples, which was why stripping te reo from the mouths of tangata whenua was a specific aim of successive New Zealand governments.

Assimilation-based education policies saw the introduction of physically violent methods to prevent the use of te reo Māori in schools (Waitangi Tribunal, 1986). Tangata whenua hold memories of the state-sanctioned abuses of children who spoke te reo in the classroom, which had a range of impacts, including parents' and caregivers' decisions to use English in the home as a means of protecting their children from the physical and psychological harm they might experience at school.

This harm has become part of our narrative. Whether voiced or silenced, it is always present. Yet, despite this history, many Māori learners of te reo shift the blame of language loss away from colonisation. In many instances, they view their state of being a non-speaker as an individual behaviour – a state that has arisen by personal choice – rather than a part of a wider historical context. When we are given time and resources to re-examine and redefine our narratives of language loss, we can shift these poorly framed narratives, which can help us to heal.

It is worth examining what this healing process involves. Sir Mason Durie (2001) provides a distinction between healing and treatment:

> Treatment is an activity designed to alleviate or remove particular symptoms or signs of ill health. [. . .] Treatment may be directed only at symptoms (for example a headache, painful movements, depressed mood) or it might be aimed at the underlying illness that has led to the symptoms. (155)

It is my understanding that trauma may be the 'underlying illness' that leads to an array of symptoms for Māori who are learning their ancestral language. These symptoms might include a desire to withdraw from painful memories, which might manifest as absences from formal Māori language classes. If memories associated with language loss are repeatedly coming up, this puts immense pressure on the learner as they try to perform language-learning tasks.

In an Indigenous language-learning context, individuals must actively engage in the process of healing. Durie (2001) indicates that healing 'demands a personal response. Even when mediated by an external agent such as a healer, the emphasis is on the person's own capacities and strengths, and their underlying beliefs and relationships.' For Durie, the term 'healing' describes 'particular restorative processes as well as holistic transformations involving the whole person. [. . .] healing is also used in a wider sense to mean the restoration of spirit or the attainment of emotional balance, especially after a period of despair or dysfunction' (155).

While it is important not to pathologise the processes that tangata whenua go through as they learn te reo, it's worth acknowledging the many resources we must draw upon to progress. Returning to Durie's assertions, language learning can help us to unblock difficult emotions that have persisted after historical language loss. We can see this loss in itself as 'a period of despair of dysfunction'. What language learning is not able to address, however, is the full cycle of harm that has diminished our full expression of rangatiratanga. Fully healing requires returning to a state of being where we can operate under our own systems of self-determination. At a minimum, this requires the return of our ancestral lands to kaitiaki and the ability of tangata whenua to assert our rangatiratanga without restraints from colonial systems of power, as agreed in Te Tiriti o Waitangi.

In our study, older participants recalled hearing elders speaking te reo Māori among themselves, as it remained their first and natural language of communication with one another. Many whānau were able to retain the use of te reo Māori in private domains, such as at home. Māori parents also made decisions to send their children to Māori boarding schools with hopes for a brighter economic future.

**Raewyn:** Yes, I heard [te reo] spoken from the time I was a baby. See I was brought up with my grandparents back in Te Araroa. Then my aunties and uncles, when they came over home that was all we heard, that's all I heard was the reo, it was beautiful really, but then they would speak to me in English and Dad told us, he said when he was at school they got strapped. When we went to Matakana our kaumātua took us to the native school there where Papa went to school, āe. So Dad knows what it's like. So Dad [. . .] was taken from the islands by his aunt and he was taken up to St. Stephens and Mum was an old Queen Vic girl. But the reo was when whānau came and, in particular, when our grandfather came, that's all that was spoken in the whare. (Tauranga, 65–69)

Some participants over 50 spoke about times when they first became aware of the colonisation of Aotearoa. The anger and grief that followed led to a stronger desire to learn te reo Māori.

**Koko:** I taua wā, kāre au i te tino mōhio nā te aha i pērā ai, engari i te wā i whakapā atu ki taua hotaka pūmamao, oh, patu te riri ki au mō ngā mahi ki ngā tūpuna, ki a mātou te Māori, nō reira, i āta whakaaro ahau, me pēhea, me haere ki te [katakata] wepua ngā mea rānei whakahōhā i a rātou pea. Koirā te take i whakaaro, 'Oh me haere au ki te ako i te reo, me pēhea te whakaako hoki.' Kātahi ka hoki ki te kāinga, he momo raru tērā ki te kāwanatanga.

———

**Koko:** At that time, I didn't really know why things were like that, however when I engaged with the pūmamao programme, I experienced rage at knowing what had been done to our ancestors, to us as Māori, therefore I thought deeply about how I should respond, or what I should do. Should I retaliate [laughs], or disrupt them. That was the rationale behind the idea, 'Oh I should go and learn te reo, and perhaps also teach.' Then I returned home, there were troubles with the government. (Taitokerau, 55–59)

Koko and Ana H. are sisters. Their shared experiences demonstrate that cultural and linguistic growth can occur in response to learning about the atrocities of colonisation.

**Ana H.:** Āe ngātahi. I kite au, i tīmata au ki te ako i te reo, engari i te tau whaimuri atu i haere au ki te pūmamao, kātahi ka tino whai au i te reo [katakata] me ngā tikanga.

———

**Ana H.:** Yes together. I saw when I started learning te reo, but beforehand, I'd been to the pūmamao programme, and that's when I really decided to get into learning te reo. (Taitokerau, 50–54)

The sisters attended a programme called Pūmamao, led by Dr Ruakere Hond. In this supportive learning environment, tauira were able to unpack the harms of colonisation. Part of their desire to learn te reo Māori arose due to a politically informed decision to reject assimilationist ideals entrenched in colonial design. In this respect, learning and speaking te reo affirms one's identity as Māori. It is a rejection of colonisation and the racist policies that were designed to remove our cultural integrity through language eradication.

With the same focus group as Koko and Ana H., we spoke about historical language trauma. Reo Māori teachers and facilitators of language learning allow classes to be a safe space for discussions of such trauma.

> **Kīngi Rākete-Tāne:** Wētahi tāngata, ahakoa te aha ka kawea tonu e rātou ērā āhuaranga ahakoa te aha. Tētahi kuia i roto i taku karaehe ka tīmata ia ki te kōrero mō ōna mātua i a rātou i te kura, kātahi ka tangi ia i roto i wā mātou akomanga, kua riro te wairua o te ako i te reo. Ki au nei, nā reira, ko te mea kē pea, me pēhea tātou e manaaki i tērā taha, ka mutu, me pēhea tātou e anga whakamua tonu ai.
>
> ———
>
> **Kīngi Rākete-Tāne:** Some people, irrespective of circumstance, they will still hold on to those challenges no matter what. One kuia in my class, she started to discuss her parents and their experiences at school, then she began to cry while we were in class. The feeling of the class was diverted from learning te reo. To me, perhaps what we need to consider is how do we act with compassion towards these issues while also moving forward? (Taitokerau, 18–23)

In some cases, older students are learning their ancestral language from younger, proficient Māori speakers who have learned te reo Māori through Māori medium education. These teachers may find themselves facilitating the emotional processes of older students. In the excerpt above, Kīngi relates how whenever the kuia in his class spoke about her father's treatment in school, she would begin to cry. The trauma that she carried affected her learning, and affected others in the class as they considered their own trauma. Kīngi also points out that it can be difficult to carry on teaching when people in the class are having an emotional response. What these excerpts demonstrate is that Māori language teachers and learners are managing many complexities in their classrooms. It requires manaakitanga and immense skill on the part of the teacher to hold the emotions of the class safely.

In these classes, kaiako and tauira can develop strong relationships due to the emotional content of the lessons. When the conditions are right (including a manageable staff-to-student ratio), kaiako can sometimes offer the support that tauira need to heal so that they can learn their ancestral language. However, not all classrooms are designed to address trauma in this way. For instance, in my own introductory reo Māori classes, unprecedented numbers of students (both Māori and non-Māori) have wanted to enrol in the past three to four years; we now consistently have over 200 students in one class. Classes of this size are normal across many disciplines in university settings. The high student numbers in university courses perhaps reflects a non-Indigenous belief about the acquisition of new knowledge. When the focus is on the task at hand (acquiring a language for the sake of learning a second language), rather than on the relationship that the student develops with the teacher, or in some instances their peers, the high student numbers are perhaps less of an issue.

However, in Māori language-learning contexts, high class numbers can come at a cost to the learning experience, depending on how a student learns and what they are hoping to receive from language learning. The size of the group impacts how likely it is that personal matters are shared. The safety of those sharing traumatic experiences is likely to dramatically decrease when the relationships in the classroom are not 'high trust'. Furthermore, the balance of Māori to non-Māori students in some of these classes is beginning to tip in favour of non-Māori students at the beginner level. Therefore, the time afforded to

Māori students must be strategically prioritised by educators in these settings. Prioritising small class numbers to allow for more high-trust relationships to develop in te reo Māori classrooms is also something that we need to work towards.

## Māori identities and motivations to learn te reo Māori

Māori identities continue to evolve based on our social and environmental circumstances. Because of our shared histories of colonisation, the access that tangata whenua have had to Māori culture and language varies considerably. With less than one in five Māori able to speak te reo Māori (Statistics New Zealand, 2013), we cannot assume that te reo is readily available to all Māori. One of our current challenges is that many Māori want to speak te reo but for a variety of complex reasons have not been able to.

It is important to recognise the other ways in which Māori can feel grounded in their Māori identity without knowledge of te reo. Māori can make sense of their identities as Māori in many ways. However, tangata whenua who view their Māori identity as connected to their ability to speak te reo are likely to be motivated to learn. Māori identity is a strong driver for learning te reo, from pre-engagement through to fluency.

The term 'Māoritanga' is sometimes used to describe Māori identity (Walker, 1989). It includes racial identity (such as skin colour or other physical features), te reo, whakapapa Māori and wairua-based belief systems. Sir Hirini Moko Mead (2003) states that values including manaakitanga, whanaungatanga (interconnectedness), and connection to whenua are all intrinsic to Māori identity. Mead argues that we are only ourselves in relation to these values, our tohu whenua (landmarks), and our tūpuna. He describes the term 'tuakiri' as having two parts: 'tua' referring to those external to the self, and 'kiri' as the skin of the individual. The role of interconnectedness is well recognised by Māori authors who reify our relationships with our environment, tūpuna and whānau (Mikaere, 2010). These theorists indicate that there is an 'other' component to Māori cultural identity. In this respect, others need to agree to the identity of an individual in order for a person to feel validated in their identity claim (see McIntosh, 2005). It is not enough for a person to claim an identity as Māori; they must also have a taituarā, or backing from their cultural group, for their claim to feel acknowledged and accepted.

Participants in our study highlighted that, as tangata whenua, even when it is not obvious that a person consciously acknowledges the connection between identity and language, that connection is implicit. Connections between identity and language were felt across participants, including older and younger individuals of varying genders. Ana H.'s and Anahera's comments highlight some of the ways in which connections were expressed.

> **Ana H.:** I feel like [te reo] connects you to your culture. Even my brother, who like never expresses any emotions or anything, like . . . 'Fuck off . . . nah.' He's younger than me, but we ended up drinking and I ended up ranting on about te reo Māori, and even he was like to my other cousins who grew up in South Auckland, he was like, 'Honestly beh, you learn your language it connects you to your culture, your sense of belonging and your identity,' and it does, it really does. (Te Papaioea, 20–24)
> **Anahera:** I cannot stress enough that even though I have grown up around, um, around-ish, you know, my marae and our family whenua. And even though, we lived in lots of places, but we would return there regularly. Um, I always felt a little bit less, you know, a little bit undeveloped, a little bit something wrong. And that was, of course, amplified by the fact that I was pale, so being able to, um, learn te reo Māori . . . [drifts into another discussion] (Te Whanganui-a-Tara, 45–49)

As Anahera's comment emphasises, many things can contribute to someone's feeling that they have a right to claim their Māori identity. While Anahera says that she had access to Māori-dominant environments, including her marae and whenua tūpuna, learning te reo affirmed her Māori identity.

Judy's ability to speak te reo Māori was perhaps less of a concern to her in her younger years, as she was surrounded by first language speakers. It was not until she was older that she developed a heightened awareness of the connection between te reo Māori and her identity. Her ability in te reo subsequently provided her with employment opportunities and helped her to grow mentally, emotionally and spiritually.

> **Judy:** Me pēnei pea taku kōrero, ko tōku reo, ko au, ko au, ko tōku reo. Ko ia taku oranga, ko ia, tuatahi, ko ia te take e whai mahi ana ahau i ēnei rā, tuarua, mōhio pai au ki te kore taku reo, mōhio au ka mate tētahi mea kei roto i au. Nō reira, kia ora tonu ai ahau ki roto i tēnei ao ā-hinengaro, ā-wairua, ā-tinana, ko te reo tērā ka whakaora i au. Yeah, koia taku ao.
>
> ———
>
> **Judy:** Perhaps what I'm saying is that I am my language, and my language is me. It's my sustanance, firstly, te reo is the reason that I have employment these days, secondly, I fully recognise that if I didn't have my reo, something would die within me. Therefore, if I am to live in this world with all of my faculties, mentally, spiritually, and physically, it's te reo that gives me life. Yeah, it's my world.
> (Rotorua, 45–49)

Other participants reported that learning te reo gave them confidence in their Māori identity. The cultural self was made meaningful through the relationships that some Māori had with those who were affirming of their culture and language. Furthermore, individuals spoke of knowing that they were categorically Māori but that learning te reo helped them to explore this identity further.

**Corban:** I suppose, gaining a bit of confidence in terms of my identity and who I am, where I come from, on a personal level. (Ōtautahi, 25–29)
**Adam:** What sort of fuelled my decisions, initially, was just because, you know, it was part of who I am, so I should embrace it, get involved, learn more about it. (Te Whanganui-a-Tara, 25–29)

Some participants who aspired to become fluent in te reo Māori said that gaining proficiency contributed to a sense of fulfilment. The concept of pride was not discussed in terms of an expression of whakahīhī, but more as a sense of ownership of their identity. Feelings of pride came through during interviews. Many tangata whenua in this study grew up experiencing racism, so feeling pride in their identity was a positive shift.

**Louise:** For me it is my true self, I feel. I wish I could speak te reo Māori all the time every day but I'm not there yet and I don't even know if Aotearoa is there yet, but when I can kōrero and be able to do that without having to think am I saying this right or first translate and then say it, if it just flows naturally then I will feel completed, there'll be a proud feeling. Yeah. (Tauranga, 35–39)

*Intersectional identities*
Our realities as Māori encompass the range of identities that we may occupy, including our cultural, ethnic, gender and sexual identities. Our identities as Māori are diverse, and our experiences as ancestral language learners reflect such diversity. African American civil rights activist and scholar Kimberlé Crenshaw coined the theory of intersectionality (Crenshaw, 1989). Intersectional identity theory helps us to understand the experiences of individuals and groups who hold multiple marginal identities concurrently. If we are trying to address issues that concern groups of society, it is important that the voices of those who are directly affected should have their voices amplified. Māori feminism has helped to identify the distinctive ways in which different parts of our Māori

societies experience the world (Awatere, 1984), which has helped to unpack some of the identity positions (Houkamau, 2010), challenges for equity in male-dominant spaces (Palmer & Masters, 2010), and political aspirations of Māori women.

This book focuses on the experiences of tangata whenua, as opposed to Māori language learners in a broader sense, because our experiences are specific to us as individuals who hold a whakapapa connection to the language. Our experiences, both positive and less so, are particular to us as tangata whenua. But they also vary: we are not homogenous, and intersectional identities occur within our cultural identity grouping. For instance, those who identify as Māori and LGBTQ+ hold a different set of identities and experiences as Māori language learners from those who identify as heterosexual and cisgender. People with intersectional identities have unique perspectives shaped by their experiences as members of diverse groups and by the discrimination they may have faced.

Learning te reo Māori can allow us to explore our identity positions, especially when we are in environments that are high trust.

> **Rangitāne:** I think, without getting really too deep about it, I think [the process of learning te reo is] really benefiting me holistically, and I know that's a, quite a, you know um . . . you know quite an obscure term to think about it. But it's, um, in terms of my own identity, not with just being Māori, but the whole [. . .] part of me. Because I'm also Pākehā, I'm also Takatāpui, I'm also many other things, but I think that te reo Māori has been one of the key elements of who I am. (Kirikiriroa, 40–45)

Hamley and colleagues (2021) indicate that whanaungatanga can act 'as an adaptive and evolving practice exemplified by takatāpui young people as they traverse new spaces, encounters and relationships' (17). Connecting these findings with Rangitāne's perspective above, it is possible that the whanaungatanga that tangata whenua experience in some Māori language learning spaces could also provide opportunities to explore diverse identities.

Intersectional identities extend to our bicultural ways of interacting. We often think of biculturalism as referring to people with both Māori and non-Māori ancestry. However, biculturalism also refers to individuals who live within two cultural paradigms. As individuals who have whakapapa Māori, we are often expected to participate in environments governed by Pākehā cultural norms, such as mainstream education systems, courts and hospitals; the list continues. In a study of rangatahi Māori, Arama Rata (2015) describes how te reo Māori has provided Māori speaking rangatahi with skills that allow them to traverse their bicultural lives. Rangatahi who were conversant in te reo Māori were more able to transition between linguistic environments that were Māori and environments where Pākehā norms were dominant. Below, Heremia talks about some of the tangible advantages of being bilingual in Aotearoa.

> **Heremia:** I mean you go back to that kōrero, 'What's good for Māori is good for everybody', and I definitely think there's a benefit for everyone learning and understanding te reo Māori. Um, not only is te reo mātāmua o te whenua nei, but in terms of just having that ability to, I guess, step away from yourself at times. I guess for some of our colonial partners, sometimes we can maintain only one line and that's all they can maintain, but because we live in both realms we easily transfer. And I guess that's been the great thing about this journey [. . .] not been submerged in te reo since I was, you know, not speaking the native tongue and then coming along and learning, I can converse quite easily in those two realms. It's a great thing to be able to do that, and I guess it's that point of view that you take from both sides. That's the benefit, or the fruit, I guess, from learning te teo Māori. (Ahuriri, 40–45)

Te reo gives individuals the tools to meaningfully participate in both Māori-dominant and Pākehā-dominant spaces, as Corban notes:

**Corban:** Koira tētahi o ngā tino hua kua puta i taku whai i te reo Māori. I can quite happily hold myself in a boardroom full of Pākehā that know absolutely nothing about things te reo, or things bicultural. And I can quite happily hang out in the kāuta at the marae. Or, you know, I'll get up and do a whaikōrero. It's something that, you know, I never really learned te reo for that. I suppose it's one of those kinds of benefits that pops up eventually. (Ōtautahi, 25–29)

Being able to speak te reo Māori fluently gave speakers unanticipated benefits, as Corban explains. Being able to operate in both spaces contributes to his Māori identity in the sense that having such skills allows him to converse with people in either cultural domain.

## Quantitative Study

The next section discusses the results from the quantitative survey data from the Manawa Ū study. The quantitative aspects of this study provide another way of interpreting motivations to learn te reo.

We asked learners of te reo Māori why they wanted to learn. They were given four set answers to select from (identity, or because it is a language used by whānau, friends or work colleagues) and the opportunity to give their own response at length. We found that most people in this study were motivated to learn te reo Māori because of its connection to their Māori identity, followed by a desire to communicate with significant others.

Of the 376 individuals who indicated that they were not competent speakers, 117 were currently studying te reo and 173 had studied in the past. Those who were not currently studying te reo and had not studied it in the past but intended to learn in the future numbered 86, while the remaining 16 stated that they had no plans to learn te reo Māori and had not learned in the past.

Fig. 5 shows the motivations of those who had begun learning te reo Māori compared with those who planned to. Notably, those who had not yet begun had fewer social groups, including friends and work colleagues, who spoke te reo. There was no statistical difference between the two groups (i.e., those who had studied te reo versus those who had not) and their exposure to te reo through whānau relationships.

The results may indicate that exposure and use of te reo Māori within social relationships external to the whānau may have an impact on a person's choice to either delay or actively engage in learning. Furthermore, those who do not have proficiency in te reo may overestimate the proficiency of others in their whānau.

We also asked participants who had attempted to learn te reo Māori but were not fluent to explain in their own words why they were motivated to learn. Although the survey included a specific question about identity, participants talked about the centrality of te reo in their connection to culture, indicating that they wanted to learn te reo 'to feel more connection to my taha Māori'.

Tangata whenua were passionate about intergenerational trans-mission and demonstrating the worth and value of te reo Māori to

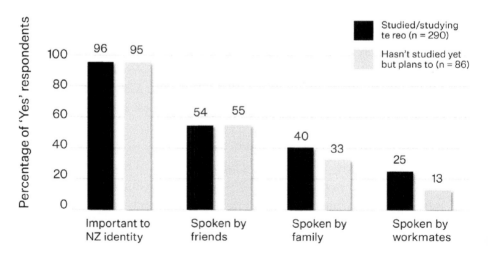

Fig. 5: Percentage of total respondents who shared motivations for learning te reo, comparing those who have engaged in study with those who have not but plan to

future generations. In other words, they wanted to pass their reo tūpuna on to their children or grandchildren. 'I want to show my tamaiti it is of value,' said one participant.

Motivations were also connected to career plans for some. This group saw te reo as important to their chosen occupation. 'It will be helpful in the field of work I want to get into,' one participant said; another shared that, as a teacher, knowing te reo would 'greatly help my ability to teach all students'.

Finally, individuals discussed learning and speaking te reo Māori as a means of decolonisation and of participating in the revitalisation or te reo. 'Te reo contains taonga in terms of world view, unique and enriching for not only Aotearoa, but for the world,' one participant said. 'I am keen to actively participate in te reo revival,' said another.

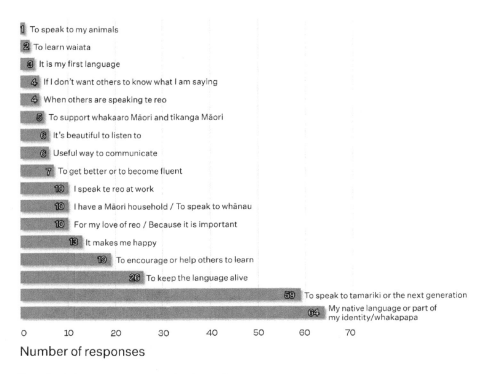

Number of responses

Fig. 6: Other motivations for learning te reo

Other motivations included seeing te reo as part of Aotearoa, observing the innate beauty of the language, wanting acceptance by other Māori, marae succession, wanting te reo in the home, being the sole non-reo speaking whānau member and wanting to change this, and wanting to speak more languages.

## Summary

The motivations for learning one's ancestral language are varied and overlapping. For instance, proficiency in te reo Māori is useful in contexts where it is the dominant language. Learners who perceive te reo Māori as beautiful may be motivated to engage with it in more complex ways. And learners may feel that they are better able to express emotion in te reo Māori – as described by participants in Manawa Ū ki te Reo Māori, who said that feelings of gratitude were easier to express in te reo Māori, particularly during hui Māori.

A desire for deeper connection with one's culture and identity was a common motivation for many tangata whenua. Through the process of learning te reo, tangata whenua found out more about their cultural selves, which was particularly healing for those who felt that a part of themselves had been missing. Knowing te reo Māori helped them to feel connected with their culture; for instance, in reo Māori contexts they were better able to understand cultural practices, which helped to reduce feelings of anxiety.

This chapter also touched on how learning te reo Māori can help us address inherited colonial trauma. Within this process, it is vital that tauira Māori are given safe spaces to explore their trauma. Knowing why we are invested in the process of language learning, and focusing on the potential benefits, can help bring us back on track when challenges arise. For some people in our study, learning about colonisation was a further incentive to learn their ancestral language. But this was not always the case: some tangata whenua are not well resourced or supported in their learning. We will explore the impacts of trauma in the next chapter.

This chapter also explored how te reo Māori interacts with the process of claiming an identity. Some saw their identity as Māori as being categorically tied to an ability to speak te reo – a belief that was more prominent among those with lower levels of proficiency.

Such beliefs are not particularly helpful, given that language learning is a challenging task for many. If a person feels they cannot claim their Māori identity because they cannot speak te reo Māori, they will likely feel marginalised. More proficient individuals were less likely to agree that speaking te reo equates to group membership, which suggests that such beliefs become less common as we become more familiar with te reo.

Tangata whenua have other reasons for learning te reo, such as a desire to support intergenerational transmission or to support career goals. We'll explore te reo Māori and employment, and te reo Māori and whānau, in later chapters.

*Questions to wānanga*

1. Why are you learning, or about to try to learn, your ancestral language?
2. How might learning te reo Māori change your world view?
3. What are some possible benefits of becoming a language speaker?
4. Who are some Māori-speaking people you would like to converse with?
5. How might you be challenged during your language-learning journey?
6. What beliefs do you have about Māori identity?
7. What life experiences have informed the ways in which you think about Māori identities?
8. In the circles you occupy, what are some common ways in which people talk about Māori identities?
9. How do these beliefs benefit you and your language-learning journey?
10. How do these beliefs limit the extent to which you are comfortable in Māori language learning or speaking spaces?

# 4. Historical trauma and language acquisition

Understanding some of the struggles that tangata whenua may experience when learning te reo Māori requires an appreciation of historical, political and social contexts. As tangata whenua, we have made immense progress in retaining and reclaiming our ancestral language in the face of colonisation. This chapter does not seek to lay out all of the ways in which colonisation has impacted on te reo Māori, as multiple authors have compiled this evidence more thoroughly (see Ka'ai-Mahuta, 2011); instead this chapter seeks to highlight how colonisation plays out in our experiences of Māori language in contemporary contexts across contexts and generations.

Colonisation is underpinned by racist ideologies of white supremacy. Ngata, Rata, and Santos (2021) highlight how structural racism (including hate crimes) in present-day Aotearoa has historical underpinnings:

> [I]n Aotearoa, as a settler colonial state, the arrival of Europeans, the ill-treatment of Māori and the violation of Māori land rights was based upon racist notions that non-white and non-Christian rights of occupancy and security were lesser than those of Christian Europeans.

[. . .] Māori have been the longest standing victims of race-based offending in Aotearoa, in addition to the process of colonisation being erased as a race-based offence. (209)

The intentional erasure of colonisation from settler memories is a disservice (to say the least) to Indigenous peoples who have suffered directly from colonial violence.

During the 1800s, white supremacist ideologies contributed to colonists' misguided assertions that Māori people would 'die out' due to colonial pressures. In 1856 the politician Isaac Featherston stated:

The Maoris are dying out and nothing can save them. Our plain duty, as good compassionate colonists, is to smooth down their dying pillow. Then history will have nothing to reproach us with. (Sutherland & Buck, 1940, 28)

The scientist Alfred Newman promoted similar beliefs in 1881:

Taking all things into consideration, the disappearance of the race is scarcely a subject for much regret. They are dying out in a quick easy way and are being supplanted by a superior race. (Sutherland & Buck, 1940, 28)

These sentiments politely reference the genocide of tangata whenua by colonialists, and while they were expressed in the 1800s, the racist ideologies that underpin them have been carried through to the present-day realities of tangata whenua (Jackson, 2020).

Our contemporary experiences of language loss can be examined within a wider system of colonial oppression, characterised by continuous, state-sanctioned violence towards Indigenous peoples over generations (Waitangi Tribunal, 1986). Intergenerational trauma that occurs as a result of colonial harm has been described as a 'soul wound' (Duran, 2019; Menakem, 2021). When one is learning one's ancestral language, these soul wounds can be accessed when least expected, with an emotional response. Historical violence that Indigenous peoples have experienced can also be understood as inherited trauma, in that the trauma that has been experienced by tūpuna in previous generations is transferred to those in their whakapapa line. This inherited trauma is closely linked to experiences of language anxiety and whakamā. These experiences are explored in this chapter.

## Colonisation and language loss

The Kenyan Kikuyu academic Ngũgĩ wa Thiong'o wrote in *Decolonising the Mind* (1992):

> The physical violence of the battlefield was followed by the psychological violence of the classroom. But where the former was visibly brutal, the latter was visibly gentle. (9)

Some of the 'visibly gentle' ways in which colonisation has subjugated our ancestral language make it difficult to articulate how the process of language loss is occurring. While the scars of brutality during periods of colonial settlement were visible on the bodies of our tūpuna, the subsequent harm is far more insidious and enduring. Analysing the ways in which colonisation continues to precipitate language loss is necessary if we are to articulate our collective experiences and responses.

Discussions surrounding historical trauma as an explanation for current experiences of disenfranchisement are not always welcome within mainstream society. A narrative still often espoused by power holders in New Zealand society is the idea that colonisation and the violent dispossession of resources from tangata whenua was 'on balance' a good thing for Māori because it brought about colonial systems of democracy and literacy (Hogan, 2021, reporting the words of politician Paul Goldsmith). This narrative downplays the negative impacts of colonisation on tangata whenua and is part of the reason why colonisation remains a barrier to ancestral language learning for Māori. Prolific narratives that present colonisation as benign or even beneficial help to maintain systems of oppression in which colonisers and dominant group members benefit from the subjugation of Indigenous peoples.

Māori are commonly used as a political football, especially in the periods leading up to elections. In 2004, then leader of the New Zealand National Party Don Brash delivered a speech to the Orewa Rotary Club which centred on a 'perceived "threat" that the Treaty of Waitangi settlement process represented for the future of the country' (Poata-Smith, 2005, 228). This divisive speech used our rights as Treaty partners for political gain. After the Orewa Speech, the National Party saw a surge in voter support. The speech makes reference to the 'grievance industry' (Brash, 2004), phrasing which minimises colonial harm and its ongoing impacts. Terms like 'grievance mode', which became normalised in New Zealand English, incentivise the silencing of tangata whenua histories and relegate Treaty-based injustices to the past in an attempt to be seen as progressive, or future-facing. Trauma that stems from historical pain has present-day implications, particularly for ancestral language learners.

Given its pervasiveness, mainstream media is arguably one of the most prolific means by which inaccurate portrayals of Māori are disseminated and embedded in New Zealand society. Māori viewpoints are silenced, and when Māori are given time to make statements in news items, mainstream New Zealanders lack the contextual knowledge to understand the points being put across (Nairn et al., 2012) . In December 2020, Carmen Parahi, the Pou Tiaki editor at news media website *Stuff*, and about 50 *Stuff* staff put together 'Our Truth, Tā Mātou Pono', a months-long investigation into New Zealand's news coverage dating back to the mid-1800s. Following this investigation, *Stuff* published an article headlined 'No mātou te hē – We are sorry', a front-page apology to Māori for 163 years of racist portrayals. In an interview with Leonie Hayden (then editor of Ātea at *The Spinoff*), Parahi said:

All of these papers were established by settlers, for settlers. That whakapapa has continued right up until this point, and we have maintained that perspective of always protecting the interests of settlers, and now their mokopuna. (Hayden, 2020)

Unfortunately, but not unexpectedly, subsequent news items have continued along the same trajectory. Changing the ways in which Māori are portrayed requires a full-scale acknowledgement of their racist colonial derivatives, and an incentive to prioritise the humanity of Indigenous peoples over the profits that are made through the vilification of tangata whenua in clickbait items. News outlets appear unwilling to make such a shift despite their intentions.

Major research undertaken by Māori in the past few years has indicated that tangata whenua experiences of criminalisation can be directly linked to historical displacement. Research into why New Zealand criminalises Māori at staggeringly disproportionate rates to non-Māori was first explored over 30 years ago, in Moana Jackson's report *The Māori and the Criminal Justice System: A New Perspective: He Whaipaanga Hou* (1987), which noted that colonisation should be considered when understanding criminal offending by rangatahi Māori. An updated study by Moana Jackson, Anne Waapu and Ngawai McGregor, including interviews with over 2000 individuals nationally, is forthcoming. About the study Jackson said:

Currently, 51 percent of men in prison are Māori, and 64 percent of women in prison are Māori. These are shameful figures. Since this issue was first highlighted 30 years ago, little has changed.

According to the findings of *He Waka Roimata*, a review of the criminal justice system released by Te Uepū Hāpai i te Ora in 2019:

[T]he effects of colonisation undermine, disenfranchise and conspire to trap Māori in the criminal justice system and that racism is embedded in every part of it. [. . .] Many Māori described colonisation and its impact on them as an overwhelming trauma: a denial of voice, opportunity and potential on an intergenerational scale; a loss of rangatiratanga, mana and dignity; stolen identity; stolen culture and language; stolen land and dispossession; a loss of place; and, for many, disconnection from whakapapa. (3–9)

When the context of colonisation is not completely understood in society, the inequalities that are present in society can be wrongly perceived. The dominant group maintains power through utilising narratives that place the blame on Indigenous people's experiences of over-representation in negative social statistics. By tracing the linkages back to the colonial conditions in which such social issues were intentionally constructed, we can alleviate misleading notions that the dominant group are those being harmed, when in fact it is they who contribute to the harm of tangata whenua.

International and local research indicate that when an ethnic group, including Māori, is seen as a threat by dominant group members due to ingrained colonial narratives, members of this group are disproportionately targeted by police. The youth-led organisation JustSpeak (2020) writes:

[W]hen first encountering police, Māori who have had no prior contact with the justice system have a greater risk of a police proceeding and are more likely to be charged by Police, than Europeans. When someone is charged they are more likely to end up trapped in the justice system. Their chance of reoffending increases with negative outcomes for whānau and communities. (1)

In the context of crime and victimisation, a 2021 study indicated that Māori are victimised at a higher rate than any other ethnic group (Ministry of Justice, 2022). These findings are as relevant now as they were in 1987.

Māori who are incarcerated have also discussed challenges relating to the active suppression of te reo Māori in contemporary times within prisons. In a qualitative study of Māori experiences in prisons (Brittain & Tuffin, 2017), participants spoke about their expressions of Māori identity, including the use of te reo Māori, being prohibited. A participant named Mickey said:

> You're treated like shit in jail by Corrections. Like you can't sit, if you sit around a table and speak te reo Māori at a table, then straight away you're instigating something, or planning something, or plotting something. Um, it's real frowned upon to like, can't sing waiatas or, they won't let you do it, but you can sit in the wing and [. . .] turn your stereo up and listen to heavy metal. [. . .] But you can't sit around with a guitar and sing waiata, not even allowed to do hakas in the wing, not even allowed to do hakas in your cell, um, so it's shit. (102)

This study further highlights how the criminal justice system continues to perpetuate harm against Māori through subtle acts of violence, which has implications for Māori language use.

Contributing to the ongoing negative impacts of colonisation are the effects of racism. In 2021, *Whakatika: A Survey of Māori Experiences of Racism* was published (Smith, et al., 2021). Incorporating the views of over 2000 Māori, it indicated that racism was a daily experience for 93% of respondents. According to the report, positive changes include the teaching of New Zealand history in schools from 2023, which has the potential to increase general knowledge of colonisation and its ongoing impacts (Smith et al., 2021).

Internationally, anti-racism activist and academic Ibram X. Kendi (2019) points out that Africans with ancestors who were enslaved should not be defined by their traumatic experiences. Kendi and others such as Duran (2019) argue that diagnoses such as PTSD are limiting and do not adequately recognise the dynamism, entrepreneurial abilities and resilience of peoples who have suffered intergenerational, group-level trauma and adversities. Indigenous peoples who fight against colonisation are a product of more than our trauma. Our traumatic history does not define us, nor does it limit the potential for excellence that Māori exhibit in a diverse and ever-growing range of contexts.

This book acknowledges historical trauma and colonial harm not to focus on our limitations, but to contextualise our learning experiences. Dominant societal narratives, which distance the impacts of historical violence that led to loss of Indigenous resources and present-day disparities in wealth distribution, have prevented Māori from vocalising our trauma. This silencing does not benefit Māori, nor does it assist in restoring the relationships between Māori and Pākehā.

Education is a central means of silencing Māori histories and Pākehā histories of violent settlement. The term 'settler' is described by Annie Coombes (2006) as having 'a deceptively benign and domesticated ring which masks the violence of colonial encounters that produced and perpetrated consistently discriminatory and genocidal regimes against the indigenous people' (2). The national education curriculum has largely excluded Māori histories (Sheehan, 2010), and has only recently gained government attention that will see New Zealand history included in mainstream compulsory education. Outside formal compulsory education, news media has provided New Zealanders with information about how to perceive Māori and our collective intercultural relationships.

Historical trauma can also impact on interpersonal violence that occurs within whānau. In a study by Pihama, Cameron and Te Nana (2019), historical trauma was found to be a central catalyst for violence within whānau. Within this context, historical trauma is 'the collective trauma experienced through "massive and cataclysmic" historical events that have been perpetrated intentionally by one group of people upon another' (1). Studies into the historical trauma of Indigenous peoples can help us to understand the present-day impacts on our health and wellbeing, as well as the impacts on our attempts to learn and sustain our ancestral language. This research can provide us with new tools to help articulate the ways in which 'traumatic events endured by communities negatively impact on individual lives in ways that result in future problems for their descendants' (Kirmayer, Gone & Moses, 2014, 307).

Hartmann and Gone (2014) present what they see as the most influential components of psychological trauma and historical oppression in an American context. Some defining attributes of historical trauma can be understood through the notion of 'the Four Cs':

> *Colonial injury* to Indigenous people as a consequence of experiences with conquest, subjugation, and dispossession by European and Euro-American settlers is the basis of the concept;
> *Collective experience* of these injuries by entire Indigenous communities or collectivities whose identities, ideals, and social lives were impaired as a result is highlighted;
> *Cumulative effects* of these injuries from continued oppression that have accumulated or 'snowballed' over time through extended histories of harm by dominant settler-colonial society is accentuated; and
> *Cross-generational impacts* result from these injuries as they are transmitted to subsequent generations in unremitting fashion in the form of legacies of risk and vulnerability to BH [behavioural health] problems until healing has occurred. (275)

While the four Cs were designed for a Native American context, these ideas apply to other Indigenous peoples, including Māori.

Part of the process of colonisation is to strip Indigenous peoples of their cultural identity, and language is central to that process. As Ngũgĩ Wa Thiong'o (1992) wrote:

> Language carries culture, and culture carries, particularly through orature and literature, the entire body of values by which we come to perceive ourselves and our place in the world. How people perceive themselves affects how they look at their culture, at their politics and at the social production of wealth, at their relationship to nature and

to other beings. [. . .] The domination of a people's language by the languages of the colonising nations was crucial to the domination of the mental universe of the colonised. (16)

Along the same lines, reclaiming te reo Māori as our ancestral language is a deliberate act of decolonisation.

One of the challenges that tangata whenua sometimes face, having lost direct access to speakers of our language in many instances, is a feeling of distance towards our ancestral language. Developing a sense of rangatiratanga or agency about the relationships we can grow with our reo is part of the decolonising process.

At the most basic level, the layers of colonisation that we have resisted and continue to resist have caused many to feel that we are in some way 'othered' from our own ancestors, and from a language that our tūpuna helped to create over thousands of years. As people with a whakapapa connection to our reo, it should not be the case that we feel distanced from the language. Te reo Māori was spoken by our tūpuna, who are part of our DNA.

Language is deeply connected to the people that own it. As Māori we are dynamic, and have survived and in many ways thrive despite the harsh conditions that colonisation has created. Despite our resilience, the enduring trauma we have suffered can be felt at a molecular level. We do not often attend to these mamae, or soul wounds, at an individual level, because our trauma has become normalised by Pākehā, which should not be the case.

The impacts of inherited language trauma on generations of Indigenous ancestral language learners is still being explored, and there is room for more research. We know from our own lives that when we hear about our old people being beaten as children, being threatened or humiliated for speaking our language, our bodies feel mamae. The weight of those experiences resides within us. This is why it is necessary to address where that mamae resides, as explored in the teachings of Duran (2019) and Menakem (2021).

Epidemiology studies are beginning to explore the trauma that our DNA may hold from previous generations. In the future, it might be possible to see how trauma associated with ancestral language learning is stored in our genetic make-up. At the current time, we can assert that learning te reo Māori can draw learners into dialogues about past trauma that might have been unaddressed for generations.

The influential postgraduate lecturer Keri Lawson-Te Aho introduced to our Māori student cohort the idea that decolonisation can occur through the unpacking of historical narratives that are tied to colonial experiences. This is complex and challenging, but we can use historical narratives to make sense of contemporary dysfunction in whānau and communities. Lawson-Te Aho (2014) writes:

> With each generation, the source of the wounding becomes more difficult to see and name, creating a necessity for de-colonisation. [. . .] The sequel to reclaiming and using historical narratives for healing is using them to further self-determination. The pathway and means by which positive reconstructions precede or follow deconstructions of trauma histories is unknown except to those who are willing and courageous enough to look for them. (183–206)

Individuals need considerable strength and support as they attempt to work through historical narratives that involve trauma, including in the reconstruction process that follows.

Duran (2017) discusses the idea that Indigenous people can heal our past through our actions in the present – which has implications for future generations. The process is similar to whakaaro Māori around the non-linear reference to wā, time encompassing past, present and future. When working with clients who are reluctant to address inherited trauma, Duran sets the task of drawing a genealogical map which includes the client and multiple generations of their descendants. He then asks his client to select which descendant they will hand over their unaddressed trauma to. In this way, Duran personalises the impacts of trauma, helping people to understand that if a soul wound is not adequately addressed in their lifetime, it will continue to be an issue for future generations. In many ways, when we learn and speak te reo Māori we are making an active, courageous choice to heal ourselves, our descendants, and hopefully, in part, our tūpuna of their trauma relating to colonial violence.

While learning te reo Māori can be healing, it can also be emotionally challenging.

## How trauma disrupts intergenerational language transmission

Participants in Manawa Ū ki te Reo Māori spoke about colonial trauma and its ability to impact on the transmission of intergenerational language. Some participants had been unaware that a parent or grandparent was fluent in te reo Māori. The combination of abuse in state schools and mainstream New Zealand's dismissal of te reo Māori as 'irrelevant' left many of our elders speaking only English with their descendants.

> **Rangitāne:** I was whāngai-ed by my nana in those early years. Um, I, I didn't know she could speak te reo fluently until much later in life. She passed away, you know, a couple decades ago, and I was talking to my mum and somehow te reo Māori came up and she said, 'Yeah, your nana could speak te reo fluently.' I said, 'She *never* spoke around me'. Um and I, I wonder, but she's from that generation [. . .] there was value placed on, on the English language you know, 'cause English was access to jobs and access to, you know, opportunities. I don't know. She didn't talk to me about it but that's what I assume and, um, perhaps that's why she didn't expose me to te reo.

Participants with Māori-speaking parents indicated that the abuse their parents had suffered in compulsory education had a direct impact on intergenerational language use. Commonly, parents and grandparents would speak te reo Māori around their children and grandchildren but not directly with them. In some instances, grandparents would speak directly with their mokopuna as this was their first language, the language that the grandparent was most familiar with, therefore communications in te reo were less hindered by English.

> **Hoana:** Both my parents were fluent and he used to come to our house for kai and you, dads and his friend and that. One day, he spoke to me in Māori and I went, 'Eh?' So, my father raised an eyebrow, but they never, my parents, you are right, they didn't speak to us. My nanny did, but I didn't spend enough time with her, even though she was there. I would go, 'What did you say nan?' 'Dahdahdahdah [speaking te reo].' 'Eh?' 'Oh, dahdahdahdah.' And if my cousin lived with her she learnt quite a bit. The only time my parents spoke [. . .] that we got the gist of was when they were talking about us [laughter]. Or talking things that they didn't want us to know about. Yeah. That's how it was. And the fact that Dad said, 'Well you know, I used to get strapped, your mother used to get strapped, I don't want you kids to get strapped.' And then, so that was us and then my youngest siblings who were about 10–13 years younger, our parents spoke to them. They were so lucky! (Waikato, 65–75)

The health and wellbeing of kaumātua has been linked to their social connectedness, including 'the capacity to serve others, being valued and [. . .] having purpose and making a contribution' (Edwards, Theodore, Ratima & Reddy, 2018, 10). Edwards and colleagues note that 'the roles and responsibilities of older Māori often increase if they are speakers of te reo Māori, are holders of mātauranga Māori, and have a wealth of lived experience' (11). Challenges can arise when kaumātua who are holders of mātauranga with considerable lived experience are not speakers of te reo, as I discussed with Ramari Stewart of Ngāti Awa, a world-renowned tohunga tohorā and holder of a New Zealand Order of Merit.

After listening to Ramari interviewed by Qiane Matata-Sipu on the podcast *Nuku*, I was compelled to contact Ramari to discuss the points she raises about kaumātua who have experienced deep-seated trauma related to Māori language use. In addition to her unmatched mātauranga surrounding tohorā, whaea Ramari is a registered nurse who is able to draw upon her mātauranga from multiple spheres to contextualise some of the language trauma responses that present themselves in kaumātua who are not speakers of te reo.

> **Ramari:** I think it is important to understand the clinical manifestations of language trauma. There is a very real intense onset of physical symptoms that are associated with sudden periods of intense fear or a sense of losing control. People with panic disorders will actively prevent future attacks by avoiding places or situations they associate with panic attacks, hence the marae etc.

The physical manifestations of language trauma can result in both emotional and physical discomfort, so much so that a person may not participate in Māori cultural contexts due to fear of experiencing a panic attack. Ramari continued:

> Māori elders are sometimes provisionally diagnosed as having cardiovascular disease (CVD) due to the acute symptoms of chest pain and breathlessness and, also because they are Māori with a higher CVD risk factor.

What Ramari reiterates is that the cultural expectations placed on kaumātua who are not speakers of te reo but who understand some of the cultural expectations to be reo speakers in Māori cultural contexts, can result in anxiety disorders and/or withdrawal from such occasions due to the stress. Edwards and colleagues (2018) write:

> Being Māori and engaging with te ao Māori are elements of positive ageing that are culturally based and distinctive for Māori. Having a secure Māori cultural identity, including a sense of connection to one's

marae, hapū, and iwi have been described as features of Māori positive ageing. (10)

Challenges arise for our old people when they feel that their participation in these environments requires an ability to use te reo Māori when they do not possess such skills. Later in this chapter, Ramari discusses why it is important to have reo Māori speakers – who in many instances are from younger generations – walk alongside our kaumātua who have a wealth of mātauranga but not always the ability to converse in te reo.

Across age groups, individuals in the process of learning te reo Māori tended to feel guilt and shame about not knowing their ancestral language as adults. In a sense, what participants were describing was a feeling of disconnection between their struggles with learning and the language loss driven by colonisation. Learning about colonisation was deeply awakening and healing. It helped Māori to put their individual learning experience into the larger story of colonisation, understanding that their difficulties with te reo stemmed from deeper issues.

> **Ariana:** Through having those sorts of conversations, my reo has increased quite quickly. And also my understanding of its whakapapa and also my own anxieties and confidence as well has grown out of those conversations because . . .
>
> **Awanui:** Acknowledging the hurt, processing the emotions as you're learning?
>
> **Ariana:** Yes, yes, yeah, umm, and being able to know that, you know, just because when we talk about intergenerational trauma or historical trauma, that sounds like trauma, because we use that word, but it doesn't have to be a bad thing. It doesn't have to be a massive weight. Of course, it is, and I'm not denying that, but inside of those things, and how we move forward, you can also find [. . .] the only place to find true, full healing of the situation. (Te Whanganui-a-Tara, 25–35)

For Anahera, seeing the larger story of language loss was helping her to move forward in her learning.

**Anahera:** For me, it's Māori who I see leaving the class, not Pākehā. And so for me, [. . .] I believe there's a thing called language trauma, you know? And it's really distressing and frightening, and you feel so whakamā because you feel like it's somehow your fault that you haven't got your language, which I totally don't believe. You know, for me that's *not* the case. It is *not* your fault and so the point at which I decided to come back and learn the reo even though I'm much older was the point at which I realised that it's *not* my fault. I did not do this to myself, you know. Oh, it makes me so upset! (Te Whanganui-a-Tara, 45–55)

Learners of te reo Māori acknowledged that learning about colonisation helped them to make sense of their situation as adult learners. For some, it provided a political motivation to learn te reo. As one group of young fluent speakers pointed out, anxiety and whakamā are common for new learners, and education can help to lessen these feelings.

**Ana:** Because they [Māori ancestral learners] are taking it on themselves, they are not realising that the whakamā isn't theirs, it was from what happened, and it wasn't even from our people, it was from them [colonisers] [laughing].
**Kōtuku:** Yeah, they are putting the blame on themselves when they should be like, 'Nah, I should be learning it because it was not my fault, it wasn't my tīpuna's fault, it was because of them [colonisers].' Why let them win?
**Ana:** Yeah, I think that education is definitely key.
**Rex:** They also see a goal of attaining te reo Māori, as opposed to being stuck in the present thinking about the now, thinking about all the mistakes you are making now, um, when you know that there is a

greater goal to achieve then you are more likely to succeed. Like, you are doing it for future generations.

**Ana:** Yeah, yeah, something more than yourself [. . .]

**Rex:** Yeah, and then ka hīkina tērā taumaha ki runga i a koe.

—————

**Rex:** Yeah, and then that weight is lifted from you.

(Te Papaioea focus group, 18–25)

Rangatahi who were raised speaking te reo discussed the mixed emotions they felt about being Māori speakers in a colonial context. Part of their reality meant monitoring when and where it was socially appropriate to use te reo, so to avoid causing feelings of mamae for older, non-reo-speaking people. They noted that they needed to be considerate towards pakeke who were non-reo-speaking, as they did not want to appear whakahīhī in the presence of elders. Rangatahi Māori also spoke about the pain they felt when seeing their elders having to learn their ancestral language as kaumātua.

Both rangatahi speakers of te reo Māori and older people face intergenerational challenges. In one instance, a group of highly proficient rangatahi working together in a professional setting discussed a sense of backlash from older people who had not been afforded the same language-learning opportunities.

**Ihipera:** [The fact that we have different levels of proficiency between age groups] kind of affects us because we feel that we are not safe, to speak [. . .] You feel that you're, you're like a bad person or you know for speaking te reo Māori, and you know our own people. So you know, you just don't feel safe in a way, and I think that's like in another way, like that's like a lot of pressure, umm, on te hunga rangatahi, because we feel that – oh, how do I say this without like disrespecting the other reanga – but, you know, for that we have to hold their, [. . .] not burden, but the mamae, the stuff that they missed out on.

**Other:** Tika, kia ora rā.

**Ihipera:** So we have to carry it, and feel their guilt, and that's something we have to live up to. And you know they are relying on us. Te hunga rangatahi, our reanga to pick that up, and umm, a lot of times I feel that it is heavy, and we don't speak up about that because we feel that, well, I don't know, but not safe, you don't feel safe [. . .] it's disrespectful in a way, and I think that is a lot of pressure, you don't want to offend our kaumātua or our pakeke. So I feel that coming from a rangatahi's perspective, that's quite a lot, eh. (Te Whanganui-a-Tara, 18–25)

What we see from these comments is that language loss has myriad outcomes for fluent reo speakers as well as for those who are learning. Being a language speaker, particularly given the cultural roles we expect of reo Māori speakers irrespective of their age or experience, can carry a heavy emotional weight.

Contrasting the experiences of rangatahi in the excerpt above are those put forward by Ramari Stewart in her discussion with Qiane Matata-Sipu (2021). Ramari talks about the intergenerational challenges she has observed for kaumātua who are cultural knowledge-holders and who have lived through periods of assimilation.

Our generation's been through the impact of, you know, not speaking the reo out in the community etc., but it was also in our homes. In the case of my father's generation, his father went to Te Aute with Ngata and he was a very close friend of Te Rangi Hiroa's and they were promoting assimilation. So it was definitely in his home, a large family, they were brought up to speak English, even though there were old people coming to meet his father for advice and they couldn't speak anything but te reo. And then we moved into another period of time where we started to get the language back, so we had young people coming out of the kura, and then my generation felt intimidated again, so many of them [kaumātua] didn't want to go anywhere near the maraes, because they thought that they were going to get bashed by the new speakers of te reo, because there was this expectation that they were older, that they should speak Māori. [. . .] My message to the younger generation, you need to stand alongside us if you want us on the maraes. Because a lot of my generation [kaumātua] have mātauranga and we were active kaitiaki, and if we are to help and participate in the things that are happening now, we're all talking climate change, but the secret to climate change is biodiversity and that requires a certain amount of knowledge.

Whaea Ramari's perspectives correspond with the writings of Dame Iritana Tawhiwhirangi (2014), who explains that in order to understand where we are in the revitalisation of te reo Māori, we need to explore the conditions that shape our present day. For example, it is important to contextualise Māori leaders' encouragement of bilingualism during the early to mid-1900s. 'When I cast my mind back, to when I was about eleven, I cannot help but ask myself why wasn't there the same panic for the Māori language that there is now?' Dame Iritana writes. 'What was the concern at the time was actually gaining English because the hapū was already in charge and in perfect control of te reo Māori.' She recalls Sir Apirana Ngata visiting her school with the minister of education and his officials, and giving a speech to the hapū in which he exhorted the other visitors: '"I want you people to teach my people English, English and more English." He said this because he had no concern for te reo Māori, it was strong, it was safe. His vision was bilingualism' (34).

Sir Timoti Karetu (1993) reflects on a shift that Ngata later made in his thinking. As whānau adopted English in the home over te reo Māori to an unanticipated degree, Ngata perhaps saw the detrimental effects on Māori language use, and in turn he encouraged Māori to re-centralise te reo by drawing on Māori identity to make these connections.

As we have seen, the taking up of English by whānau hapū and iwi cannot be attributed only to encouragement from Māori leaders. While their views surrounding the use of English may have contributed to this shift, the conditions imposed by colonial governments pre-empted the encouragement towards English – and should be our focus.

If tangata whenua had continued to hold control and rangatiratanga over our lives, including our ability to sustain ourselves and the mana whakahaere to use our language without restraint (including at school), it is highly unlikely that we would now be attributing Māori language loss in part to the use of English. Bilingualism without the loss of te reo Māori might have been achieved, if not for the overarching devastations caused by colonisation.

The colonial context creates the foundations for some of the miscommunications and harmful dialogue that are currently occurring in Māori language discussions. These discussions are taking place within our online communities in particular. Online forums are not safe spaces to deal with some of the issues that we see arising given that these platforms do not adhere to customary tikanga, or ways of managing conflict effectively in a public domain.

The differences in experiences between speakers of te reo Māori and non-speakers of te reo continue to be a point of tension, which has come to the forefront prominently in recent times. The conflicting views that Māori voiced during Te Wiki o Te Reo Māori 2021 with the release of the reo Māori of Lorde's EP *Te Ao Mārama* highlighted some of the strains in our speaker and non-speaker communities, covered in more depth in Chapter 8. Though a series of opinions were put forward, there were very few avenues to hold constructive and meaningful conversations in safe spaces.

In 2022, comedian Kajun Brooking's twitter meme 'How Te Reo speaking Maori look at the rest of us Hori's', alongside an image of men dressed as European aristocrats gazing disapprovingly down, prompted further responses. The meme communicates a growing feeling among some Māori (particularly non-reo speakers) that there is an 'elite' class of Māori language speakers whose ability affords them certain privileges. This was followed by a meme by Te Taura Whiri i te Reo Māori, with Kajun's image of aristocracy on the left and an image of a person exhausted from reading/studying on the right, and the words: 'What people think being fluent in te reo Māori is like vs what it's actually like'.

Both memes demonstrate the tensions of navigating this space in which some Māori can speak te reo but the majority cannot. My take on Te Taura Whiri i te reo Māori's meme is that it demonstrates a misunderstanding from the perspective of proficient speakers about how they are seen by critical non-speakers. Depicting te reo speakers as hard-working and exhausted from language learning can also be interpreted to mean that non-speakers are not hard-working or do not understand that, to be proficient, we need to work hard. While it's unlikely that the creators of the second meme were intentionally promoting harmful dialogues, the post highlights the need for us to understand where both sides are coming from so that we can find common ground.

The idea that a person can become a proficient speaker of te reo from merely working hard, or through individual merit alone, stems from notions of meritocracy. The tensions we are currently experiencing are born of a set of colonial conditions that have placed us in opposition with one another.

## Summary

Research indicates that the violence our tūpuna experienced on the battlefields and the violence that their descendants experienced in the education system are linked. As a nation, we cannot continue to downplay the negative effects of colonisation on our whānau hapū, iwi and communities. *He Waka Roimata* (Te Uepū Hāpai i te Ora, 2019) and *Whakatika: A Survey of Māori Experiences of Racism* (Smith et al., 2021) both describe tangible ways in which tangata whenua are facing the impacts of colonisation. These impacts extend to interpersonal violence within whānau (Pihama et al., 2019). Acknowledging the ongoing nature of colonisation will help us all to understand why ancestral language learning is incredibly challenging for many.

Esteemed social justice leader matua Moana Jackson (2020) repeats the message time and again that the colonisation of Māori in Aotearoa is not tied to a particular time or event, and that it does not have an end date:

> [E]ven the greatest injustice need not destroy hope. Colonisation is an
> injustice that is often too painful to be fully told; and the relationships
> it has damaged and continues to damage can seem beyond repair. Yet
> the stories and their hope may be a guide to resolution.

One of the points Jackson makes here is that our historical trauma can feel too painful to speak about, but that hope is available to us through the sharing of our stories, memories and histories.

On a personal note, I remember one of our koroua talking about a racist encounter that he and his kuia experienced in the streets of Te Awamutu when he was a child. After listening, I probed in my naïve manner, 'So did you talk about this when you got home? Was there any debriefing about these types of encounters?' But the acts of aggression that our people so often experienced were not talked about at home in the 1950s. Perhaps it was seen as impolite or was merely discouraged to discuss such matters at the time. However, given that our koroua was recalling this incident 70 years later, it had clearly had a deep and lasting impact on him.

The intergenerational challenges caused by colonisation and living in a colonial context require a collective wānanga. Rangatahi are indicating that they have been gifted te reo Māori, but a condition of receiving te reo within a colonial context is to use it with humility. Kaumātua who are not Māori speaking but who are knowledge-holders from a different time can contribute in a wealth of ways to the learning of younger generations of reo speakers. When we understand the vulnerabilities of both groups from a place of aroha, the most beneficial outcomes are likely to occur across generations.

If the stripping of language was key to domination of the mental universe of Indigenous peoples by imperialists (Wa Thiongo, 1992), then understanding how to reverse this process is key to our future aspirations. As we reclaim te reo Māori, we begin the process of reinviting the language into our bodies, minds and hearts. During the process of ancestral language learning, we absorb the language to the core of our being. From a cognitive psychology perspective, we are encoding our language from our short-term into our long-term memory. It is my untested assertion that colonial-based trauma creates a layer of fog in the encoding process. If left unaddressed, this fog can prevent learners from engaging with their reo tūpuna. Therefore, before we begin learning, we must accept whatever proficiency level we are currently at and hold tight to our aspirations for higher levels in the future. Ancestral language learning is tied into our experiences as Māori and all that these experiences encompass, including our relationships with those who speak te reo in our time and our tūpuna who spoke it in theirs.

Tangata whenua who are experiencing mental health challenges may find that learning te reo Māori helps with their healing, as acknowledged by Durie (2001):

> Provision for patients to learn Māori as part of a rehabilitation programme is increasingly recognised as relevant to longer term goals of identity consolidation and preparation for greater involvement with whānau and the Māori community. The implications, therefore, are that some staff in a mental health service ought to have a degree of expertise in Māori language and the service itself may be expected to provide opportunities for language development as part and parcel of an integrated approach to treatment and rehabilitation. (233)

As the value of learning te reo is recognised by health practitioners, a joint approach to supporting learners through this journey would be welcomed. Kaiako reo Māori tend to be exposed to some of the challenges that learners experience, which extend to challenges in psychological wellbeing. Kaiako reo Māori are not necessarily trained in mental health, which could be addressed. There is a need to improve the ways in which we can support ancestral language learners as they work through challenges which often have historical roots.

In the next chapter, we will explore te reo Māori and identity, and some of the ways in which relationships can support learners of te reo Māori. We will also explore reasons why individuals who share a level of proficiency and those who differ in proficiency relate to one another.

*Questions to wānanga*
1. What aspects of our history have been silenced?
2. What are some stories of resilience that you can draw upon and relate back to being an ancestral language learner?
3. When was te reo Māori last used between parent and child in your whānau?
4. What healing can come from learning about interruptions in Māori language transmission in your whānau?
5. How do collective experiences of language loss affect your individual learning experiences?
6. What are some ways that we can attempt to heal pain surrounding intergenerational language loss?
   a) Who is supporting you in this process?
   b) What steps can we take in seeking additional support as we explore some of these mamae?
7. How might learning and speaking te reo help us to address some of the challenges related to colonisation?

# 5. Encountering barriers

Ko te reo te taura here i te tangata ki tōna ao, ki tōna tuakiritanga. Ko te reo te whītau rangitāmiro i te tangata ki tōna taiao, ki āna tikanga, ki tōna mātāpono, ki tōna ao.
—Ngapo (2014), 182

There are many reasons why learning te reo Māori in a colonial context is challenging for Māori, and why it often takes multiple attempts to become fully conversant. In our communities, we have many positive examples of Māori who have become exceptionally skilled communicators in te reo. However, the path that they took was often filled with trials and tribulations, just as it is for learners currently struggling. The Manawa Ū ki te Reo Māori study found four overarching reasons why Māori found the process difficult: racism, intergenerational trauma, personal constraints and educational constraints. Many of these related to the learner's particular environment and set of circumstances.

Racism, which is pervasive at structural as well as interpersonal levels, affected Māori experiences of language learning immensely. Racism towards Māori people, culture and language impacted on how valuable Māori saw learning and using te reo, and their ability to speak, hear and learn te reo in daily life. Racism was experienced by Māori in all age groups. This finding is discussed more in later chapters.

Intergenerational trauma and authenticity beliefs tended to lead to feelings of whakamā, language anxiety, and lack of self-confidence.

Personal constraints included limited time and resources to dedicate to learning. Other constraints were related to education, including teaching methods and classroom dynamics. The limited number of people available to practise using te reo Māori with was a major constraint for learners, particularly those at intermediate and conversational levels of proficiency.

While touching on each of these points, this chapter focuses on the intersections between conceptualisations of Māori identity, whakamā, language anxiety, and the limitation of resources. We will look at participants' longer answers to the Manawa Ū ki te Reo Māori survey questions to explore some of the challenges that tangata whenua experience during their language learning. As we hear people's stories, alternative narratives and interpretations emerge that show that Māori ancestral language learners are not to blame for the challenges they have faced while learning te reo.

## Language anxiety and whakamā

Language anxiety is a very common experience for learners of second languages. Language anxiety can impact negatively on our ability to process new words and language structures, and can prevent us from verbalising words that we feel we know when not under stress (MacIntyre & Gardner, 1994). The impact of language anxiety is heightened for ancestral language learners, as the multiple pressures placed upon us make learning or speaking the language tense in many situations.

As ancestral language learners, we are also often processing the language experiences of our tūpuna. What our interviews indicated is that people with a whakapapa relationship with te reo Māori and who were learning as a second language often struggled to gain confidence using te reo. These struggles were characterised by a fear of failure. At the crux of their descriptions was a feeling of whakamā, particularly in the inability to speak a language that they felt they should already know because they identified as Māori. It is important to explore how identity interacts with language learning in order to resolve some of the challenges that Māori ancestral language learners face.

Māori identity is diverse, complex and ever-evolving. Our experiences and the myriad changes we encounter in our daily lives lead us to our understandings of what it means to be Māori. In Chapter 2 we looked at how identity was often described by participants in our study as a motivation for learning te reo Māori. In this chapter we will explore how our desire for belonging and our investment in being perceived as Māori may lead to experiences of language anxiety.

While whakapapa Māori remains the most widely agreed upon requirement for claiming a Māori identity, other factors contribute to individuals feeling that they have a right to claim this identity (McIntosh, 2005). What makes rangatahi identities distinct from previous generations is that they are far more likely to whakapapa to two, three or four cultures (Statistics New Zealand, 2013). The diversity in our Māori identities continues to change, and these changes have a relationship with te reo Māori.

## Tangata whenua and identity quantification

'Tangata whenua' can be translated as 'people belonging to the land'. Our relationships with our tribal lands shape our identities. Our identities as tangata whenua highlight the interconnections that link us as kaitiaki to the responsibilities that we have for our lands. However, the connections that we have with our taiao have been interrupted by the restrictions that have been placed on how we care for our whenua as kaitiaki.

Cultural erasure and forced assimilation are characteristics of colonising practices, and Indigenous populations internationally have experienced them (Oliver et al., 2015; Haque & Patrick, 2015). One aspect of these practices is land confiscation, which has had a significant impact on Māori access to 'traditional' methods of making sense of our tribal, place-based identities, as Moeke-Pickering (1996) writes: 'Alienation from ancestral lands resulted in reduced opportunities for Māori to be exposed to living, working, playing and developing an economic base from their tribal lands' (4). Despite land confiscation and land alienation at the hands of the British Crown, Māori continue to demonstrate that our connection to our whenua as kaitiaki can be maintained across generations.

A major way in which land confiscation has been carried out is through attempts to 'measure' tangata whenua identity, a process which began during the colonial settlement period. The antiquated technique of blood quantum, used by European colonisers both before and after their arrival into Aotearoa, has contributed to the homogenisation of tribal identities, as Ngāi Tahu descendent Alvina Edwards (2020) writes: '[F]rom an historical and cultural perspective, blood quantum standards divide and alienate communities and perpetuate a discourse that promotes internalised self-hatred, alienation, and fractionation' (12). When identities are measured in ways that align with values and beliefs from a different culture, issues are inevitable.

In Aotearoa, the quantification of Māori identity included blood quantum measures, fractioning systems and lifestyle descriptions. These methods required a person to identify their supposed proportion of Māori ancestry and non-Māori ancestry. Māori identity was also quantified by 'lifestyle' – as in, how 'Māori' a person's way of living appeared to be. Our whakapapa has always been an important way of recognising who we are and who we come from, and of recognising that as individuals we belong to a wide set of human and environmental connections (Mikaere, 2010). Notions of whakapapa are unique to a Māori world view of connectedness – a world view that differs considerably from Euro-centric methods of identity quantification.

Moana Jackson (2011) writes of how European notions of identity

were weaponised against Māori, leading to land loss and, ultimately,
loss of a sense of identity.

> The colonisers enthusiastically imported the idea here with definitions
> such as a 'real' Māori only being someone with more than three-quarters
> native blood. They divided us according to this blood quantum,
> and if in that definition you had less than three-quarters, then, for
> example, you could not have an interest in native land. By redefining us
> according to a scientific untruth they effectively removed thousands of
> acres of land from our people and thus began over a century of defining
> and redefining who we are as a people. Between 1841 and 1990 there
> were in fact 33 different blood definitions of who a Māori is. Some said
> you were a Māori if you had a certain degree of Māori blood and lived
> as a native. Others said you could not be a Māori if you had a Māori
> mother and a Pākehā father because obviously the Pākehā man's blood
> was quantifiably worth more than the Māori woman's blood, and so
> you miraculously became Pākehā. [. . .] In my view, the imposition of
> that whole discourse is one of the most damaging things that has been
> done to our people because it has altered the very notion of our identity
> and worth. (74)

Each of these colonial notions of identity categorisation has
contributed to the policing of Māori identities. These essentialist beliefs,
colonial in design, have narrowed society's understandings of what it is
to be Māori, and have meant that some Māori do not feel entitled to
claim an identity as Māori. Furthermore, when we adopt essentialist
beliefs about who is Māori and who is not based on these strict criteria,
we can end up agreeing to concepts that have the impact of excluding
ourselves or those who we love from feeling 'Māori enough' by merely
not being critical about where such essentialist beliefs have come from.

The introduction of the Native Land Court in 1865 meant whakapapa
Māori was called upon to assist in the process of land dispossession
through legislated colonial practices. In court proceedings, Māori were

required to recite their whakapapa to prove their relationship with Māori land. Crocker (2016) describes the Native Land Court as a 'source of breaches of the Treaty of Waitangi':

> The Native Land Court investigated claims to the customary ownership of Māori land brought before the Court and sought to transfer that land into individual ownership through a statutory system. [. . .] [T]he Native Land Court interpreted customary rights to land, the limitation on the number of owners who could appear on the resulting title, the costs incurred with the process, and the resulting fragmentation of Māori land holdings. (82)

By limiting the number of individuals who could appear on land titles, the Crown made it easier for themselves to purchase land at extortionately low rates, leading to the dispossession of lands from tangata whenua.

The New Zealand Census now poses identity questions in two ways: 'Do you have Māori ancestry?' and 'Do you identify as Māori?' As Durie (2001) points out, a difference in response – when Māori answer 'Yes' to the first question and 'No' to the second – is a cause for concern. Why do individuals who have Māori ancestry choose not to identify as Māori? Two reasons are: racism, and claims making. Racism, both historically and today, can make individuals who have whakapapa Māori feel that they want to dissociate from being Māori. This dissociation is an effort to escape the threatening ways in which the state punishes Indigenous peoples for existing at both a local and global level.

Identity quantification works in favour of colonising belief systems. Claims that there were no longer any 'real Māori' alive helped to extend the unfounded assertion that it was possible to extinguish Māori from existence. Featherston's assertions that encouraged colonisers to 'smooth the dying pillow' followed the Darwinian theory of 'survival of the fittest'. Extinction was thought to be a pending reality for Māori through to the early 1900s, a belief which stemmed mostly from the devastating impacts of land confiscations, which diminished the ability of tangata whenua to self-govern and self-sustain. The idea that there are 'no real Māori' alive persists today. It is used to disqualify claims for equality between us as tangata whenua and our Treaty partners, tangata Tīriti.

## Māori identity claims

Just like Māori identity itself, the relationship between identity and language is complex and ever-evolving. Rewi (2010) writes that Māori identity can act as a form of protection: 'Ko te tangata kāore ōna tikanga, he rite ki te rākau kāore ōna pakiaka. Ka pūhia e te hau, ka hina noa, ka maroke, ka popo, ka hanehane' (57). A translation of this text could include: 'People without identity are like the tree with no roots to establish itself firmly. It is constantly at the disposal of the elements.' Having a cultural identity includes participating in that culture. For some, there is a connection between feeling entitled to claim an identity as Māori and feeling entitled to learn our ancestral language. When we feel othered from our ancestry as Māori, we may also feel unable to claim ownership of our reo.

McIntosh (2005) explains that identity is part of a process of claims making. When individuals state their cultural identity, they are making a claim to that identity. McIntosh provides three ways in which we might understand Māori identities: fixed, fluid and forced. Fixed identities incorporate identities associated with 'traditional' notions of being Māori. The reference to 'traditional' is less about describing identity in pre-European times and more 'a contemporary identity that is articulated by Māori and can be characterized as presenting particular identity hooks as markers of identity' (43). Knowledge of whakapapa, mātauranga Māori, te reo Māori and tikanga are central to the fixed identity position.

In McIntosh's definition, fluid identities take on elements of surrounding culture, including hip-hop culture or local identities, as opposed to a whakapapa relationship with the land. Together, this makes up a fusion of what it means to be Māori, based on the lived realities of Māori as they incorporate elements of their social and material environments to make sense of who they are. This identity position adapts to accommodate traditional and modern aspects, and generally it describes rangatahi Māori, most of whom are not schooled within Māori medium education settings.

Finally, McIntosh describes a forced identity position. Forced identities include marginal identities 'formed under conditions of deprivation [. . .] these are identities that are cast upon individuals and groups rather than having been formed by them' (48). For language learners, it is the fixed identity position that is likely to cause the most tension.

Te reo Māori continues to be highly sought after and prized by many members of our Māori society, particularly those who see te reo as a core marker of Māori identity. The fixed identity position incorporates views of authenticity, or specific views about criteria that must be met in order to claim an identity. Houkamau and Sibley (2015b) describe authenticity beliefs as:

> The extent to which the individual believes that to be a 'real' or 'authentic' member of the social category Māori one must display specific (stereotypical) features, knowledge and behaviour *versus* the extent to which the individual believes that Māori identity is fluid rather than fixed, and produced through lived experience. (281)

When individuals feel that they can claim an identity only once they have met a set of criteria, the desire to meet these criteria becomes a goal in and of itself, irrespective of whether the criteria are colonial derivatives in nature. We may then ask: how does claiming an identity relate to language anxiety? The stakes for learning te reo Māori are higher for ancestral language learners because of the layers of social meaning attached to the language. Knowledge of te reo Māori (among other knowledge sets) has become attached to how justified some Māori feel in claiming a Māori identity, irrespective of their whakapapa Māori.

When language becomes a prerequisite to Māori identity reclamation, Indigenous learners may be less willing than non-Māori to put themselves in situations that expose their identity to risk. When learning any language, we need opportunities to practise, but like all language learners we will make mistakes. Beliefs that link Māori identity with proficiency in te reo contribute to a heightened sense of risk for learners; making errors can lead them to feel identity vulnerability. The pressure to be correct relates to assumptions about what it means for our identity if we are incorrect.

There are three interacting components to identity and language learning (Fig. 7). These include a) having fixed ideas about what it means to be Māori, so that te reo Māori is equated with ingroup

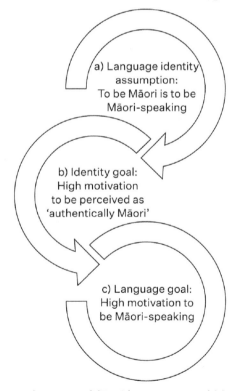

Fig. 7: Interactions between Māori language and Māori identity

membership; b) wanting to be a Māori person who can speak te reo Māori, but who is not at their self-set desired proficiency level; and c) wanting to be perceived as Māori (including fulfilling fixed criteria) by others who share similar authenticity beliefs. When a person has fixed identity beliefs (a) but is not at their desired reo Māori proficiency level (b), they may feel less confident claiming their Māori identity (c).

Almost all participants in the Manawa Ū study had experienced some language anxiety, irrespective of their proficiency. While more proficient individuals reported lower levels of anxiety, they still reported feelings of anxiety. This tells us that anxiety is part of the ancestral language journey. It is important that our anxiety does not reach a point where we are put off learning altogether. Seeking out strategies for managing anxiety can be helpful.

Below are six of our findings relating to our participants' experiences of language anxiety.

1. Speaking to those with more fluency was anxiety-provoking.
2. Speaking to those with less fluency was uncomfortable.
3. The expectation that a Māori person would also be a speaker of te reo Māori was a common experience.
4. Some Māori non-speakers of te reo had internalised the idea that Māori should speak reo Māori. These individuals expressed that they were unlikely to feel welcomed (unconditionally) into Māori-dominant spaces where te reo might be used.
5. Having fun with te reo, using games in low-stress environments, reduced anxiety around Māori language use.
6. Both male and female participants experienced anxiety when they were asked to perform ceremonial roles. Anxiety was heightened in situations where their language capabilities did not match the formality of the occasion.

## Lack of time and resources

Time and resources are a major barrier to Māori who want to learn te reo Māori. The availability of 'free time' to focus on formal study is a luxury for many Māori. Findings from Te Kupenga (Statistics New Zealand, 2014) based on over 18,000 responses from Māori indicate significant changes in the ways that te reo Māori is being learned. People aged over 55 tended to indicate that they learned their reo Māori from whānau (71.2%) or at hui (73.9%). For these generations, te reo Māori was traditionally transferred through whānau (intergenerational transmission).

Those aged 15–34 were more likely to have learned te reo Māori formally, such as at kura or school. Considerably fewer Māori aged 15–24 learned te reo through kōhanga reo, kura kaupapa Māori and wharekura (42.4%) than those who attended other non-Māori-medium education options (65.1%). These results indicate that incidental learning of te reo Māori is becoming less available to younger generations, who rely on Māori medium education to develop language fluency. More Māori are learning te reo at mainstream schools than in Māori medium education. In mainstream education, the limited time and resources for the specific teaching of te reo Māori, as well as a lack of language normalisation outside of the classroom, mean that students' reo Māori proficiency is lower than that of students in Māori medium education. In the future, Māori who attended mainstream schools are likely to need additional Māori language training to reach high levels of proficiency.

Those who have not had an opportunity to attend Māori medium education, and do not have whānau or fluent reo speakers to teach them, are likely to be learning through formalised methods. In the Te Kupenga study, those aged 35–54 were more likely than other age groups to be learning te reo Māori through wānanga or other tertiary institutions. This suggests that Māori learning te reo as adults need to be afforded the time and resources to commit to learning te reo.

In terms of unpaid labour, there are also discrepancies between Māori men and Māori women. Māori women are responsible for carrying the heaviest loads at home and in the whānau. The 2018 census data shows that Māori women are more likely than Māori men to undertake unpaid labour within every category offered to survey respondents. Household labour is an additional area where Māori women contribute at greater levels than Māori men, with Māori women undertaking more work such as cooking, repairs and gardening (88.5% of women compared with 82.2% of men).

Not only do Māori women carry a heavier load of unpaid labour than Māori men, but the distribution of work between Māori women and Pākehā women is also unequal. Māori women are more likely than Pākehā women to look after a child who is a member of their own household (44.3% compared with 29.7%) or a child who is a member of someone else's household (27.7% compared with 20.1%). Māori women are also more likely than Pākehā women to help or volunteer at organisations, groups or marae (21.7% versus 17.8%). In the Manawa Ū study, Māori women indicated that a lack of time and resources were a considerable barrier to their learning te reo. But it is no wonder that finding time to study is difficult for many Māori women. Even when she is highly motivated, the practicalities of language learning might be considerably complicated by her responsibilities to whānau.

The availability of whānau to engage in language learning is also likely to be tied to time spent in paid work. In 2018 the median income of Māori men and Māori women combined was $24,300, while the median income for Pākehā was $34,100. The amount of disposable income that Māori have to spend on learning te reo Māori is likely to impact on their availability to formally study te reo. With this said, Māori rates of engagement in formal study of te reo are higher, at 29.9%, compared with Pākehā, at 21.3%. The value that tangata whenua place on education is seen in these high numbers. The challenge for many Māori, however, is in having the time and resources to dedicate to learning their ancestral language in formalised ways, in addition to other stressors that they may be experiencing.

Given these struggles, how can we support the learning of te reo in ways that do not further limit learners' time and resources? One example of how this can be achieved is Pūniu River Care (PRC), an environmental organisation based at our pā, Mangatoatoa, who are restoring our tūpuna awa, Pūnui. An evaluation of this organisation's cultural impacts on staff wellbeing showed that employees at PRC were supported financially, linguistically and culturally within their daily work lives (Te Huia, Maniapoto-Ngaia & Fox, 2022). Pūniu River Care pays its kaimahi equitably and builds te reo and tikanga meaningfully into its work programme. Learning te reo during work hours (and including work that is meaningful) allows kaimahi to learn te reo in ways that are less focused specifically on the action of language learning. Taking the focus off the task of Māori language learning was helpful for some tangata whenua, particularly older people, who had had negative experiences of trying to learn previously. Furthermore, learning at work, especially where the culture of the organisation was founded on tikanga Māori, allowed kaimahi the opportunity to see the relevance of te reo in their daily lives. Learning within a supportive workplace also meant that kaimahi did not need to spend their time outside of work completing formal studies.

## Survey results on barriers to learning te reo Māori

In the Manawa Ū study, we wanted to understand the kinds of barriers that learners were facing. We asked participants about the barriers that they had experienced. The responses listed in the findings below include summaries of the long-answer survey responses. These responses included views from learners in three groups: a) those who had not formally studied te reo Māori in the past, b) those who had studied te reo Māori but did not identify as competent speakers, and c) those who were competent speakers.

*Those who had not yet begun learning*
Results showed that the strongest barrier for learners in this group was managing their commitments, particularly work commitments. Being declined from a course (due to courses being full) was not a significant

contributor to barriers for this group, which was unexpected. We also asked these participants to explain why they had not yet begun learning te reo Māori. Their answers were summarised and grouped (Fig. 8).

All three groups indicated that a lack of time and resources were the greatest barrier to learning te reo Māori, with one respondent from the first group saying: 'No babysitter to go [to] classes, online options not available at required level.' Growing up abroad was also a barrier, and those overseas indicated that they had strong motivations to learn but that opportunities were limited: 'I live in Australia but yearn to learn te reo for myself and my family.' Respondents' self-beliefs about their language learning abilities alongside fear of judgement and failure were also barriers: 'Fear of being judged for not fluently knowing our language' and 'Being called dumb' are examples. Finding the right course could be challenging: 'Connecting with a course that is appropriate stops me from enrolling.' Technology problems such as unreliable Wi-Fi were issues for some.

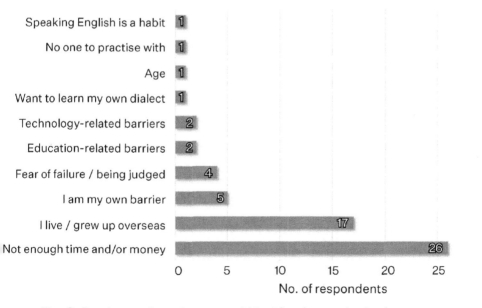

Fig. 8: Barriers to learning te reo Māori for those who had not yet begun learning

Some responses included ideas about future fear-based realities, such as not having a community of te reo speakers to engage with: 'Retaining the reo would be hard because I will need to apply it consistently to be confident to speak it and fear that I may speak it incorrectly.'

Interestingly, a sense of needing to learn one's own dialect also came up: 'I want to learn my own dialect of Māori from Ngāti [iwi name] before learning another Māori dialect.' Although this point was raised only once in the long answers, it relates closely to the idea encapsulated in the whakataukī 'Hoki ki tō maunga kia purea ai ngā hau o Tāwhirimātea'. Those who are interested in learning may hold views that it is more 'authentic' to focus on learning one's own dialect. However, accessing one's own dialect is likely to to be difficult for individuals not residing in their own tribal region, thus introducing more barriers to learning.

*Speakers who had attempted learning but were not competent*
For learners in this group, time and/or money were once again the main barriers to learning te reo (Fig. 9). This included work commitments, followed by whānau and personal commitments. Costs associated with study may have moderately deterred people from continuing to learn. Not having courses available or having their applications declined was not a barrier for this group of participants.

Whānau are juggling multiple commitments, and language learning on top of everything else that they are managing can be too difficult. Some responses about lack of time and/or money included:
- 'Not having access and the money to learn.'
- 'I just struggle to prioritise studying it.'
- 'Te wā!'
- 'Finding the time to commit to learning.'
- 'Time. I work every day and get home in time for my second job as a housewife and mother.'
- 'I often work shift work and so having the ability to learn course material at different times (from home) is crucial.'

Participants in this group came with a range of previous learning experiences, and these were reflected in their responses about education-related barriers. The right fit between learners and teachers was important, and when individuals had a poor learning experience, including during compulsory education, this tended to negatively impact their decisions to learn te reo. Some responses about education-related barriers were:

- 'My teacher scolded and made us stand in front of the class if we got anything wrong which was very humiliating, discouraging and obviously has stuck with me up to now.'
- 'I don't like being told to play games and act in classes, nā te mea ka haere au ki te kōrero noa iho.'
- 'I would prefer to learn Māori in a small familiar group rather than a large university class.'

A more extensive discussion of factors relating to education and te reo Māori is in later chapters.

It's clear from these responses that having support to overcome the challenges associated with study would help learners. One participant responded: 'I just struggle to prioritise studying it every day. Classes are really long and go until late on weeknights – it makes it really hard to keep going and I didn't want to take up a place in the year-long class when I knew I'd end up missing a lot, so I didn't re-enrol this year or last.' This point indicates that people are cognizant of their ability to commit for the full year, and if they are unable to make all of the classes, they may think they are taking the spot of someone who could have participated more fully. Some long-answer responses included:

- 'Access to all forms of learning is high importance as no one method works for all.'
- 'It takes time, effort and to let yourself be vulnerable to making mistakes and being embarrassed when doing so.'

A significant number of participants in this group indicated that they were their 'own barrier'. Examples of these responses include:

- 'Myself really. I just need to be persistent and make time to learn.'

- 'Self-sabotage.'
- 'Self-limitations.'
- 'My own discipline, commitment, focus and dedication to studying/learning te reo was lacking.'

Having ordinary, everyday contexts in which to speak te reo Māori was a challenge for both competent speakers and those aiming to gain competence. This long answer is a familiar scenario for learners who are not competent but who are wanting to improve: 'Not enough contexts

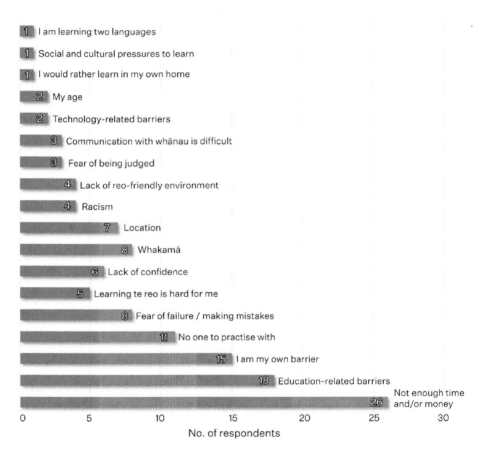

Fig 9: Barriers to learning te reo Māori for those who had attempted to learn but were not yet competent

in which to practise. I'm not very good but in most contexts, I now speak better reo than others.' It is likely the case that the social groups of new learners do not speak te reo Māori.

Fear of failure was another theme that came through in the long answers, such as: 'Many people like myself are scared of failure, which makes it harder for people to actively participate in the learning of the language.' This comment encapsulates why fearing failure can be debilitating to one's learning. Other participants, including those who did not fit stereotypical ideas of what it means to be Māori learning te reo, expressed a fear of judgement: 'Perceived racism/privilege. As a white Māori I feel like others are judging me "not speaking my language" and nervous to make mistakes in front of others.'

Generational differences also came through in the long answers. Adult learners are often learning te reo Māori at the same time as their children, so the re-establishment of te reo Māori as a means of everyday communication at home can require attention. This comes with its own challenges: 'Communicating with my kids is difficult because they don't understand or dismiss me because I don't speak the way they have learnt.'

Some older reo speakers shared ways in which they perceived younger speakers to hold certain privileges. Furthermore, older people felt that there were some unhelpful ways in which younger, proficient speakers of te reo treated them:

- 'I have found that younger reo speakers are less encouraging and supportive of my learning than older reo speakers.'
- 'The young can be very judgmental of non-reo speaking elders.'
- 'There is a lot of insecurity amongst Māori and I find some of those with great reo use it as a tool of power over those without.'

The points raised by this participant group spoke to some of the experiences described in Chapter 4. These comments highlight the need for concepts like aroha ki te tangata to be encouraged and embodied by competent speakers, who are often the power-holders in cultural contexts where te reo is normalised, towards non-speakers of te reo.

*Competent speakers*

Time and money presented challenges for competent speakers too (Fig. 10), with one participant saying: 'My solo mum lifestyle doesn't always allow me time out to learn at night or with noho.' Noho marae with children may mean that noho-based courses are limiting for sole parents or whānau who are juggling childcare arrangements.

The costs associated with study were also raised: 'I need to work, there are currently no scholarships for low-level teachers to learn te reo. I have some ability but can't go to he kāinga mō te reo because I have to work.' As adult learners of te reo were also household income earners, finding time outside of work to complete studies was a challenge: 'Time after working to support a whānau'; 'Ko te wā me taku mahi i ia rā, ia rā, kāore au i te wātea.' Having free time in which individuals were not exhausted from working was a luxury, and fatigue was one reason for switching from Māori to English: 'Inā ka kōrero Māori au, ā ko te reo Pākehā te whakahoki mai. Inā tino ngenge au he uaua ake te ū ki te reo Maori.'

Even competent speakers of te reo struggled with fears of making errors, which prevented some from speaking te reo: 'I get caught up on thinking I'm making mistakes or cannot correctly articulate what I want to say.' In some instances, individuals had received discouraging remarks from Māori speakers who had higher levels of proficiency: 'When Māori ridicule you and correct you while laughing at you.'

The way in which people were corrected also had an impact on competent speakers' willingness to use te reo Māori: 'People correcting my mistakes in a rude or disruptive way puts me off.' Persistent corrections were also off-putting to some: 'People correcting every single mistake.'

A number of competent speakers of te reo had limited access to other competent speakers in their immediate settings, including at work and with whānau, as one person shared: 'No one in my family speaks or understands te reo. My immediate colleagues at work aren't speakers of te reo, and don't understand.' Individuals also expressed that they weren't able to meet up regularly with other speakers: 'Not many people to korero Māori with regularly.'

Competent speakers also sometimes struggled with vocabulary. Some shared that, in instances where they did not know a particular word or phrasing, they would switch from Māori to English:

- 'I might not be able to finish the sentences because there might be a few words I can't translate into Māori.'
- 'Just don't feel my vocabulary is expansive enough, and I think faster in English than in te reo Maori. English keeps creeping in like a virus.'

Younger generations who have had the opportunity to learn te reo Māori were cognisant of their privilege, and one participant shared that their position of privilege felt like a barrier: 'Don't want to offend elder peoples who were deprived the opportunity to speak/learn te reo.' While

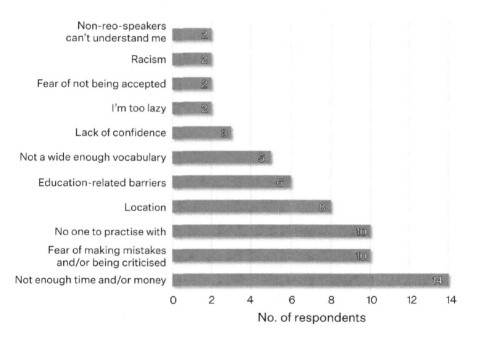

Fig. 10: Barriers to learning te reo Māori for competent speakers

this point was a one-off, it relates back to the focus group interviews with rangatahi who expressed similar concerns.

Competent speakers also spoke about racism and its impact on Māori language use: 'when Pākehā send bad vibes upon it when spoken freely'. The issue being raised here refers to the use of te reo Māori in Pākehā-dominant spaces, including in public spaces. Racism and its impacts on language learning are explored in the chapters ahead.

## Summary

Māori face many barriers in learning and using te reo Māori. Three of the most significant barriers – not having enough time and resources, not having access to environments where te reo Māori is normalised, and fear of failure or of making errors – stem from learning an endangered Indigenous language in a colonial context. Our reduced ability to be self-sustaining is a direct result of our landlessness, which costs us our time. As tangata whenua, we are not only managing the impacts associated with language loss, but we are also directing time and resources into multiple areas to combat the impacts of colonial violence.

The small number of environments in which te reo Māori can be spoken freely, and in which we can listen to and engage with te reo, shows the degree of control that a Pākehā-dominant society holds over our language. Due to the systemic processes of colonisation, we rarely encounter Māori-speaking environments by chance; rather, we are intentionally placing ourselves in reo Māori-speaking spaces. Investing in environments where te reo Māori is normalised, such as Māori language employment options where people can learn on the job, will support beginners as well as competent speakers. As a part of this, policy makers need to focus on providing options for whānau to study te reo while also managing their other commitments.

Importantly, fear of failure needs to be explored within our communities. The necessity of ingraining aroha ki te tangata in all of our interactions fits with notions of manaaki tangata, arguably a central

Māori cultural value. There is a need to address the concerns of those who are in the process of learning (or anticipating learning) so that their fears are not actualised. Given that some of our whānau anticipate feelings of whakamā about learning te reo, it is in the best interests of our language revitalisation that these potential future language speakers are nurtured in Māori language-speaking spaces. Aroha ki te tangata between speakers and learners needs to become the norm – so much so that any variation on this experience is deemed socially unacceptable. If a goal of Māori language revitalisation is to grow the number of Māori who can kōrero Māori, those who have the power to nurture our future reo speakers need to see the value in supporting them, which may mean constructing alternative narratives and ways of interacting.

Given the considerable resources required to gain proficiency, the feelings that non-reo-speaking whānau have about being in reo Māori-speaking spaces or engaging in reo Māori interactions have an impact on numbers of future Māori language speakers. Fear of failure is likely to be linked to feelings of not belonging in Māori language contexts.

Māori identities have been up for scrutiny for generations, and given that they are so highly politicised, it is not surprising that Māori feel vulnerable when learning a language that has been equated with our right to claim membership of a group. Narratives that incorporate te reo Māori into fixed notions of Māori identity may be contributing to these fears, which makes supportive, mana-enhancing language engagements even more necessary.

Some of the challenges we've explored in this chapter can be addressed at an individual level; for instance, we can work to understand the roots of our fear of making language errors. Other issues, such as racism and the wage inequities between Māori and Pākehā, require attention at a policy level. The labour inequities between Māori men and Māori women also affect our ability to work towards our Māori language aspirations.

In the next chapter we will explore the creation of Māori language speaking environments.

*Questions to wānanga*

1. What are some policy changes that would positively impact on the ability of Māori to participate in Māori language learning?
2. How is it possible to lobby governments for some of those changes?
3. How is your time structured, and how manageable would it be to formally engage in Māori language education?
4. What are some ways you can incorporate te reo Māori into your daily life at your current proficiency level?
5. What are your underlying beliefs about Māori identity? Do they fall into one or more of the three categories described by Tracey McIntosh: fixed, fluid, or forced?
6. How do fixed Māori identity beliefs affect your desire or ability to use te reo Māori freely, without reservation?

# 6. Ko ngā tūhononga: The importance of interpersonal relationships

Languages do not thrive in isolation; they require communities where those languages can be spoken. As Bauer (2008) explains:

> [I]t is communities rather than individuals that speak languages: if you can speak a language, but have nobody to speak it to, you do not speak it. For a language to survive, what matters is not who *can* speak it, but who *does* speak it. (63)

This chapter focuses on the importance of relationships in our reo Māori learning. Developing and maintaining Māori language relationships helps to normalise reo use and allows us to sustain or improve our proficiency over time. In this chapter we'll also explore behaviours that improve language speaker outcomes between two individuals who have Māori language competence, a desire to use te reo Māori over English, or a combination of the two. We can draw on the 'Zero – Passive – Active' model (ZePA) proposed by Higgins and Rewi (2014) to support Māori language use in relationships, helping us to move from being a passive language 'knower' to being an active user. Societal Māori language norms can help to provide environments where learners are free to engage in te reo Māori in mana-enhancing ways.

This chapter also describes the Tūhono model, which helps us understand how the decisions we make during social interactions can enhance or inhibit opportunities for language growth. Within this model are two focus areas: a person's ability to converse in te reo, and their preference for doing so within a language partnership. In our discussions with participants, my colleagues and I explored how Māori who have limited access to environments in which to use te reo can maximise the potential of the interactions that they do have.

My colleagues and I were interested in whether Māori language speakers preferred speaking with people who shared their level of proficiency over people with higher or lower levels of proficiency. This chapter explores some of the conditions that encourage speakers of te reo Māori to extend their comfort levels. Tuakana teina approaches can help us to conceptualise some of the roles that we engage in as ancestral language learners.

### Preference of conversational partner

Competent reo speakers (N = 315) were asked how likely they were to use te reo with people of proficiencies different from theirs (Fig. 11). Responses were on a 5-point Likert scale, from 1 (*strongly disagree*) to 5 (*strongly agree*). The strongest preference was for conversing with someone of the same proficiency (M = 4.12), followed by someone with higher proficiency (M = 3.83), and lastly with someone of lower proficiency (M = 3.50).

There are many reasons why a competent reo speaker might prefer to speak with someone who shares their proficiency. Firstly, it is comfortable. Social engagements that are awkward make most people want to change the situation so that the interaction is pleasant or relaxed, or avoid the interaction altogether. When we speak with

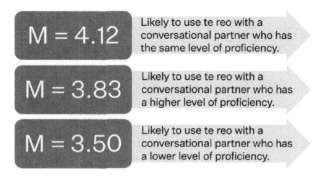

Fig. 11: Who te reo Māori speakers prefer speaking with

people whose language proficiencies are similar to ours, we likely have a shared understanding about vocabulary, kīwaha, and whakataukī/whakatauākī, which makes it possible to take conversational short cuts. While whakataukī/whakatauākī are not always used regularly in conversation, this shared lexicon or knowledge set in te reo is likely to make speaking with each other more enjoyable. Secondly, those with the same proficiency level as us may have similar learning experiences, which may increase a sense of connection.

In our interviews for the Manawa Ū study, competent speakers often described feeling uncomfortable when speaking te reo with more proficient speakers. Those with intermediate levels of proficiency indicated that they actively sought out spaces where te reo Māori was used, but before entering these spaces they engaged in preparation to mitigate feelings of mauri rere. Usually, this meant understanding that they would be going into a slightly uncomfortable space but that, ultimately, they would benefit from engaging with more proficient speakers. Below, Ariana discusses her decision to attend Te Matatini, knowing that te reo Māori would be a normal language of communication there:

**Ariana:** [At Te Matatini] it was kind of like almost, like I need to be on guard about, um, how much reo fluency I indicate to others that I speak with. And that was interesting to me cause I'm used to being the teina, I mean [. . .] I've moved from teina to tuakana in certain spaces.

And then I kind of flip back into teina with tuakana around me in that [Matatini] space, which generally feels safe. But I did note that there was a little bit of a wariness of that within me. And I actually had really positive conversations everywhere. None of that [fear-based anxiety] actually came to fruition but [. . .] I do note that that was something that I felt. So for me, the anxiety that came in [. . .] as a kid [. . .] despite all the stuff I've worked on, there is still this underlying, um, not so much anxiety, but a wariness around that [. . .] and a carefulness of how I then walk and put things into this space around me [. . .] It's a protective factor, so that I don't, um, get anything slammed back. Yeah. So that anything that happens in those [reo Māori dominant] spaces, and especially Te Matatini, that I just wanted it all to be quite positive and moving forward. And that was my experience. Yeah, that was my experience of that space, and I expected it to be safe and it definitely was. And it was very empowering and inspiring to me, and just felt like this is what Aotearoa New Zealand could be. It could have been this decades ago, and this could be just our norm everywhere. (Te Whanganui-a-Tara, 30–34)

Speakers at intermediate levels spoke about different phases that they went through as learners. Below, Anahera indicates that as a new and enthusiastic learner, she wanted to speak to everyone who spoke Māori, irrespective of social context. However, once she learned more about the socio-political context of te reo Māori, she became more discerning, given the array of language experiences that exist in our community.

**Anahera:** I went through a phase of feeling really proud and excited and wanting to talk, to speak te reo constantly to anybody. Even a little bit, even whatever limited amount I had [and then transitioned] to a sort of deeper, slightly deep, I think deeper, understanding that actually this is still a painful journey for everyone, even though I'm on a bit of an excited kick right now, and so there are a lot of people around me

who this is very painful for so, be more gentle, save face, and manaaki them, you know, and they can feel welcomed to, to come and find their way towards that language as well without feeling excluded. So kind of shifting into a space that's more caretaking, after my own excited phase, you know, moved off. [. . .] But I developed, on the going home, much more of a sense of pride about myself.
(Te Whanganui-a-Tara, 45–49)

The point above highlights the sense of excitement and joy that some new reo learners experience. For Anahera, excitement was then paired with a sense of caution or intentionality in her Māori language use. Understanding the socio-political history of Aotearoa helped her to consider how to manaaki others who may have found language learning challenging into a language speaking state.

In the following discussion, young language learners describe some of their anxieties.

**Ana:** It's that confidence and that comfort. Because even I'm fluent, but I still have trouble finding spaces where I feel like I can openly speak te reo Māori. Like which I know you should be able to all the time but, there is still that fear of like, even judgement from other Māoris for not being able to speak like up to par, or like matatau, or like Panekiretanga. Like there's that fear of making mistakes and getting judged for it.
**Piripi:** Colonisation.
**Ana:** Not feeling Māori enough, kind of thing?
**Piripi:** Colonisation. (Te Papaioea, 20–24)

Ana and Piripi are Māori-medium-educated, competent speakers of te reo Māori, but the anxieties that Ana expressed were shared by other participants, including those at lower levels of proficiency. As Māori language use is so closely tied with our identities as Māori, using the language is less straightforward, especially when we consider the many internal negotiations we make before vocalising our language with someone we might feel uncomfortable speaking with.

**Shirley:** Ko te nuinga o te wā kei te whakamā au ki te kōrero Māori i te mahi nā te mea he whakamā au ki te kōrero ki ngā tāngata tino matatau. He pōturi kia mārama ētahi wā, ki te whakautu, nō reira ka huri mai i te reo Pākehā ki te reo Māori, he uaua ake.

———

**Shirley:** Most of the time, I am whakamā to speak Māori at work because I'm embarrassed to speak to those who are highly proficient. It takes a while to understand sometimes, and to respond, so I revert to English, because it's more difficult [to speak te reo Māori].
(Te Whanganui-a-Tara, 60–64)

Even speakers with high levels of conversational reo Māori sometimes struggled with self-confidence. In some instances, not having a clear language-speaking community was not the only barrier. The decision to use te reo Māori came down to other factors, as Anahera says:

**Anahera:** I don't have a big reo Māori community in which I can speak te reo and practise. Not an everyday constant sort of place, you know, or way, even though I wish for it desperately. But I also think it's more complicated than that, because some of my friends who do speak te reo, we don't speak te reo to each other which is a really interesting thing, which I can't quite grasp why. (Te Whanganui-a-Tara, 45–49)

We asked Māori with high levels of proficiency to describe some strategies that could help to support learners with low levels of proficiency. Some responses included an appreciation of the difficulties of being a beginner and having few people to speak with. They also had an understanding of the whakamā that people might feel as learners of their ancestral language.

Te Rangihau: Hei āwhina i a rātou ki te kōrero? Āe, he uaua, he
mahi uaua nā te mea me kaha tonu te tangata ki te whakamahi te
reo mehemea kei te hiahia ia kia kōrerohia i ngā wā katoa nā te mea,
he maha tātou kāre i te mōhio ki te reo. He maha anō tātou ka āhua
whakamā mehemea ka kōrero Māori ki a rātou. Kei reira anō ngā mea
e mea ana, 'Hei aha tēnā reo, me kōrero Pākehā tatou.' Engari he iti
noa iho ērā kua rongo I ahau. Ko te whakamā tētahi, koirā tētahi mea
e patungia ana e tātou e te whakamā. Whakamā nei ki te, ahakoa he
aha nei te kaupapa, ko te whakamā.

———

Te Rangihau: How to support learners to speak? Yeah, that's challenging,
that's difficult, because the person themselves needs to have conviction
to use te reo for that person to speak it all of the time, because there are
so many of us who don't speak te reo. There are also a lot of us who are
whakamā if we speak to them. There are also those who say, 'Never mind
that language, we should just speak English.' However, there are fewer
individuals with those views to my knowledge. Whakamā is one of the
things, whakamā is something that really gets us down. Embarrassed to
. . . irrespective of the circumstance, whakamā is a deterrent.
(Ahuriri, 55–59)

Te Rangihau refers to the whakamā that is specific to language
learning and also the whakamā that Māori experience in other settings.
He discusses why the emotions associated with whakamā can be
detrimental to us all, and alludes to some negative views about the use
of te reo, which he sees as becoming less prominent.

Most confident speakers in this study indicated that they were
supportive of others who were learning te reo, and that they tried to
encourage them to speak te reo conversationally. They indicated that
they understood the impacts of whakamā and how it inhibited the use
of te reo, and therefore tried to guide others to kōrero Māori. Ihipera
provides an example:

**Ihipera:** I te nuinga o te wā, or i ngā wā katoa i au e kōrero ana ki tōku whānau, or ki aku hoa. Ko tāku, he āta akiaki i a rātou, ahakoa kāre rātou i te tino, he āhua whakamā ki te whakahoki kōrero mai, reo Māori mai ki au. Umm, ka kaha akiaki tonu i a rātou. Nō reira, i te nuinga o te wā ka kōrero Māori au ki te kāinga, ki te mahi, I ngā wāhi katoa.

———

**Ihipera:** Most of the time, or all the time that I am speaking with my family, or my friends, what I do is carefully support them, even though they're not really, well, somewhat whakamā to reply to me in Māori. I will still support them. So, most of the time I speak te reo Māori at home, at work, and all places. (Te Whanganui-a-Tara, 20–24)

An older person from our study who grew up around te reo Māori decided to relocate to a place in Te Waipounamu where te reo Māori loss had occurred prolifically. As a proficient speaker, she noticed that whakamā was integrated into her interactions with the community.

**Iritana:** I was brought up [with kaumātua and kuia who were native speakers of te reo and rarely spoke English] and [then I] decided to come down here. And when I came down here I just lost it all, because it was really hard, there was nobody here to [speak with]. When I first came here, I met some of the old people and I started talking Māori to them and they looked at me. It was really embarrassing, and I really felt the aroha because they didn't know what I was saying. It was just simple, you know, 'Kei te pēhea koe,' just real simple, but they just had no [. . .] So I think I was determined then to, um, try and teach my kids to keep the reo. (Hokitika, 65–69)

A point raised here is that others can experience whakamā when a person makes an assumption about their language abilities. Iritana's interaction is an example of why many individuals avoid using te reo in case they put others into a situation where their lack of te reo is highlighted. This point is also made by Olsen-Reeder (2017), who writes that individuals who could quite easily converse in te reo Māori across multiple contexts, such as in shopping centres and libraries, would not be understood.

In the Manawa Ū study, speakers least preferred speaking with those with less proficiency than themselves. It is quite likely that reo speakers do not want others to feel 'less than' in social interactions, and a way of 'saving face' of those with less proficiency is not to use the language at all. A Māori language learner from our qualitative study explained why a learner might switch to English.

> **Ariana:** In Pākehā or more mainstream spaces I'm wary of other learners and being able to quickly identify them and not . . . because I, I would say my level of fluency now is about intermediate, and so recognising a few years back if I engaged in a kōrero with someone and then they, they carried on, I'd be like 'Oh shit, I don't understand what you're saying,' and the whakamā that comes with that. So, um, I'm always careful to not put a person into that space too much but to not also make it like, 'Okay, well, we'll code switch back into English now because probably you won't be able to have this conversation.'
> (Te Whanganui-a-Tara, 30–34)

A commonly held belief or narrative is that by code-switching from Māori to English, more proficient speakers are enacting manaakitanga towards the English speaker. But such a narrative is unhelpful for progressing language shift and needs to be re-examined. The way that we include language learners in ordinary reo Māori interactions is a work in progress. When someone with less proficiency joins a group, the group can 'manaaki' their language journey by continuing to provide them with exposure to the language and allowing them to participate as they feel comfortable or able. Such behaviours are more prominent in rūmaki reo learning situations, where the assumption is that everyone speaks te reo Māori all the time.

Fluent speakers of te reo spoke about the importance of creating environments that are safe for learners to use their reo and where they can make the necessary mistakes prior to progressing to higher levels.

> **Tihou:** What I see on people's faces and have experiences that have arisen to be in a position where a person does not know your reo, it can be quite confronting for you personally, and a space of shame perhaps. So, one thing you can do as a Māori language speaker, or kaiako, is you can create a safe environment for them to come into and explore that, but as soon as they go out of that safe space, I think we have quite a judgemental community outside of the places we have with each other.
> **Mere:** Yeah.
> **Tihou:** So, safety probably yeah. A safe space to express or try and fail.
> (Hokitika, 30–34)

The discussion above raises points that also came through in the survey responses. As individuals with high levels of proficiency, we can do our best to create interpersonal environments where learners feel safe using te reo Māori.

The ZePA model proposed by Higgins and Rewi (2014) offers insights into some of the factors that push speakers towards the use of te reo Māori or pull them away from it. When people are supported to use te reo Māori in high-trust engagements (including interpersonal relationships), it is more likely that that they will progress to a more active state of Māori language use. Conversely, when people are restricted in their support for language use (including the language being relegated to a particular domain, or positioning te reo as antiquated), the likelihood of active engagement with te reo is lower.

*Interpreting the challenges between individuals of varying proficiency*
When competent speakers use te reo Māori, this supports its revitalisation. However, the conditions are not always set for using te reo. As Bauer (2008) writes:

For there to be a reasonable chance that Māori will be spoken, there has to be a reasonable chance that those spoken to will also speak Māori. Every time a te reo speaker begins a conversation, they have to make a decision about whether it will be in Māori or in English. If they know that their interlocutor speaks Māori, they have a real choice. If they do not know, then they have to make a guess. (63)

Hinton (2001) suggests that we can assume that speakers of endangered languages can also speak the society's dominant language. Māori language speakers can assume that their interlocutor (the person with whom they are communicating) will also be able to speak English To learn more about when or why a competent bilingual person might opt for English over te reo Māori in a conversation, we asked survey participants who self-identified as competent speakers of te reo why they were *unlikely* to use te reo Māori more often. Response options included:

- 'I'm not sure whether people will want to speak back to me, because of my proficiency level.'
- 'I'm not sure whether people will be able to speak back to me, because of their proficiency level.'
- 'I'm not sure that I'd understand the person's response in te reo.'
- 'I don't have many people to speak with.'
- 'It would be a bit awkward.'
- 'I feel like people will think that I'm too hard out.'
- 'I find it hard to switch to te reo Māori from English.'
- 'I'm too tired.'

All four statements in Table 5 were over the midpoint, indicating a moderate agreement with the statements. (For instance, if participants were asked to rank their response from 1–7, the midpoint was 3.5.) The statement that competent speakers agreed with least was 'I am too tired'. This supports the notion that reo Māori speakers are not māngere but are evaluating the social conditions that encourage the use of English over Māori. The choices we make are complex; a range of interactions inform our decisions to use or refrain from using te reo (Fig. 12).

Table 5: Interpersonal barriers to te reo use by competent speakers

| Statement | Interpretation |
| --- | --- |
| *I'm not sure whether people will be able to speak back to me because of their proficiency level.* | The other person has less language proficiency than the competent speaker. Their language abilities are too dissimilar. |
| *I don't have many people to speak with.* | Limited community of competent Māori speakers. |
| *I'm not sure whether people will want to speak back to me, because of my proficiency level.* | The competent speaker could be limiting their reo Māori use because they have either more or less language ability than the other person. |
| *I'm not sure that I'd understand the person's response in te reo.* | The other person might have low levels of proficiency, so interpreting them could be difficult. Another possibility is that the competent speaker is thinking of a scenario in which they are speaking to someone with higher proficiency and finding them difficult to understand. |

The questions relating to language anxiety were combined and averaged to create what is termed a 'language anxiety measure'. We were then able to correlate this measure with other items to determine the strength of the relationship. The most common response related to language anxiety is a functional challenge: 'I'm not sure that I'll understand the person's response in te reo.' This was followed by a social challenge: 'It would be a bit awkward', then a cognitive challenge: 'I find it hard to switch to te reo Māori from English.' Responses also included: 'I'm not sure whether people will want to speak back to me, because of my proficiency level.'

From a positive perspective, being perceived as 'too hard out' was the lowest item related to language anxiety. Only one participant gave a long answer indicating that the idea that they were 'too hard out' was a barrier for them. This may suggest that Māori are not experiencing 'othering' simply from being Māori language speakers.

*Kia tūhono ki te reo: Theory for understanding Māori language interactions*
A combination of factors can interfere with our ability to use te reo Māori. We often see speakers of te reo Māori opting to use English in some social interactions. There are also individuals with low levels of proficiency who wish to use te reo Māori regardless of their competence.

Language planners have focused on the language use, rather than other factors, such as attitudes, that occur within endangered language communities. Language use is a central factor in language revitalisation; it is necessary that communities who are attempting to achieve language revitalisation use the language (Hond, 2013; Chrisp, 2005; Muller, 2016). Creating environments in which te reo Māori is an ordinary

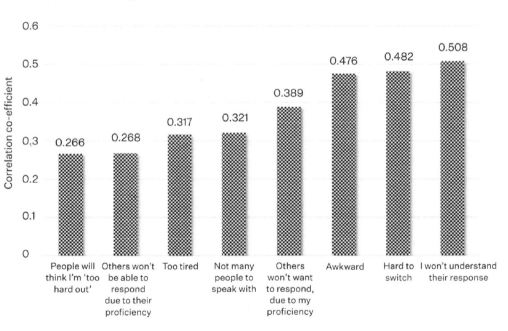

Fig. 12: Correlation coefficients between language anxiety and barriers to speaking te reo. All correlations are significant at p < .001.

part of our social interactions is crucial in promoting language use. But a big part of achieving Māori language revitalisation also includes understanding how interpersonal communication functions. Language choice plays a role in which language we will prioritise in a given situation (Olsen-Reeder, 2017). As Hond (2013) writes, 'If bilingual speakers are indifferent about the use of the minority language, the value of revitalisation efforts is diminished' (121). The choices that individuals make to prioritise te reo over English are important for achieving language revitalisation.

The concept of translanguaging might be useful for Māori bilinguals who are navigating the conversational needs of both interlocutors. Translanguaging allows for greater levels of flexibility between speakers, particularly when one has less proficiency than the other. Vogel and Garcia (2017) write that translanguaging theory:

> posits that rather than possessing two or more autonomous language systems, as has been traditionally thought, bilinguals, multilinguals, and indeed, all users of language, select and deploy particular features from a unitary linguistic repertoire to make meaning and to negotiate particular communicative contexts. (1)

Translanguaging allows for a broader range of language negotiations to take place, as bilingual Māori are not forced into an 'all or nothing' approach.

To understand why two people with some Māori language proficiency might prefer the use of te reo Māori over English, we need to explore some of the contextual information that helps Māori language communication take precedence. This is where the Tūhono model comes in. The Tūhono model can help us to understand, at a micro-level, the likelihood of two individuals engaging in a reo Māori interaction. Learning from the findings in the previous section relating to barriers to Māori language use, we can see three core challenges to language use: functional/utilitarian conditions, social conditions and cognitive conditions.

The Tūhono model groups some of these challenges into two questions (Table 6):

- Do the speakers have similar levels of proficiency, or do they differ? (cognitive/functional)
- Do the speakers both prefer to speak te reo Māori in this interaction, or does their preference differ? (social/functional)

Four descriptive categories result from the combination of proficiency and preference for using te reo Māori. Each indicates the likelihood for reo Māori use in the interaction, and ways in which the individuals might adapt their behaviours to support conversational reo Māori progress.

*Attuned:* This profile describes two speakers who have similar language abilities and a similar preference for reo Māori use. The likelihood of sustained reo Māori use is relatively high, as the most basic conditions for language use are available to this pair.

When both speakers have moderate to high proficiency, te reo Māori is likely their normal language of communication. Challenges may arise when they need to discuss a highly technical topic that they can discuss more easily in English. Expanding technical vocabulary may help them maintain reo Māori use.

Table 6: Model for understanding language use between two reo Māori speakers

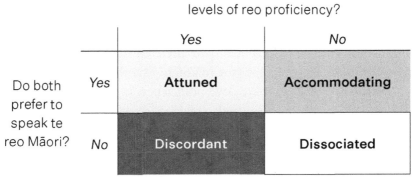

Do the speakers have similar levels of reo proficiency?

|  |  | Yes | No |
|---|---|---|---|
| Do both prefer to speak te reo Māori? | Yes | **Attuned** | **Accommodating** |
|  | No | **Discordant** | **Dissociated** |

When both speakers have low to moderate proficiency in te reo, their goal is to extend reo Māori interactions over time. They will need to work on improving their proficiency to make their preference for reo Māori more beneficial.

*Accommodating:* This profile describes two speakers who have differing language abilities but a shared goal for reo Māori use. The likelihood of sustained reo Māori use is moderate. This pair is likely a teacher/learner or parent/child, or two friends, with one supporting the other to improve reo proficiency.

This pair can transition towards 'Attuned' if the person with lower proficiency can progress their reo to match the proficiency of their language partner. The more proficient speaker will also need to sustain their motivation to use te reo despite the differences in proficiency. There is a risk of code-switching if one person (or both) becomes less tolerant of the conversational pace or of the other's ability to convey complex concepts. Translanguaging could be beneficial for this pair.

*Discordant:* This profile describes speakers who have the same level of language ability but different preferences for reo Māori use. Sustained reo Māori use is challenging for this pair; their preferences need to align for reo growth to occur. Conversational progress is likely to increase when they can adapt their preferences for using te reo Māori.

When two individuals both have moderate to high proficiency but different preferences for reo Māori use, chances are high that they will revert to the language of most functional ease. In some cases, they might not have made explicit their preference to use te reo Māori. Conversations that shift the pair to kōrero Māori might be helpful.

When a pair both have low proficiency in te reo and different preferences around its use, both conditions need to change to allow for a conversational reo Māori exchange. This pair will likely require a third, more proficient individual to support their reo Māori aspirations. Working on aligning their preferences to use te reo with each other will also increase the number of occasions in which they use te reo.

*Dissociated:* This profile describes two speakers who have different proficiency levels and different preferences. These two states are unlikely to entice this pair to kōrero Māori; both conditions need to change for reo use to occur. For the moderate to high proficiency speaker, a shift towards wanting to speak te reo with the lower proficiency speaker is necessary. For the low to moderate proficiency speaker, an increase in proficiency and an increased desire to use te reo Māori is required for language outcomes to improve.

The Tūhono model can help us to understand why it is more challenging to speak with some individuals than others. Many factors feed into our decision to speak te reo with others, including our level of comfort, trust, investment and enjoyment.

## Summary

Strong interpersonal relationships are crucial as we work to overcome emotional barriers to ancestral language learning. Individuals who can act as taituarā, or support people, through the journey can help to provide an environment for growth. As reo Māori speaking environments can cause us stress or anxiety, it is useful to prepare ourselves emotionally prior to entering these spaces. When we feel prepared, we are more likely to engage in positive Māori language interactions – and the more positive Māori language interactions we have, the more our brain is primed to view these interactions as rewarding.

Our language preferences are linked to functionality ('Will this person understand me? Will I understand them?'); social dimensions ('Will this interaction be enjoyable or awkward?'); and cognitive decisions ('Am I or my language partner able to switch from English to Māori at this time?' / 'Are we tired or cognitively impaired?'). As described in the Tūhono model for Māori language use, our decision to speak te reo with another person relies on us having similar preferences to them, and the ability to do so. When both have a preference for te reo and share similar language skills, the Māori language benefits are positive. When two speakers are attuned to each other's preferences, and they have similar abilities to kōrero Māori, the barriers to speaking te reo can be greatly reduced.

Other factors that can affect our decisions to use te reo Māori relate to feelings of confidence and safety in a relationship. In Manawa Ū ki te Reo Māori, we found that confidence often increased in relationships that were characterised as having high levels of manaakitanga. Learners were then more likely to want to express themselves in te reo.

As we have seen, a person's sense of security in their Māori identity contributes to feelings of confidence and/or vulnerability in Māori language contexts. Our participants who were raised in Māori language speaking environments, including in kura kaupapa Māori/ā-iwi, shared that regardless of their proficiency in conversational reo Māori, they continued to feel uneasy when using te reo with more proficient speakers.

Public spaces in which te reo Māori is the dominant language of use is vital for the shift towards language normalisation. For instance, at Te Matatini, participants spoke about feeling an expectation to use te reo Māori. Public engagements, too, are important for providing us with exposure to reo Māori. They can allow Māori language learners the opportunity to practise language negotiations that happen in real time, outside the confines of the classroom. The importance of environments that support Māori language use will be explored in Chapter 9.

Experiences of whakamā or shame about language proficiency were prolific across participant groups regardless of proficiency level. Learners indicated that they felt vulnerable in Māori language speaking contexts due to the personal nature of ancestral language learning. This tells us that learning te reo Māori is challenging for almost all ancestral language learners. When asked how more proficient speakers could support less proficient speakers to reduce feelings of whakamā and increase confidence, they were unanimous about the importance of whanaungatanga and manaakitanga. It is clear that, while individuals can engage in self-directed learning, interdependent learning is likely to have the greatest benefits.

Relationships provide us with the support that we need not only to learn the language at a functional level but also to learn it at a cultural level, and an identity level. Returning to the assertions of Mead (2003) and his interpretations of tua-kiri, those who make up the external parts of ourselves make the 'self' meaningful. We are reliant on others to support the development of our confidence in Māori language learning settings. Again, this chapter demonstrates why relationships between speakers and non-speakers of te reo Māori are interdependent. As Māori, we want our people to use te reo Māori. For competent Māori speakers, this means shifting the narrative of manaakitanga. Instead of trying to show manaakitanga to non-speakers by speaking English, we can show manaakitanga by offering avenues to use te reo, and giving time, patience, and support to learners to help them gain confidence.

We also need to be more explicit in encouraging the use of te reo Māori, particularly in situations where it is unclear whether a learner wants to engage in te reo. If a te reo speaker assumes that the learner is ambivalent about speaking in te reo, they will most likely chose to speak in English in order to avoid discomfort.

Furthermore, language learners may need to actively give *permission* to more competent speakers to use te reo Māori in their relationship. As speakers, we are often hesitant to use te reo Māori with non-speakers, because we understand the shame that they might experience if they're put on the spot, so to speak. As a result, we often revert to English in an effort to protect the non-speaker and preserve the status quo in our relationship. Permission-giving can help us to overcome this tension. Permission-giving is especially important between generations, including between older people who are non-speakers and younger people who speak te reo. Even though younger people may want to encourage te reo use with older people, this might seem inappropriate unless permission is clearly given and behaviours that encourage reo communication are shared by both parties.

*Questions to wānanga*

1. Who are your taituarā in a language-learning context?
2. What qualities do they have that help you feel safe or comfortable entering Māori language contexts?
3. How do you currently voice the challenges that you experience in language-learning contexts?
4. What would need to happen for you to share your language-learning vulnerabilities with others whom you trust?
5. What are some benefits to vocalising some of these vulnerabilities?
6. How might you go about addressing some of the barriers that prevent you from engaging in te reo Māori with those who are more competent speakers?
6. What are ways in which you might encourage others to speak te reo with you?
7. What behaviours might indicate to others that you would prefer to use te reo Māori as your main language of communication?

# 7. Te reo Māori i te kāinga: Whānau reo Māori – Māori at home and within whānau

Speaking te reo Māori in the home is one of the key strategies to achieving Māori language revitalisation and normalisation. Māori language theorists encourage whānau and Māori language communities to focus on 'micro-language planning' as a means of achieving Māori language revitalisation (Hond, 2013; Muller, 2016).

This chapter has three main sections: quantitative research findings, conversations with interviewee participants, and strategies and ideas for whānau to develop their own language plans and increase reo Māori use within the kāinga. The dynamism of our kāinga mean that reo strategies and policies that attempt to support the development and maintenance of te reo in homes need to take into consideration our varied and flexible living arrangements. In this chapter, we'll explore some of the options for increasing reo Māori language use at home. Your interpretation of the results presented in this chapter will vary depending on the composition of your household.

Most of the kāinga in our study had at least one Māori-speaking adult. Typically, an adult interviewee was a speaker of te reo in their household. Most of the interviewees were parents or grandparents. Younger interviewees (including those aged 18–30) were more likely to be in flatting situations where te reo Māori was used either in the kāinga or with friend groups outside the home.

In two-parent homes, one parent usually had stronger reo Māori abilities than the other. In instances where a non-Māori-speaking parent lived at home, having them express their support of te reo, or at least not being resistant or negative about its use at home, helped the Māori-speaking parent maintain Māori-language-speaking behaviours with children. Creating 'reo Māori talking time' was important for instilling and normalising whānau reo Māori use.

We also found that hearing te reo Māori being spoken by others who were not competent speakers was motivating for these non-Māori speaking whānau members. Discussions with participants in the 50+ age group revealed that they were highly motivated to use te reo Māori due to their relationships with their mokopuna and tamariki. Both older (50 and over) and younger (under 30) acknowledged that older generations often faced challenges relating to language acquisition.

There were two prominent instances in which individuals were less supportive of whānau language use. These included situations where there was a sense of devaluation of te reo Māori, which presented as apathy or indifference. Secondly, intimate partners sometimes found it difficult to be supportive when their partner/spouse was learning te reo. Language-related challenges or frustrations were often conflated with other issues in the relationship.

Other findings relating to whakapapa whānau language use indicate that Māori-speaking whānau provided opportunities for language use among those attempting to improve their reo capabilities. Whānau who were proficient in te reo, and those who encouraged te reo use irrespective of their fluency, also had a positive impact on reo learning motivation. Our study highlighted that a number of learners did not have other speakers or learners of te reo Māori in their whānau. Language loss and reduced accessibility to tohunga tikanga was a reality for many whānau.

## Te reo Māori in the home

Language behaviours outside the home have an impact on language behaviours inside of the home. As part of our quantitative study for Manawa Ū ki te Reo Māori, we asked participants to tell us how much te reo Māori was spoken in their daily lives and by whom. Once again, we were able to compare our results with those of Te Kupenga (Table 7).

Māori participants in Manawa Ū were more likely than those in Te Kupenga to speak Māori in a range of whānau relationships, including with parents, a spouse or partner, and with a pre-school, primary-school or high-school-aged child (Fig. 13). Te Kupenga shows that when data collection is not situated in a kaupapa Māori space like Te Matatini, or in Māori language learning environments as in Manawa Ū, the average Māori respondent used te reo Māori to a far lesser degree.

Table 7: Comparison of te reo Māori use by whānau members in Te Kupenga (TK) and Manawa Ū ki te Reo Māori (MŪ)

| Person spoken to | All / mostly Māori | | Māori equally with English | | Some Māori | | No Māori | |
|---|---|---|---|---|---|---|---|---|
| | TK | MŪ | TK | MŪ | TK | MŪ | TK | MŪ |
| Parents | 1.6% | 11.3% | 10.5% | 19.4% | 40.8% | 52.8% | 47.1% | 16.5% |
| Spouse/partner | 2.4% | 12.3% | 7.6% | 14.1% | 46% | 48.9% | 44% | 24.8% |
| Pre-school children | 7.2% | 55.5% | 11.1% | 16.8% | 63.4% | 18.1% | 18.3% | 9.6% |
| Primary school children | 5.5% | 28.7% | 11.7% | 20.4% | 62% | 33.9% | 20.9% | 17% |
| Secondary school children | 4.7% | 18.6% | 9.5% | 21.4% | 58.4% | 37.4% | 27.4% | 22.7% |

Māori participants in the Manawa Ū study typically used te reo Māori more often, signifying that this group were exposed to te reo more often than the average Te Kupenga respondent.

A total of 717 people responded to a question asking whether they were parents or grandparents, and of these, 436 were either parents or grandparents, while 281 were not. Those identifying as non-parents had relatively similar proportions of competent speakers and non-competent speakers (Fig. 14). In comparison, those who identified as parents or grandparents had fewer competent speakers than non-competent speakers. This finding could indicate that non-parents in our study were likely to be young people, and the differences in language competencies between members of this group were less stark in comparison to one another. The other point of note is that a spouse/partner was the group that participants were least likely to speak with. This indicates that specific strategies need to be used to encourage the use of te reo between romantic partners.

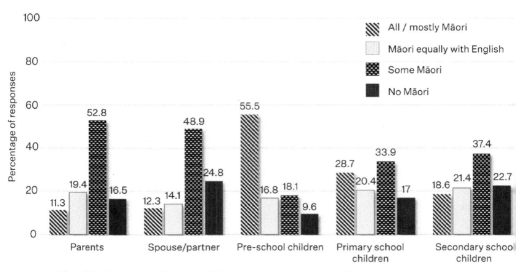

Fig. 13: Amount of te reo Māori spoken at home by whānau members

Our findings also showed that for parents and grandparents across all age groups, English is the dominant language being spoken. Although parents/grandparents reported having more reo in their homes, they were significantly more likely than non-parents to report difficulty in managing commitments to study te reo.

In Manawa Ū, the most common reo Māori interactions that whānau had were at marae, followed by when visiting whānau, at hui, with friends, at work, at a club or interest group such as kapa haka, at school, during religious activities, and lastly at sports (Fig. 15).

The results also showed that those with higher proficiency have more exposure to te reo. This shows a cyclic pattern: the more exposure a person has to te reo, the more likely they are to gain proficiency. Likewise, the more proficiency a person has, the more likely they are to be in environments where te reo is used. The types of Māori language

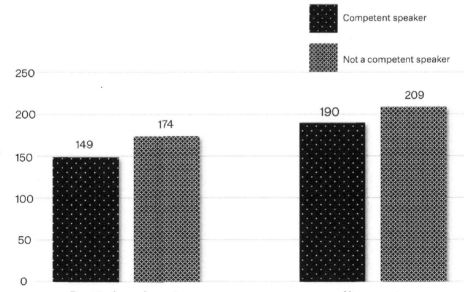

Fig. 14: Individuals who reported their competency in te reo, with comparison between parents/grandparents and non-parents

domains that they are privy to may also grow. One condition appears to reinforce the other.

The marae continues to contribute meaningfully to te reo Māori revitalisation by offering opportunities for Māori to hear te reo Māori. Social engagements also provide these opportunities, particularly for those with whānau who use te reo Māori. Friendships, hui, workplaces, clubs, religious activities and some sports that utilise te reo Māori all offer us opportunities to hear te reo outside of a formal learning context. For this reason, it is vital that we expand our opportunities for engaging with these places.

Urbanisation – an outcome of colonisation – has resulted in marae nationally experiencing challenges in ensuring tangata whenua are supported to maintain meaningful relationships with their marae. Results from Te Kupenga (Statistics New Zealand, 2013) indicated that 29% of all participants were unable to name their ancestral marae,

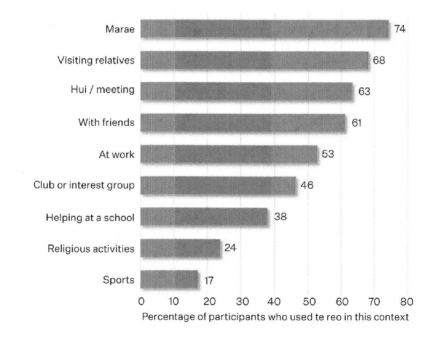

Fig. 15: Contexts in which participants spoke te reo Māori

while 52% had not been to their ancestral marae in the past 12 months. These findings illustrate that a large proportion of our population need both informal and formal occasions (hui ōpaki and hui ōkawa) to access their marae outside of ceremonial occasions, such as tangihanga. Te Kupenga also demonstrated that 60% of those who did not live near their ancestral marae wanted to go more often. Older Māori, including those aged 55 and older, were far more likely (45%) than those aged 15–24 (23%) to have visited their marae in the past 12 months. When tangata whenua are supported to access their marae, this provides opportunities for individuals to participate in te reo Māori contexts. We need to think strategically about ensuring that younger people have access to their marae, which brings with it a wealth of opportunities for cultural and linguistic exposure and the potential to build mutually beneficial relationships. Through their shared whakapapa, younger people are likely to receive guidance from these connections and positively contribute to them.

It is possible that the amount of exposure we have to te reo Māori outside the home affects our language choices and behaviours in the home. Our daily realities and interactions vary considerably depending on how we spend our days and who we interact with. When we have a lot of contact with Māori speakers, or kaupapa Māori, te reo Māori might seem highly relevant. In such cases, its benefits are immediately reinforced because the language has a functional purpose outside the home.

However, while some whānau benefit from daily exposure to and participation in te reo outside the home, this is not the reality for many. The opportunity to speak te reo Māori as a functional language in the workplace is not afforded to many Māori. When whānau are outside kaupapa Māori employment, the urgency of learning and speaking te reo might not seem as pressing. Furthermore, the ability to learn and normalise te reo use through daily informal conversations is reduced when we work outside of kaupapa Māori employment. This highlights a need for more contexts outside the home in which te reo Māori is required, including in workplaces. The reo Māori activities that occur outside the home can directly impact the likelihood that individuals will perceive te reo Māori as useful and relevant.

## Qualitative research findings

This section highlights excerpts from discussions with reo Māori speakers who were part of whānau with varying levels of Māori language proficiency and language use. Our discussions had five main themes:
- the positive impact of language socialisation on new learners;
- the support that whānau provide;
- the different time frames in which whānau begin learning te reo;
- the importance of environments that support whānau reo development outside the home; and
- managing work and whānau commitments.

*The positive impact of language socialisation on new learners*
Exposure to te reo Māori was important for those considering learning te reo Māori. When family members spoke te reo Māori for functional reasons, this demonstrated its relevance to those who had limited daily exposure to te reo.

> **Te Reimana:** I really am inspired by like [Māori language speaking whānau members] when they speak te reo to their kids, I think that's the coolest thing. You know, to just, you know, raise your kids in the reo, yeah. So, like, yeah if I could, if I was fluent, I'd try, you know, use it whenever, wherever. (Ōtepoti, 20–24)

Māori language use among whānau members had a direct impact on other whānau members' decisions to become active learners, even when te reo was not directed towards them. Learners who had whānau members with whom they could converse in te reo Māori experienced positive outcomes. For these individuals, learning te reo meant that they could increase their participation in reo Māori-speaking interactions with Māori-speaking whānau.

> **Raewyn:** I just felt it was a good time for me to have an understanding, especially going back to Matakana and Te Rangiwaea and being around whānau down here where reo is really their first language, and then to hear even in our hāhi the reo is spoken, we've got Māori family. (Tauranga, 65–69)

Whānau who had begun learning te reo Māori were encouraging of other whānau who had not yet formally begun. Some whānau who had never learned te reo Māori were hesitant about learning and required encouragement to build their confidence to transition to active learning.

> **Heather:** 'See, you can kōrero Māori, do a class, keep your mind active.' So hopefully that's encouraged her, because I'm finding her starting to kōrero Māori more. Yeah, she didn't really wanna do it at all but now she's talking about it and I says, 'Yeah, you go.' (Rotorua, 40–44)

Our findings indicated that, for whānau who are considering learning, exposure to the language and encouragement to speak it are necessary. Tangata whenua with Māori-speaking whānau found learning te reo particularly rewarding: knowing te reo Māori opened new avenues for connecting with whānau members.

### The support that whānau provide

Learners benefited from having Māori-speaking whānau living nearby or in regular contact with them. Whānau were able to help learners to practise the reo that they knew as well as provide gentle corrections.

For individuals who were raised overseas, exposure to te reo through whānau was limited, but the impression that Māori language had on the individual was enduring. Terrence describes the influence of his whānau.

Terrence: Being born and raised in Australia, I wasn't around our te reo Māori, however I had lots of whānau that came over and they taught us songs, I think, 'A ha ka ma na pa ra ta wā ngā whā' [laughter]. I think I was like six or seven years old when I learnt that, and then when I was in high school all us Māori crew back in Sydney, we would sing that, chant that at the beach, wherever we are. I grew up with a lot of Māori students who came from New Zealand. So, there was quite a few of us so, um, we weren't shy about our culture. (Te Papaioea, 18–25)

Terrence spoke about singing a song typically used to help people at introductory levels of their reo journey to become familiar with pronunciation. The idea of singing a song like 'A ha ka ma' outside of a learning context might seem humorous (as we can tell by the laughter in the focus group), but for those living abroad, anything remotely Māori can help to reinforce a collective identity as Māori. Terrence notes that he and his friends 'weren't shy about our culture', which differs from the experiences of some participants, who were encouraged to hide their Māori identity through assimilationist pressures. Freedom from the pressure to assimilate is likely to affect a person's decision to explore and embed their Māori language practices. At the time of the interview, Terrence had been living in a flat with all-Māori language speakers and was making significant progress in his reo Māori development, despite having had little exposure to te reo during his childhood and adolescence.

Māori raised in Aotearoa also discussed the importance of whānau who could help them practise the reo Māori they were learning formally, such as in a class.

Louise: Language support for me is whānau. I know that I can always go to whānau to say, 'Oh, how do I say this?' It only takes a text or a call or anything. Another thing that I have started using, it was a lot last year, is I'll take snaps or Instagram and I'll use what I know and I'll just say the conversation in te reo Māori. A lot of my friends don't speak te reo Māori so I'm sure they get hōhā with a lot of my snaps [laughter] and my Instagram, but that's fine. What I'm trying to do is to use the reo so I've reached out to whānau who do speak the reo and I always say to them, 'Please tell me if I'm saying it wrong,' so I can correct myself and get the structure right or however it's wrong. That's the support system I have in that aspect. (Tauranga, 35–39)

Louise was motivated to actively use te reo Māori, but not having a lot of Māori-speaking friends meant that she was reliant on supportive whānau. High-trust whānau relationships meant that learners like Louise could ask for help, which included receiving constructive criticism. Such relationships provided some of the necessary conditions for Māori language progress.

Like Louise, Tai talked about the positive role whānau play in providing opportunities to speak te reo. As someone with a higher level of proficiency in te reo than other participants in this study, Tai engaged with a wide range of reo Māori speakers and contexts in which te reo was spoken.

**Tai Rakena:** Marae, when I'm back home, when I'm with my whānau, usually on the marae I go to . . . waiata, karanga, kōrero ki ngā kaumātua, at work 'cause I work with reo kaiako so we use it at work as well, at home with my mokopuna trying to teach him . . . he's two, trying to teach him te reo, or just some kupu Māori . . . wānanga, wānanga back home, wānanga at work. With friends who kōrero te reo Māori, with whānau who kōrero te reo Māori, āe.
(Waikato, 55–59)

Tai talks about the marae as a place where whānau come together to use both ceremonial reo Māori and casual reo Māori. Her comments show how many opportunities she has to use te reo, which may indirectly impact on her ability to maintain her proficiency. Being able to speak te reo with friends and whānau, including mokopuna, allows fluent reo speakers to normalise te reo Māori in the whānau.

Participants also spoke about holding wānanga in their whānau to directly increase the attention given to te reo Māori. Direct contact with marae, or with other Māori-speaking whānau, provides some learners with an advantage. Their Māori-speaking relationships (and domains such as marae where te reo Māori is still used, particularly for ceremonial occasions) provide them with occasions and contexts in which to kōrero Māori.

Some of the challenges participants raised involved staying motivated to use te reo and encouraging other whānau members to use it. Some participants commented that they encouraged the use of te reo Māori but sometimes inhibited it due to lack of knowledge about kupu. Some strategies to try when limited vocabulary is an issue include:

- setting specific times and locations for using te reo Māori in the whānau;
- anticipating barriers that might arise, such as a lack of kupu;
- gathering kupu that might be needed for an activity, or looking up kupu in a dictionary as you go, building in time to collect new kupu;
- keeping track of kupu needed during the 'reo Māori talking time', and recording these in a book; and
- memorising new kupu during down-time.

*Different time frames in which whānau begin learning te reo*
Whānau members in our study chose to learn te reo Māori at different times of their lives. Some active learners were learning in isolation in a household setting. People in this group indicated that their ability to use te reo Māori was sometimes siloed within the home. Huria provides an example of this kind of situation.

**Huria:** I like to turn the TV on and on to the Māori programmes and lessons, 'cause my whānau don't kōrero, my tāne and my tēina, so

I'm there, 'Āe!' And I'm doing the lesson there you know, and they're looking at me.

**All:** [Laughter]

**Huria:** 'Don't turn it off!'

(Rotorua, 55–65)

It is possible to see that others in the group were sympathetic to Huria's situation. Her comment 'Don't turn [the TV] off!' gives us an insight into her home. Firstly, it is likely that Huria has authority in the home and perhaps can mandate what is being shown on the TV. Secondly, when she remarks, 'They're looking at me', we can infer that others in her home might think that te reo Māori on TV is not the norm. For people who are the only reo Māori learner or speaker at home, it is challenging to create new norms that encourage the use of te reo Māori. Individual whānau members who were able to instigate change at home and increase reo Māori use did so by being a dominant voice (a power holder) and being consistent in their reo Māori use.

Whānau members differed in terms of their exposure and abilities in te reo Māori, sometimes within the same generation. However, differences in proficiency levels within a generation sometimes left those who did not have knowledge of te reo Māori feeling that reo Māori skills were meant only for particular individuals and not others, as opposed to skills that anyone could acquire. Below, Raewyn speaks about challenges she experienced.

**Raewyn:** I would really love to learn more and to really put my heart into it because I think . . . the stumbling block has been me. I'm not as confident as the rest of my whānau. My sister [name], no trouble, 'cause she went to hui with papa, went everywhere with papa and my younger siblings, yes, because by the time they were at high school of course the reo was already in the school so they already had that, but for me, no. So, part of me is longing to get that again, you know . . . then it'll make me feel good about myself as Māori. (Tauranga, 55–65)

Raewyn describes how her confidence to learn te reo was impacted when she compared her own language abilities with those of other whānau members. The age gaps between siblings also meant that opportunities for exposure to te reo varied in her whānau. Some of her siblings received more reo Māori instruction in the education system than others. Irrespective of the efficacy of teaching methods in schools, attributing one's limited abilities in te reo Māori to not being taught in school was disempowering to some Māori, as they felt that they had missed their opportunity to learn.

The differences in opportunities to attend Māori-medium education had a similar impact on rangatahi participant responses. For instance, within one whānau, children attended either Māori-medium or English-medium schools. Those who attended English-medium schools said that they saw te reo Māori as a skill reserved for those in Māori-medium education, as Mania says:

> **Mania:** When we were growing up, [a close family member] could speak fluent Māori, and she didn't know any English. She didn't know how to write in English, I guess. So whenever I wanted to learn, it was like I'm always like way lower than her. Um, because she'd grown up with it and I felt like I wasn't supposed to learn, I guess. Um, I felt like it wasn't only supposed to be people who went to kōhanga for the whole year, and yeah, and the kura, and everything. And because I went to a white school it wasn't, I wasn't supposed to learn it. So, yeah, growing up, I thought that there was always that expectation that I wasn't supposed to learn it. But um . . . now I'm like oh, actually, I'm, I'm exactly like you, I'm the same. (Waikato, 18–23)

Talking directly with study participants about their experiences of Māori language learning was helpful in addressing some of the widely held beliefs about who had the right to learn and use te reo Māori. Interviews with whānau highlighted a need to talk through some of the assumptions held by individuals on their path to learning te reo Māori.

Dispelling misunderstandings requires reframing our understandings of how te reo can be learned. The importance of a sense of rangatiratanga, or agency, about one's own learning capabilities and the right to learn te reo Māori came through in these discussions.

While the previous comments tended to focus on those who were still becoming speakers of te reo Māori, we also heard from te reo speakers who were one of a few speakers – or in some cases, the only speaker – in their whānau, which held numerous challenges. Māori language advocates have needed to fight to change negative beliefs about te reo Māori, an Indigenous language that has suffered generations of direct violence and subjugation, by promoting te reo Māori as something that benefits its people. Given the racist policies and political practices that have been imposed on te reo Māori in efforts to reduce its worth, it makes sense that some Māori would not be completely aware of the benefits of speaking it. Not being conscious of the benefits was one reason why some whānau did not actively seek out reo learning opportunities for themselves.

> **Rakihi:** My family isn't very conscious around how te reo Māori can positively affect our life, and especially having my brother who has two daughters now and knowing that they won't grow up in a te reo Māori environment and that if none of the rest of my immediate family learn te reo Māori I will be the only one that will speak to them in te reo Māori, it's just, I can see how difficult it will be for them to nurture their children in te reo Māori, but, um, I don't think a lot of my family and cousins are very conscious of the benefits of learning and speaking te reo Māori on a daily basis? (Te Papaioea, 20–24)

It often fell to the few reo Māori speakers in the whānau to create opportunities to experience the direct benefits of speaking te reo Māori. However, support for te reo Māori from outside the home reinforced the positive experiences that ingroup-whānau members had when socialising within their whānau.

*The importance of environments that support whānau reo development outside the home*

Some individuals spoke about wānanga or hui that they would attend which were held in te reo Māori. Such hui provided opportunities for whānau to use te reo Māori together outside of their familiar whānau environments. At home, whānau members responded in more predictable ways when speaking te reo than in wider reo-speaking environments, where individuals were not always sure how others might respond to them. There was anxiety around 'real life' language interactions given the uncertainty about whether their language use would be positively received.

Māori-medium education provided ways for whānau to kōrero Māori with others in their community. Attending kōhanga reo provided some people with another place to be immersed in te reo.

**Huria:** At the kōhanga when I'm visiting with my other mokos . . . I try and bring it out there too. So, yeah. I avoid sometimes going to [place where te reo Māori is spoken fluently] [laughter].

**All:** [Laughter]

**Huria:** Yeah. I'm inclined to sit and listen. I love it, yeah. And I try, and I know the ones that I'm going to, where I'm going and I can't help it sometimes, now it just comes out. Yeah, strangely enough I find myself um say, oh, 'Kōrero Māori ki a tātou or koutou,' and [. . .] they look at me in surprise and I say, 'Oh, aroha mai kei te haere au ki te kura, he kāinga mō te reo,' 'Oh, ka pai whaea, ka pai,' you know, I'm encouraged.

**All:** Mmm.

**Huria:** So yeah, hui, um, going to kōhanga and I try in my household to kōrero to my sister, my tāne [. . .] more so at the table you know, simple basic commands. I try and tell them – try and encourage them so I can have some mates to come to kura with me . . . Sitting there shaking, ya know.

**Rebecca:** Kei konei, kei te kōhanga aku tamariki kei te haere aku tamariki ki te Kōhanga Reo o [name of kōhanga reo], ā, kei te haere taku um pēpi tuatoru ki te kura kaupapa Māori o [name of kura], tērā wāhi, me taku kāinga ināianei, he nui ake ināianei.

------

**Rebecca:** Here, my children go to the kōhanga, my children go to [names kōhanga reo], and, my third child goes to [names kura Kaupapa Māori], that place, there are more options now.
(Rotorua focus group, 35–65)

Some of the points raised above demonstrate the importance of places where learners can go to learn and practise te reo Māori, given that there are sometimes few whānau members using te reo Māori at home. Learners who were active in their reo Māori pursuits were supported to use te reo Māori at home, even though they were usually outnumbered by monolingual English-speaking whānau.

The dynamics playing out in the interaction above show that older people who are learning te reo Māori can find solace in attending kōhanga. As Te Ripowai Higgins (2014) writes, when kōhanga were initially established in 1982, very few communities did not have kōhanga reo: 'Ko te pai i taua wā, ko te tokomaha o te hunga taipakeke matatau ki te kōrero, me te tautoko nui hoki a te Tari Māori, ā, tau ana tērā o ngā kaupapa' (279). A challenge that she highlights about kōhanga at that time was that few parents or children could converse in te reo. Kōhanga provided a place for whānau to learn te reo Māori together.

The late Te Wharehuia Milroy (2014) wrote: 'Ko te reo kaumātua, ko te wairua o te reo kaumātua he momo nōna anō' (199). The examples he gives demonstrate the importance of intergenerational learning – when older generations teach younger. There are still benefits when older people who are non-reo Māori speakers participate in kōhanga, as their way of relating to tamariki is likely to differ from younger generations.

*Managing work and whānau commitments*
Our quantitative study showed that, for those with children, managing
work and whānau commitments was the primary barrier to learning
te reo Māori. These issues have been described in previous chapters, so
here we are merely reiterating that learning te reo Māori is especially
trying for whānau who are juggling commitments.

The changes that would allow whānau the time and resources to
prioritise learning te reo Māori need to come from multiple directions,
including policy. At a national level, government-funded programmes
with te reo Māori learning options could allow whānau to study more
flexibly and be resourced to do so. These are not our current reality but
would be extremely helpful for supporting whānau language aspirations.

## Challenges associated with whānau reo use: Loss of reo and tikanga-related anxiety

Throughout our interviews for Manawa Ū ki te Reo Māori, participants
expressed their awareness of the direct loss of te reo Māori and tikanga
Māori within their whānau. The responsibilities surrounding the
upholding of tikanga and te reo Māori had begun to fall on the shoulders
of a few Māori-speaking whānau members, which led to feelings of
unease and anxiety, as Koko says:

> **Koko:** Kua mate taua reanga katoa. [**Others:** Āe.] I āwangawanga
> mātou ka aha? Mā wai? Mā wai e mahi ngā mahi? Engari te tokoiti i
> roto i te whānau e mōhio pū ana ki te reo me ngā tikanga, ko ērā atu
> kāre i te mārama.
>
> ———
>
> **Koko:** That generation have all passed away now. [**Others:** Yes.] I
> worry about what we'll do. Who will do it? Who will carry out those
> [cultural] roles? However, there are few whānau members who truly
> know te reo and our customary ways of being, others are unaware.
> (Taitokerau, 55–59)

Older participants were directly responsible for upholding ceremonial tikanga roles in their whānau and marae. As certain roles are deemed most suitable for older kaumātua and kuia, the strain of being one of a few speakers able to perform these roles was a heavy load to carry for many. Participants with these roles expressed often feeling a deep sense of grief and loneliness.

Below, whaea Judy explains that she was one of the few speakers of te reo Māori in her whānau, and that this caused her sadness. However, she also makes the point that her relationships with friends, and with reo Māori learners, fulfilled some of her needs to speak te reo. Whaea Judy explains that even as someone who was raised speaking te reo, she was unable to use te reo Māori 100% of the time since only a few people could respond to her.

**Judy:** Ko taku pouritanga, he nui te wā e noho ana ki ōku whānaunga, tē taea te kōrero Māori i te mea kāore rātou i te mārama, tē taea hoki te whakaiti i a rātou i runga i tērā kaupapa, ko te reo Māori. Nō reira kei ngā wā e noho ana ki ngā hoa e mātau ana ki te reo Māori, e ako ana i te reo Māori, e whai ana i te reo Māori. Ahakoa te iti te nui rānei o tōna reo, ka ngana kia kotahi ōrau, ka nui ake taku wā kōrero Māori. Engari, ki te hunga kāore e whai pānga ki te reo Māori, he rerekē anō tērā taha. Ko te nuinga o te wā ka ngana au kia kōrero Māori, engari me pono, kāore anō kia kotahi rau ōrau taku whakapaunga ki te kōrero Māori i ngā wā katoa.

——————

**Judy:** What I'm sad about, [is that] I am often with relatives who cannot speak Māori because they don't understand, I also don't want to belittle them because of their level of understanding of te reo. Therefore, during the times when I am with friends who are familiar with te reo, or with those who are learning or on a reo Māori path, [is when I'll use te reo]. Regardless of how much or how little reo Māori a person has, I will try and speak to them completely in te reo to increase the amount of reo Māori spoken. However, to those who haven't connected with learning te reo, that's another side of the story. Most of the time I will try and speak te reo Māori, however, if I'm honest, I haven't reached a point where I can use te reo all of the time. (Rotorua, 45–49)

Younger participants were also cognisant of the loss of te reo Māori in their whānau. They understood the impacts of that loss in the inability of whānau to express themselves at ceremonial occasions where only te reo Māori was permitted. In some instances, knowing that whānau reo capacity was low motivated younger members to learn and to improve their whānau reo Māori competencies.

Terrence: I want to represent my whānau. The house of [whānau name], I'm the last male [whānau name] in my line so to be able to whaikōrero on the paepae. It's embarrassing to go home and see Dad talk in English and all the kaumātua are just like, 'Who is this Mozzie?' Really, really, really like it's really embarrassing and I'm like, 'I'm so sorry for one' and for me to represent [. . .] the [name] whānau on paepae and off. And also inspire the younger generation as well. (Te Papaioea, 20–24)

*Intergenerational challenges: Younger people afforded more opportunity than older learners*

Kōrero with rangatahi (those under 25) who were confident reo speakers indicated concerns about using te reo Māori in the presence of older people who had not been afforded the same learning opportunities due to the processes of colonisation. In one organisation, we spoke with rangatahi who had been given cultural leadership roles within the business, largely prematurely, due to the limited number of reo Māori speakers in the organisation. These rangatahi felt that there was a push-and-pull tension from older Māori who were not speakers of te reo Māori. On the one hand, rangatahi indicated that older people had encouraged them to attend kōhanga and kura kaupapa to learn te reo. However, now that these children were young adults, they expressed feeling that their use of te reo in the presence of non-speakers was viewed as whakahīhī (boastful). Rangatahi indicated that they needed to tread carefully when using te reo Māori in the presence of older non-speakers as they were keenly aware of the privileges that they had been afforded. While the example here is not specific to te reo o te kāinga, these tensions were present in some whānau with varying proficiency levels of reo Māori.

Older participants in this study did not express that they viewed younger people as whakahīhī. Instead, older learners of te reo Māori generally described a sense of fulfilment when they heard their young people speaking te reo. Pakeke tended to discuss being observers of te reo, rather than engaging in discussions with rangatahi or tamariki due to the differences in proficiency levels. The following focus group discussion provides an example.

> **Louis:** No, I'm still an ongoing learner, um, after we had our first daughter, our first child, um, I think it would've been about two–three years after we had our first child, I began Te Ataarangi classes in Christchurch and from there just going to the marae and listening to ngā kōrero and also going back to Tūhoe and how they are just so fluent in te reo and I'm sitting round and listening te reo and going, hmmm, I'm going to get it one day. [Laughter]
> **Hoana:** I still do that. I'll get it one day. [Laughter]
> **Louis:** So, yes. So, now you know my children, my grandchildren, barring two . . . are all fluent in te reo Māori and ngā tikanga and ngā kawa. And I'm still learning.
> (Waikato focus group, 65–74)

Parents and older generations made concerted efforts to ensure that te reo Māori was accessible to future generations, often understanding that they themselves might not become confident reo Māori speakers in their lifetime. However, older generations had clear intentions to support te reo Māori revitalisation by nurturing a desire to use te reo with their children and grandchildren.

*Te reo o te kāinga versus te reo o te whānau*
Te reo o te kāinga and te reo o te whānau are potentially two separate speaking groups. Language shifts can occur more broadly for whānau who are not necessarily residing in the same household. The needs of whānau and kāinga can overlap, but some elements remain distinct.

In this section, we'll talk about te reo o te kāinga (including whānau who might be kaupapa-based) as well as te reo o te whānau i te kāinga (including whakapapa-based whānau). When I refer to the whānau in the home, I'm referring to whānau with shared whakapapa as well as households who reside together, all with the goal of increasing te reo Māori at home. In some situations, it may be easier to redefine the language norms of a kaupapa-based whānau than a whakapapa-based whānau, and vice versa, depending on the group's goals and their access to language support.

The group communication norms of kaupapa whānau may be less embedded and more flexible than the norms of whakapapa whānau. This untested assumption is based on the understanding that whakapapa whānau roles and language norms may have taken longer to develop, so readjusting them may require a break in the social systems of the whānau. There are likely pros and cons to creating language shifts within both whakapapa whānau and kaupapa whānau.

*Te reo o te kāinga: Diverse household needs*
Our research for Manawa Ū ki te Reo Māori did not extend to whānau living in precarious housing situations. The uncertainty and insecurity associated with precarious living situations likely means it is not a priority to have wānanga about language choices. This is not to say that those living in precarious situations are unable to transition from English to reo Māori dominant use, but that such a transition requires a good deal of time and resources, which are likely to be less available. The current housing crisis in Aotearoa is likely to impact on Māori into the future – which also has an impact on whether te reo o te kāinga can compete with the other pressing housing-related issues that we collectively experience.

*Creating boundaries around language behaviour changes*

In 2021, before the Delta variant of COVID 19 arrived in Aotearoa, I attended a reo symposium where Dr Ruakere Hond gave some very helpful advice for learners and speakers of te reo Māori more broadly. His advice is also particularly helpful for whānau who are transitioning to Māori speaking. Dr Ruakere Hond is a life-time advocate of te reo Māori and has spent a considerable amount of time understanding the complexities of ancestral language learning. These three letters have many years of thought behind them: T – Time, L – Location, C – Context.

*Time:* What I understood from Dr Hond's advice was that, as whānau, we need to set out specific periods of time in which we speak or learn only te reo Māori. The length of time will vary depending on the proficiency levels of whānau members. Whatever you can commit to, it needs to be achievable and regular to maintain a change in behaviour.

*Location:* It is helpful to associate your language use with particular places when starting out. By repeatedly engaging in te reo Māori in certain locations, the brain begins to make a connection between that place and te reo Māori. This location could be the dinner table, the car, or anywhere the whānau regularly meets.

*Context:* Creating language domains in contexts where whānau regularly congregate for a shared purpose, such as at sporting events, is Dr Hond's third strategy. Creating vocabulary lists or phrases in preparation can also help to lessen a reliance on English in such contexts.

## Summary

Where research is collected, and how, is important for how we interpret the results. Comparing our quantitative findings with those of Te Kupenga, it is clear that participants in Manawa Ū ki te Reo Māori were far more likely to use te reo Māori at home with all members of their household than in the general population.

This tells us that the findings of the Manawa Ū study are perhaps articulating the experiences of people who have more access to te reo Māori than the general population. Among our participants, it was most likely that te reo Māori was spoken to children (primary-school-aged and pre-school-aged). The challenge we continue to observe is that as children become teenagers, they are less likely to engage with te reo Māori. We also see challenges for increasing te reo within romantic partnerships. Creating strategies to increase te reo within romantic relationships, both before and after having children, will increase opportunities for language use and language modelling by parents in the home. If we are to see substantial shifts in Māori language use in the home, it is not enough to speak te reo Māori with children; we need to think strategically about extending our reo Māori use to older tamariki and other adult whānau members. In this way, we model ideal behaviours to our future generations of reo Māori speakers.

The Manawa Ū study also demonstrated that marae and hui Māori are crucial for providing occasions for whānau to hear and use te reo Māori. There is a dual positive impact here: as we increase our participation in te reo Māori, we increase our engagement with marae. With fewer people living near or having access to these vital spaces, strategic planning needs to explore how whānau and hapū can meaningfully engage with marae. Furthermore, marae-based employment such as Pūniu River Care (see Te Huia, Maniapoto-Ngaia & Fox, 2022) has demonstrated that te reo Māori can be learned outside a formal setting. With this said, we should not consider te reo Māori relegated to certain domains only, but focus on using it across many domains (Higgins, 2016; Higgins & Rewi, 2014). As Prof. Higgins (2016) writes: 'Promotion of, or restricting, the language to specific domains such as the marae, impacts on the use and relevance of the language in our society. We must be cautious not to allow the marae to become the "museum" that houses our "relic language"' (34). We can continue to see the value that marae have in supporting our language, while acknowledging that te reo Māori can be normalised in many other settings.

Our qualitative findings demonstrate that support from whānau was crucial for many learners. In many instances, whānau relationships were an incentive to extend one's knowledge and use of te reo Māori, as well as providing context for language use. Of note, participants indicated that combining formal learning with informal support from whānau was useful. Whānau who may not have had the technical skills to teach te reo could still provide language support, manaakitanga and occasions for learners to speak te reo outside of the classroom.

Many of our whānau live abroad, particularly in Australia, and some are unable to return home regularly. For those living overseas, te reo Māori offered a means of connecting with their identity, which also meant feeling a connection to their whānau.

Creating social norms for the use of te reo Māori in the whānau was sometimes challenging for our participants. Power holders were able to help, and having a pou reo helped motivate whānau to keep on track with their whānau reo Māori goals. We found that when proficient speakers used te reo Māori with their children or around non-Māori-speaking whānau members, it showed them what was possible and gave them the opportunity to practise what they were learning. From this, we know that it is important that te reo speakers use their reo Māori. Even though it may not be obvious when others are listening, whānau often find motivation for te reo Māori learning through exposure.

Environments that support whānau who speak te reo Māori are critical. As we have seen, te reo Māori was most likely to be heard on marae, but te reo was most likely to be used by both competent speakers and non-speakers at hui Māori. For reo Māori normalisation to happen, it's vital that we create more opportunities for whānau to extend their participation in te reo Māori outside the home.

Below, I suggest some practical ways for whānau to explore their language behaviours as well as come up with new strategies that might grow te reo Māori use within the whānau.

## Wānanga relating to whānau reo strategies

*Understanding the goals of whānau members*
Identifying the reason behind the decision to become Māori-language-speaking can help to redirect whānau members to stay on track when the goal of learning becomes burdensome. As a whānau, set aside time to wānanga what a whānau who kōrero Māori might look like. Setting specific goals with specific time frames can help your whānau to monitor progress and feel rewarded for their efforts.

Part of this process means interrogating our intentions and digging deeper into our answers. When we are asked, 'Why do you want to become Māori speaking?', at first the answer may be, 'I want to speak Māori at home so that I can improve my language fluency.' From here, reframe the question as: 'Why you want to develop reo fluency?' For instance, do you want to be able to communicate with others more fluently, or do you want to feel comfortable in Māori-language-speaking spaces? Do you want your children to see te reo Māori as normal at home? If you don't have children, why do you want to grow te reo Māori use in your home? Do you want to have a home where te reo Māori is comfortable to see, hear and use? Once again, dig deeper into your answer. Why do you want this to be a reality? What state of being do you hope to achieve by increasing te reo Māori use at home and among your whānau?

*Questions to wānanga*
1. Why do you want your kāinga to be a kāinga kōrero Māori?
2. Why is it important to you that you kōrero Māori with your whānau?
3. Why is it important to you that your whānau kōrero Māori with you?
4. How will you feel about yourself as a member of a whānau who kōrero Māori?
5. How can you contribute to making this goal a reality?
6. What behaviours will you need to change to make your home a kāinga kōrero Māori?

7. What behaviours will others need to change for your home to be a kāinga kōrero Māori?

*Understanding roles and contributions*

Te Ataarangi use the term 'pou reo' to describe a whānau member whose role is to support, encourage and motivate the use of te reo Māori in the whānau. Dr Maureen Muller (2016) explored the use of te reo Māori in whānau for whom it was the dominant language. Her research indicates that children often occupy the role of pou reo. Children are usually non-threatening in their use of te reo Māori with adults who might be on their reo journey. This makes a child's encouragement of the use of te reo Māori at home endearing rather than off-putting to adults. In a household, it is useful to identify who might assume the role of pou reo.

Alongside the pou reo, we need to think about which members of the household support the shift towards more Māori language use in the home. Identifying how these support members help the pou reo will keep the household on track with its goals.

Finally, every kāinga has a power holder or holders. The power holders will vary based on the structure of the home. For a kāinga that consists of parents and young children, the power holders are likely to be the parents. In a flatting situation it may be less obvious, as power may be shared among members of the kāinga. Identifying the power holders and their willingness to make and sustain reo changes can help to drive language norm shifts in a kāinga over the long-term.

When whānau choose to change the language of a household from English to Māori, it is helpful to understand some of the limiting beliefs or behaviours that might prevent this from becoming a reality. As te reo Māori is closely tied to our identity as Māori, it is vital that when we discuss our language behaviours we do so with aroha – including empathy, consideration and compassion. Working through our own beliefs and behaviours that might interfere with sustained whānau reo Māori use will help us to avoid putting blame on others.

*Questions to wānanga*

1. Who are the pou reo in the kāinga and how can other household members support them in their role?

2. Who are the power holders in the household and what are their language goals? What are the ways in which they can support the Māori language goals of the home?

3. If you are a power holder in your whānau, how can you adapt your behaviour to support the wider whānau to become reo Māori speaking?

4. What are some potentially limiting beliefs that you hold about yourself that might prevent you from sustaining te reo Māori use in the whānau?

5. Are there people in your kāinga who are likely to resist reo changes?

6. What behaviours might come up in the whānau that might be limiting for our reo Māori use?

7. If an individual in the kāinga is resistant to reo Māori use at home, what are some ways in which you can negotiate with these attitudes and/or accompanying behaviours to support the reo Māori goals of the kāinga? What strategies can you use to ensure that those who are resistant do not negatively impact on the language goals of the kāinga?

# 8: Kia tangata whenua anō ai te reo Māori: Creating a shift in societal perceptions and behaviours

Kia tangata whenua anō ai te reo Māori relates to the normalisation of te reo Māori within the self and within our communities. The previous chapter focused on te reo o te kāinga, noting some conditions that help us to create a Māori-language-speaking home. Following on closely, this chapter focuses on the factors that shape societal perceptions of te reo Māori. Racism towards Māori, still widely experienced in Aotearoa, muddies perceptions of te reo. Although there have been some significant positive shifts in attitudes towards te reo Māori over the past five years at least, there are still members of Pākehā society, including those in positions of power and influence, who have held tight to some racist views towards te reo. Mainstream society's reluctance to change its racist thoughts and behaviours means that it is challenging to shift societal thinking about the value of te reo Māori. We will explore these challenges and consider what is needed to shift societal perceptions of te reo Māori so that it is understood not as foreign or unusual but as belonging to Aotearoa.

The relationship between te reo Māori in the home and outside of the home is an intimate one. Participants in our study talked about attitudes and values they have encountered which have affected their decisions to use te reo Māori and seek employment using te reo Māori. There were three overarching themes to our discussions: the impact of societal attitudes and racism on Māori language use; the need for specific Māori-language-speaking communities; and the impact of Māori-language-reliant employment on Māori language use.

Language revitalisation and normalisation refer to slightly different processes. Revitalisation includes the wider contextual struggles that help to bring te reo Māori into a state where we have speakers from multiple generations who can confidently use te reo Māori, across a range of contexts, with a degree of complexity. Normalisation refers to seeing and hearing te reo Māori used in somewhat benign ways in everyday contexts. As we are not at a place where te reo Māori has been normalised in public settings, the path towards normalisation is still in progress and requires critical reflection.

## The impact of societal attitudes and racism

*Managing complex relationships between Māori, Pākehā and competing ideologies*

Over the past ten years (and the past five in particular), we have seen a considerable increase in numbers of Pākehā in Māori language classes. The implications of Pākehā participation in te reo Māori have recently been the topic of media debates. The most notable recent debate occurred during Te Wiki o te Reo Māori 2021, with the release of the songwriter Lorde's EP *Te Ao Mārama*, which includes five songs in te reo. This debate was highly polarising. Not all of the viewpoints that were expressed are captured in this section, but given the significance of the debate to the overarching theme of this book, a brief summary is included here.

Commentators in favour of *Te Ao Mārama* argued that Lorde's large audience might mean that many more people would become sympathetic towards te reo. Some people expressed the idea that Pākehā use of te reo (across genres) is necessary to achieve normalisation of reo Māori, noting that if we wait for the perfect conditions before Pākehā can participate, we may run out of time (Godfery, 2021). In this argument, the time pressures associated with language revitalisation and the shift towards normalisation are highlighted. Others in support of Lorde's reo Māori EP pointed out that she was faced with more scrutiny than other Pākehā artists, due to her being young and a woman.

The loyalty and immense gratitude that large parts of our Māori speaker community hold towards those involved in translating the EP was also a factor, and perhaps this extended to support for the artist Lorde. Without the support of these highly influential Māori language leaders, who have transformed the lives of many Māori language learners through decades of hard work (myself included), the EP may have received a different response from some who were vocal in their support.

Commentators less in favour of Lorde's EP argued that Lorde, as a Pākehā pop musician, was not being held to the same standards as Māori artists; research has indicated that Pākehā learners of te reo are not held to the same standards as Māori who have a whakapapa connection to te reo, even though Māori are more likely to feel shame for making errors or breaking tikanga publicly (Te Huia, 2016). Others pointed out that Lorde, the individual, as opposed to her brand, had not previously demonstrated any meaningful commitment to te reo Māori, nor was she aware of how whiteness infiltrated her approach (Gray, 2021). Criticism was also angled towards her previously expressed 'hate' for reggae. The connection between anti-colonialism, and the liberation of oppressed peoples, is a strong theme of reggae, and her dislike for this genre, which is popular among some Māori, was perhaps an additional point that did not work in her favour.

The responses to Lorde differed from responses that other Pākehā artists have received when translating waiata from English to Māori. For instance, the 2019 compilation *Waiata / Anthems*, which included non-Māori artists who had rewritten their English language songs as te reo Māori for Māori listeners, were received rather positively. This difference in reactions was perplexing for some. But Rangimarie Sophie Jolley (2021) pointed out:

> To put it simply, the artists who collaborate through Waiata Anthems are invited in and they take a risk on that kaupapa. There is no such risk for Lorde. She's got a team of suits who know exactly how profitable indigeneity is right now, and that's what the criticism is really about. It has nothing to do with Lorde, or the translators, the intentions of those involved or even those who think it's a good idea for non-Māori to be praised for creating Māori content.

In this case, Lorde was perhaps seen as the human embodiment of a corporate brand. Jolley argues that when it seems as though Pākehā corporations are being extractive about the ways in which they engage with Māori and te reo Māori, their projects are unwelcome. Furthermore, as Jolley notes, some viewed the EP as a ploy to gain plaudits from international audiences, who might view Lorde as being pro-Indigenous – a position for which the brand that is Lorde would receive social recognition and, potentially, financial reward.

Seeing responses of support for the EP caused additional stress among some non-speakers and some reo speakers, who were offended by the direction of criticism towards pillars of our reo Māori community who they perhaps felt were being unfairly targeted. Some individuals were concerned by Lorde's access to translators, noting that 'seeing a privileged person gain such easy access to reo experts deepened language trauma among Māori who didn't have te reo or were struggling to learn' (Middleton, 2021). Vini Olsen-Reeder (2021) responded to these perspectives by noting that language trauma should be acknowledged, but that it should not prevent engagement with te reo. He also wrote that seeing friends criticised in the media and on online platforms caused him and others to react. 'Some of the criticism was fair, some was careful, and some was unkind – and just about all of us did a mix of all three.'

Lateral violence through comments such as 'What have you ever done for our reo?' and 'Don't complain if you're not the one doing the mahi' (Jolley, 2021) offered in support of Lorde's EP were triggering for some of our non-reo-speaking whānau who are working through issues related to historical language trauma discussed in Chapter 4 of this book. The tone of such comments act to silence the concerns of non-speakers, by asserting that only individuals who are 'doing the mahi' have the authority to contribute to discussions about te reo Māori use.

The commentary about Lorde's EP was illuminating to me because it demonstrated the need for better spaces in which tangata whenua who have varying views and lived experiences can deal with challenging issues – in particular, issues that involve differing perspectives about non-Māori engaging in reo spaces. From my perspective, these discussions among tangata whenua were not handled particularly well, because most of the conversations took place on public online platforms. Online platforms leave those who participate in such conversations in positions of considerable vulnerability. These discussions were not contained by the usual practices of wānanga in person, which would have helped to guide them.

Another example of Pākehā participating in Māori language on a public platform is that of Sir Dave Dobbyn's song which was translated to te reo Māori as 'Nau Mai Rā' during Te Wiki o te Reo Māori in 2017. This hardly raised an eyebrow at the time, despite some of the lyrics being slightly problematic from a tangata whenua/tangata Tiriti standpoint. Lyrics include lines such as 'Nau mai rā, tēnei rā tō kāinga', translating as 'Welcome, this is your home.' The song's title and lyrics suggest that the singer, a Pākehā man, is in a position to claim the role of haukāinga, or the person with authority to welcome manuwhiri, despite not being tangata whenua. With this said, the anti-racist intentions of Dobbyn's song, to welcome new migrants and refugees to Aotearoa (Oliver, 2017), may perhaps align with Māori values. Furthermore,

Dobbyn was approached by the singing group Maimoa to have a song translated, as opposed to Dobbyn making a direct request to translators – a dynamic which contributed to support of (or apathy towards) the song, as Jolley (2021) mentions. Dobbyn's previous work with Māori, including his role on the Māori TV series *Songs from the Inside*, in which artists like himself mentor imprisoned people, including Māori, could have added to his appeal. None of these assumptions have been tested; they merely aim to highlight the complexities in our interpretations of public Pākehā displays of Māori language use.

A final example of Pākehā participation in te reo spaces is that of the chocolate company Whittaker's, who in 2022 revealed new packaging for their milk chocolate block, with 'Creamy Milk' translated as 'Miraka Kirīmi'. Responses tended to fall into one of three categories. The first, most dominant response was that of racism toward te reo (and Māori more broadly), with some Pākehā boycotting Whittaker's, which posed a potential financial risk to the company. The second response was scepticism towards Whittaker's for using te reo Māori as a

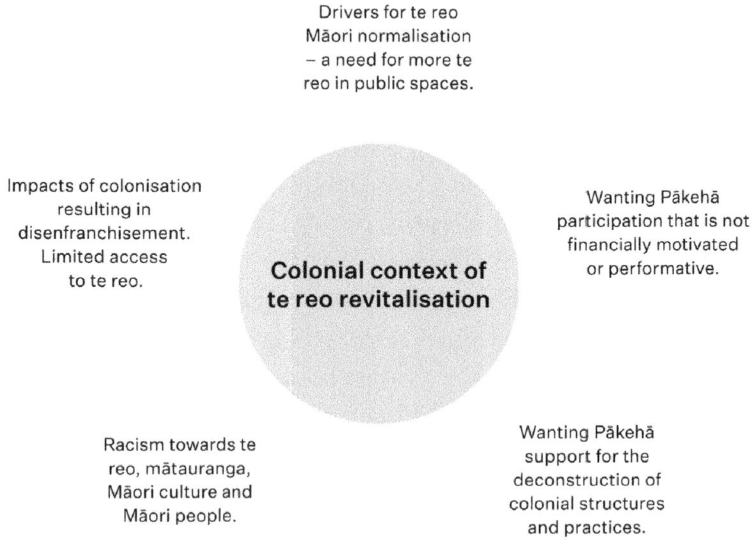

Drivers for te reo
Māori normalisation
– a need for more te
reo in public spaces.

Impacts of colonisation
resulting in
disenfranchisement.
Limited access
to te reo.

**Colonial context of
te reo revitalisation**

Wanting Pākehā
participation that is not
financially motivated
or performative.

Racism towards te
reo, mātauranga,
Māori culture and
Māori people.

Wanting Pākehā
support for the
deconstruction of
colonial structures
and practices.

Fig. 16: Factors contributing to contested space: Te reo revitalisation in a colonial context

marketing tool, with profits as a driving force. The third response was to support te reo Māori 'normalisation', seeing Whittaker's Miraka Kirīmi as a benevolent act of support for te reo. Though Lorde's songs and Whittaker's chocolate are separate cases, they are related in important ways. What we see in the most recent example is that because we are consistently responding to racism, we are drawn away from other parts of the conversation. The dichotomous nature of the debate can oversimplify some of the concerns that Māori in our community have about Pākehā in te reo spaces. Some of the factors that are challenging for te reo Māori normalisation are outlined in Fig. 16.

We also need to consider the possibility that Pākehā corporations are motivated to use te reo due to a genuine interest in supporting te reo – as well as to position themselves as pro-Indigenous/pro te reo.

[A Whittaker's spokesperson] said it was too early to comment on the sales of the blocks, and if sales of the rest of its range had increased. 'But for us this is not about sales. As a proudly New Zealand family-owned company that makes all of our world-class chocolate at our one factory in Porirua, we're proud to celebrate Te Wiki o te Reo Māori.' (McIlraith, 2022)

Companies that position themselves as pro-Indigenous/pro te reo have the potential to profit from doing so. If celebrating te reo is a strong motivator for Pākehā corporations, then non-performative offerings would be welcomed in their organisational strategies. For instance, offering Māori staff opportunities to learn te reo during work hours, or incorporating Māori language incentives in their staff performance processes to incentivise te reo use within the workplace. These actions would demonstrate that the organisation's intentions were more than simply performative or financial.

In 2022, what we can observe is that if we are to achieve Māori language normalisation, the path towards it must be critical, reflective and considered. This path is not only about more Pākehā speaking te reo Māori, but about breaking down the political structures that favour Pākehā and increase inequities in our society.

*Negotiating two spaces*

There have been some quite drastic changes in who we now see learning te reo Māori and why they are learning. However, casual racism still exists in Aotearoa. Participants in this study who were highly proficient in te reo explained that they often took on the role of cultural advisor or educator for those who held racist attitudes towards Māori and te reo. Some individuals were motivated to progress in their reo Māori studies by a desire to challenge such racism.

Creating space for te reo Māori to exist sometimes requires Māori language speakers to directly acknowledge the presence of racism and to navigate anti-Māori social contexts.

> **Ariana:** Why I continue to, to move along my, my reo path is so that I can speak reo in spaces and feel confident with it in how I *whiua* my reo so that a) I can sort of be a push-back to those people who feel like this might be a safe space for them to be racist. I show them that, actually, it's not. And to lead a space and show that, [. . .] this is actually a safe space for te reo Māori, and lead and show for others who might just, just be kind of neutral [. . .] but to show them that this is an empowering thing that you could be a part of. Showing that it's quite easy to weave between English and Pākehā in say, like hui space that aren't, um, especially Māori, but that, because they are happening here in Aotearoa that this could actually just be a natural part of what we do in recognising official languages of this country, and especially one that's born of the whenua. (Te Whanganui-a-Tara, 25–35)

Rata's (2015) idea of Māori identity migration was also highlighted in some of the discussions with Māori language speakers. Knowledge of te reo Māori allowed reo Māori speakers to become embedded in spaces that were relegated to other Māori, who generally held anti-racist views.

Being in such environments allows Māori to thrive in ways that are not always possible when in mainstream spaces, which may have undertones or overt forms of racism. Corban discusses some of these points:

> **Corban:** They're not always aware of their own prejudices or, you know, they've got a particular mindset or standpoint that informs how they view the world. I think having te reo and that kind of ability to move between both worlds, it allows you to look at things from multiple standpoints and so you can put yourself [. . .] like I can totally get why some people are so kūware and white sometimes, because [. . .] even my parents' attitudes have changed to the point where, you know, my dad's even started learning te reo somewhere along the way. I kind of want to get as many people as I can on our kaupapa because I think once you're in and you get things it changes your whole outlook on life. (Ōtautahi, 26–35)

As Corban notes, Māori ancestral language learners often need to operate in two separate language domains, which can strengthen their ability to negotiate who they are in various contexts. But Corban also notes that prejudice can operate at a subconscious level, especially when it is accepted and perpetuated by the dominant culture. Working through generations of colonial devaluation of mātauranga Māori and te reo Māori requires considerable shifts in thinking. As ancestral language learners, we are often working to move away from racist modes of thinking towards a healthy relationship between the self and our ancestral language.

These ideas correspond with points made by Olsen-Reeder (2017):

> Ehara i te mea he tino kī atu kia kaua e kōrero Māori. Heoi anō rā he momo whakahau tērā nā te hapori whānaui, he whakaatu atu ehara te reo Māori i te reo tika mō ngā wāhi tūmatanui nei. (178)

> _____

> It's not as though individuals must be explicit in their instructions not

to speak Māori. Instead, it is possible to for wider society to instruct or demonstrate their view that te reo Māori is not the appropriate language for public domains.

Below, Anahera talks about trying to adapt to 'both worlds', Māori and Pākehā, when she was growing up.

**Anahera:** Even though [my Māori mother] spoke some reo at home and tried to teach us some things, I was really obstinate and really anti. And one of the important kaupapa for her was to send us to fancy white schools if she could – sorry for the answers and generalised statements – but sent us to fancy white schools because that was the way. (Te Whanganui-a-Tara, 45–49)

Being in a Pākehā school and a Māori home meant Anahera was forced to adapt to both environments. There were considerable wealth disparities between her whānau and the other children at her school. These differences, and the cultural differences, meant that growing up Māori but passing as Pākehā presented several challenges. She continues:

**Anahera:** [My whānau] had no idea so it was just such a weird environment [at school]. And only as I've got older and had my own kids and become you know, made my own decisions and forays into the world have I come to understand how really difficult that must have been for my family, for my mother, to make that decision and see her children grow away from her. (Te Whanganui-a-Tara, 45–49)

Since the beginning of colonisation in Aotearoa, Māori parents have had to make decisions on behalf of their children to protect them from the realities of living in colonial society. Some of those decisions have meant that, as adults, Māori have had to try to understand their parents' decisions and unlearn some of the ways they were made to feel about their culture, language and identity during childhood.

More positively, moving between two worlds requires a great deal of cognitive skill and flexibility. When I was living in Japan, I began a study that explored how Māori and Pākehā interpret being 'othered' in some Japanese contexts. Pākehā in this small-scale study often described their experiences of being 'othered' in negative ways. This was partly because they had very few experiences to relate back to when making sense of why they hadn't been perceived as ingroup members. In Aotearoa, Pākehā have few opportunities to practise cultural negotiation skills, which reduces their flexibility in other cultures.

Some authors (McGhee, 2021, and Ting-Toomey, 2005) suggest that, unlike dominant group members, those who are part of a cultural minority (including Indigenous peoples) are more adept at engaging with ways of being that are different from their own, and this was borne out by the study in Japan. Māori participants in Japan used their past experiences of being 'othered' to interpret situations in which they were classed as 'outgroup members' (Te Huia & Liu, 2012). Māori were far more comfortable than Pākehā with being considered 'not part of the group', as they were able to utilise their understanding of Māori customary concepts (such as manuwhiri/haukāinga roles and responsibilities) to validate their position in Japanese contexts. Applying these findings to Māori in Aotearoa, the requirements to navigate Māori and Pākehā spaces allow us to develop our relationship skills.

## Intentional reo Māori use in communities

Creating 'safe' zones where te reo Māori can be used was essential for Māori language learners. Part of creating safety in a language use context involved being intentional about where and when individuals used te reo. Learners in the Manawa Ū study discussed how learning te reo Māori with like-minded people gave them a social group with whom they could freely begin conversations in te reo Māori. These Māori language ingroups provided shelter from some of the discriminatory views about te reo Māori outside of Māori language spaces.

For some students, learning te reo provided a Māori language community. This was also the case for those with conversational fluency who tended to use te reo Māori at their workplaces. However, opportunities for meeting other speakers outside of work and the classroom were often limited. As Anahera points out, there can be issues with not having a set community outside of those set relationships.

> **Anahera:** I don't have a big reo Māori community in which I can speak te reo and practise. Not an everyday, constant sort of place, you know, or way, even though I wish for it desperately. But I also think it's more complicated than that, because some of my friends who do speak te reo, we don't speak te reo to each other, which is a really interesting thing which I can't quite grasp why. I know about the research that you did that says, you know, that if you begin by speaking Māori to that friend then possibly you will continue to speak in te reo Māori to that friend, heoi anō. (Te Whanganui-a-Tara, 45–49)

As Anahera says, and as discussed in Chapter 6, the reasons we choose to speak te reo Māori to one another are complex.

Bringing together individuals who do not share whakapapa or an educational group or workspace but who do have a shared goal of using te reo Māori, and shared interests in other areas, is helpful for creating language communities. In our research, we heard from individuals who had tried to create such communities, but unless there was consistent buy-in from members and regular availability, they were difficult to maintain. Some whānau spoke about their efforts, like Hiria.

> **Interviewer:** Who provides you with the most support to use te reo Māori?
> **Hiria:** Um ... nobody. [Both laugh.] At the moment, nobody. Yeah. Why is that? Because I haven't really created a solid language community where I can bounce off somebody. So I was trying to do that on my maternity leave, um, with our reo pēpi sessions, but that kind of

dwindled. So we gotta, we've gotta start that back up again, so, yeah. So, creating a language community. (Te Whanganui-a-Tara, 25–35)

In the past, language communities were more likely to form incidentally. But as Hiria points out, many language speakers, including parents, are now responsible for creating language communities for themselves and their children. Parent groups can provide such support, but it requires time and commitment from the parents to come together and intentionally use te reo Māori with one another.

Having a community who could support Māori language learning was useful, especially for people with some degree of proficiency who were looking to further improve. However, finding a language community for those at the beginning of their learning journey was difficult, particularly for people in friendship groups where te reo Māori was not the normal language of communication. Some Māori indicated that before learning te reo Māori, their friendship groups were not only non-Māori-speaking but were comprised mostly of non-Māori who did not share their goals for becoming reo Māori speakers.

**Te Reimana:** So, like, all your friend groups are Pākehā and you know none of them speak te reo, you know, so like, you're not sure if you kinda wanna go out there and learn it yourself. I feel like that's a barrier. (Ōtepoti, 20–24)

In a few cases, people who had learned te reo Māori during childhood were looking to re-engage with learning; they shared that they already had communities of language speakers from childhood educational settings. These communities made the goal of re-engaging in language learning feel more achievable.

**Whaitiri:** I know that there are like lots of different communities, especially here, in Hamilton. In Tainui, there are heaps of communities, like quite a few of my friends, they went to Te Ara Rima and stuff, so

I've met them a couple of times [. . .] their parents all belong to the community of Māori speakers, and so even at the events still now, they're 20 years old, my friends, and there's lots of different whānau that all kōrero hard out. So that, I could just probably look for groups like that because they already exist. (Waikato, 20–24)

### The challenges of speaking te reo in public

The subtle and overt ways in which te reo Māori is minimised by strangers in public can cause us to choose English over te reo Māori. To achieve revitalisation and ultimately normalisation of te reo, it needs to be spoken in as many contexts as possible. However, many of our participants indicated that when speaking te reo in public, they were made to feel like this was 'not normal', to say the least. When we feel uncomfortable using te reo Māori in public, it is pushed into more private spaces, which means we are unable to access the full range of experiences of te reo.

Racist attitudes that compel Māori language speakers to use less Māori and more English are another reason why the normalisation of te reo Māori in public spaces remains aspirational. As Georgia says, in some regions of Aotearoa, using te reo Māori freely, including with children, is uncomfortable.

**Georgia:** [Te reo is] not everywhere, [and] not everyone speaks te reo Māori. Even sometimes when I'm out in the supermarket and I'm talking to my kids sometimes to be honest I feel like certain people look at me like, why are you speaking that language to your kids? I feel judgement. But I still [speak te reo]. That doesn't stop me from speaking it. But there are still people who say, 'We're not a racist country.' We still are very much so. So those things are barriers. But they don't stop me, they actually make me more keen to speak Māori. [Laughter] (Waikato, 30–34)

Though Georgia had been made to feel that speaking te reo Māori was not normal, this did not stop her from speaking it with her children. Parents who are dedicated to raising Māori-speaking children need to model ideal behaviours both publicly and privately, regardless of potentially negative opinions, to normalise te reo Māori.

With this said, the 'othering' that we can experience in public can be off-putting, especially for those who do not have solid language proficiencies or who may be exhausted from experiencing discrimination. The accumulated impacts of discrimination may stop us from wanting to speak te reo Māori. Kiri gives an example of the othering that can occur in public for reo Māori speakers.

> **Kiri:** Yeah, sometimes when I talk to my dad on the train, I have all these people stare at us, and then we are just like, oh we will just whisper. (Te Whanganui-a-Tara, 20–24)

This instance relates to breaking social norms. The first norm being tested is the one of silence on public transportation: Kiri and her dad are speaking on the train, which others might discourage. The second norm being tested is that of language. The fact that Kiri and her dad speak te reo on the train intensifies the breaking of the first norm. It would be reasonable to assume that the stares that Kiri and her dad receive from fellow train-goers are a reaction to their use of te reo in a confined public space, as opposed to the mere act of speaking. What this demonstrates is that te reo Māori receives unwanted attention when it is spoken in public.

> **Mere:** One time [friend's name] and I were talking Māori to each other, and we were laughing, you know, all this sort of stuff, and this one lady stood up on the other side and she thought we were talking about her. You know, [. . .] 'Yous are sitting there, you fullas think you are better than all of us.' I was like, 'We weren't even talking about you, actually.' We were just having a conversation in and amongst ourselves.

We don't want anybody else to know what we are talking about, but it wasn't anything to put anybody down, or anything like that. So, I probably get a lot of that. (Hokitika, 35–39)

From Mere's story, we see the fragility of some Pākehā non-Māori speakers who feel that their preference for English should be catered to across all public domains. Pākehā are accustomed to their cultural norms and language being dominant in public places, and the idea that reo Māori speakers are using te reo as a means of 'othering', of intentionally excluding non-reo-Māori speakers, is 'white centring' at play. This speaks to a deeper insecurity that some Pākehā experience when they are unable to participate in – and therefore, unable to control – an environment (Jones, 2001).

When English-speaking Pākehā other te reo Māori, this has a negative impact on Māori who are learning. Below, Eru articulates the normative nature of racism about te reo Māori by Pākehā.

> **Eru:** So mō te hunga whakapeto ngoi kia kōrero Māori, ka raru taua tangata ki roto i tēnei momo taiao, e hia kē rānei kua kite, kua rangona te tangata e mea ana, 'This is New Zealand speak English.' You know, wērā momo tāngata e whakaweti nei i te hunga e whakapau wera ana. Koirā noa.
>
> ———
>
> **Eru:** For those who have exerted energy to speak Māori, those individuals would struggle in this environment. How many individuals have we seen or heard who say, 'This is New Zealand, speak English.' You know, those types of individuals who are disparaging towards those who have put in effort [to revitalise te reo]. That's all.
> (Te Whanganui-a-Tara, 20–24)

Notice that Eru references the racist comment 'This is New Zealand, speak English' without hesitation. This demonstrates his familiarity with such sentiments. Eru then continues his conversation, implying that the audience to whom he is speaking is also familiar with the racist tone of the statement. This indicates to us that racism about te reo Māori in New Zealand society is normative, and in many respects it is socially sanctioned (Spivak, 1988) by Pākehā power holders.

Georgia spoke about the reactions of people around her when speaking te reo:

**Georgia:** To be honest I wonder sometimes if they think to themselves, 'Why does she waste her time with that? It's just a dead language. Why is she bothering?' It feels like that sometimes, because you can tell none of them speak Māori. (Waikato, 30–34)

Corban also spoke about the challenges of using te reo Māori in public. During the discussion below, Corban and his interviewer are bilingual. When Corban is describing experiences of racism, he switches to te reo Māori, perhaps as a way of protecting the conversation from the interruptions of Pākehā who might disagree.

**Corban:** Still a lot of, I don't want to call them red necks but te hunga kūware. Kei reira tonu rātou. Ko rātou pea tētahi o ngā tairo nui a Kupe. Mutunga kē mai o te kuware. You definitely notice it in Christchurch. Yeah, I think um, well even here. Kāore e kore kua rangona ēnei nā e kōrero ana tāua i te reo Māori. Engari, ehara i te mea kua pūkana mai tētahi or kua waea haere. Kei te waea haere a Aotearoa whānui ki te reo Māori engari, ka pōhēhē ētahi kāore he reo Māori i Te Waipounamu. He mate nui tēra. Ki te pūkana mai tētahi, ki te whakaiti mai rānei, ka mutu ki te rangona ngā tamariki ka . . . ka whakamā hoki rātou ki te kōrero i te reo.

———

**Corban:** Still a lot of, I don't want to call them red necks but the ignorant ones. They're still there. They are perhaps some of the biggest obstacles of Kupe. Just the absolute epitome of ignorance. You definitely notice it in Christchurch. Yeah, I think um, well even here. Without a doubt, these people have heard you and I speaking in te reo. However, none of them have batted an eyelid at us speaking or perhaps they're used to it. Aotearoa more broadly is becoming more accustomed to hearing te reo Māori being used. However, there are some who think that te reo Māori is not spoken in the South Island. That's a considerable issue. If they glare, or if they belittle the language, and what's more the children hear them, the children may become embarrassed to speak te reo Māori. (Ōtautahi, 25–29)

If children are to see te reo Māori as a normal language of communication, te reo Māori needs to be spoken in public and not only at home and in classrooms. It is important, too, that adults who perpetuate racist views are made aware of how their behaviour affects our children, and the language use of our children.

*How perceptions of Māori are connected to te reo acquisition and use*
Racism towards te reo Māori is tied to the racism that we experience as Indigenous people. If we feel that being Māori is valued, we may make the sacrifices that are required to learn te reo Māori. When Māori people, culture and language are devalued by power holders, there is less incentive to learn.

> **Te Reimana:** I feel for some [Māori], they might feel as if, you know, they kinda wanna [shy] away from showing their Māori side, 'cause they don't wanna be in that class of perceived as Māori people. I feel like that would, yeah, affect people learning the reo. (Ōtepoti, 20–24)

Pākehā New Zealanders vary in their interpersonal interactions with Māori people. Some have little interpersonal contact, and we can see the ways in which they perceive Māori people and culture in the dominant narratives around us, such as historical representations and mainstream news media, which tend to silence Māori voices and vilify Māori bodies. The challenge that Pākehā need to address is how to deconstruct and eradicate colonial ideologies and practices that dehumanise Māori.

Māori participants who worked in Pākehā-dominant environments, particularly in which Māori use social services, reported feeling that their co-workers viewed Māori culture as consistent with the lives of the people using their service. For example, in sectors that provide assistance to those in need, Pākehā workers tended to express the idea that conditions such as homelessness were indicative of the general character of Māori people and our culture and values, and not a symptom of landlessness and deprivation, which are at the heart of colonising practices.

**Marlana:** How are Māori people perceived? [. . .] I refer to this morning's conversations with this range of professionals, so we are talking about people who are trained in social work and psychology and they work with communities of families and whānau and tamariki where abuses have occurred, so they are finding care options and trying to keep kids in homes and looking for safe-placements [. . .] The stories that they hear are negative stories, they see us saturate the statistics with negative statistics. Top of every negative stat that you can think of in Aotearoa. So what they hear, that's kind of their, I would say, 'become normal'. It was cool to point out some really cool stories, like actually, the way that I and the circles of people I connect with are thriving, doing well, are safe – we nurture, we love, we support, we care, we educate, we are educated, that is how Māori are experienced in the kinds of communities that I'm also involved with. In a personal kind of context? I think, generally speaking, I think Māori are often looked at as not good enough, or whatever. If we think, what are some of the dominant voices that are heard, or dominant stories that are told, [they] come from a very white, colonial lens, which influences the way that society as a whole sees Māori. Yeah. But, yeah, some of our stories are starting to be told – oh, not be told, be heard. Because they've been told for many, many, many years. But now we are starting to be heard. Yeah. So, flipping the script I suppose. (Kirikiriroa, 40–44)

Here, Marlana points out that when Pākehā do not see a full range of healthy depictions of Māori, they revert to dominant narratives about our culture and people without thoughtful interrogation into such assumptions about who we are. This is the 'standard story', a phrase coined by Pākehā allies Nairn and McCreanor (1991, 2021) to describe the contradictory views that Pākehā hold about Māori people as demonstrated through historical and contemporary depictions.

In their work examining anti-Māori themes in New Zealand journalism, Moewaka Barnes and colleagues (2013) describe patterns we see in the media. These include:

- Pākehā as norm: Constructs Pākehā as the ordinary normal citizen and culture of New Zealand.
- One people: New Zealanders are represented as a single culture in which all are to be treated the same.
- Rights: Individual Pākehā rights take precedence over Māori collective rights.
- Privilege: Māori are portrayed as having resources and access denied others.
- Ignorance and hypersensitivity: Pākehā offend Māori because of ignorance. Māori responses are unduly sensitive.
- Good Māori/Bad Māori: Māori are seen as good or bad depending on the argument of the speaker, Pākehā are rarely described in this way.
- Māori crime, violence: Māori are more likely to be seen as criminal or violent than Pākehā.
- Māori culture is depicted as primitive and inadequate for modern life, and inferior to Pākehā culture.

These stereotypes present as dominant discourses. Reid (2011) notes: 'The focus on Māori as "the problem" ensures that the outcomes of non-Māori are never closely examined and Pākehā privilege is never considered' (43). Furthermore, Nairn and colleagues (2011) assert that derogatory narratives about Māori 'encodes a social positioning that separates Māori and Pākehā assigning the latter normality and some superiority' (169). When Pākehā are consistently positioned as superior, their discriminatory behaviours are presented as reasonable or justifiable.

Studies have shown that people understand that racist and derogatory thoughts or comments about marginalised groups in society are politically incorrect (DiAngelo, 2018; McGhee, 2021). Diangelo (2018) highlights that those in the dominant culture are aware of how they talk about race and racism. The act of not naming race when making derogatory references towards specific racial groups allows individuals plausible deniability if questioned about their racism. Individuals who attempt to appear informed about the dehumanising effects of racism may have intentions of appearing more enlightened – when they are functioning well. However, when someone who holds underlying racist beliefs is emotionally strained or tired, we may see these beliefs emerge as the individual reverts to widely held stereotypes, due to the accessibility of such schema. The term 'aversive racism' is used to explain the contemporary forms of racism that present themselves in more covert ways. Aversive racism is described by Gaertner and colleagues (2005) as the 'conflict between the denial of personal prejudice and unconscious negative feelings and beliefs, which may be rooted in normal psychological processes' (377).

'Flipping the script', as Marlana says in her quote above, involves having Māori stories not only told but *heard* in dominant cultural spaces. She puts the onus back on the Pākehā audience by indicating that, as tangata whenua, we have told our stories numerous times; the audience needs to be ready to hear what we have to say.

The extent to which our people are affected by the devaluation of Māori culture, knowledge and language does vary across groups. As discussed in acculturation literature, when people who are not part of a dominant cultural group (such as Māori) are invested in becoming part of the dominant group (such as Pākehā) but are not accepted by them, the less dominant group experiences negative emotional consequences (Rata, 2012). However, when individuals from minority groups are less invested in acceptance as ingroup members, the feelings associated with that rejection are less severe (Nesdale, Rooney, & Smith, 1997).

Social psychology also provides theories and examples of individuals from marginal positions in society creating alternative ingroup criteria. In her research, Rata (2012) describes how Māori who are racially discriminated against can redefine positive ingroup identity based on a new set of criteria that they themselves create. In Manawa Ū ki te Reo Māori, we saw that for Māori language speakers who predominantly occupied environments in which Māori language and culture were valued and normalised, the impact of racism was less than for Māori in direct contact with racist views. This is not to say that a Māori person living in Aotearoa, even a person in a supportive Māori environment, is ever completely sheltered from racism. All Māori experience racism, because we were colonised under the white supremacist regime of the British Crown, and because the impacts of this colonisation are ongoing.

In our discussions, rangatahi participants showed an acute awareness of the impacts of colonisation. As DiAngelo (2018) has written, repetitive and narrow representations of who we are as Māori told from non-Māori perspectives has aided the process of sustaining negative framing of Māori. Ana and Kōtuku, two university students with a strong Māori student support system, spoke about how positive narratives towards mātauranga Māori are necessary for combating dominant negative narratives about Māori.

> **Ana:** Our people, we've just, there's just become so much negativity towards what it is to be Māori, that we've forgot our greatness. We've forgotten what we came from and how great our culture really is, you know? How great our men were, we weren't just a statistic. They [colonial settlers] were amazed at our mental health. 'How are these Māori so healthy?' 'Why are they treating their kids so great?' And then now we've lost that and, because of that, that gap.
> **Kōtuku:** [whisper] Colonisation.
> **Ana:** That gap, our people just think we are a statistic now. That's all that is portrayed about us. You are not going to hear that we were

fucking great navigators, that we did all this great stuff.

**Kōtuku:** They were the meanest scientists in the world. Our tīpuna were great scientists. We forget that.

(Te Papaioea focus group, 20–24)

Ana and Kōtuku point out that long-held colonial narratives have minimised the skill and expertise that have existed in Māori knowledge systems prior to European arrival – and that continue to exist in the present day and into the future.

*How racism affects willingness to be seen as Māori*
The cost of racism is high, and Māori continue to experience it to an unacceptable degree. The Manawa Ū study showed that racism was a major factor in discouraging Māori from investing in their language learning. The racism that many had experienced and internalised throughout childhood and adolescence needed to be unlearned during adulthood. Participants who shared that they were less impacted by racism tended to be fully immersed in environments where te reo Māori and Māori people were highly valued and normalised; in other words, they had little daily involvement with mainstream society.

Participants in Manawa Ū ki te Reo Māori described how, growing up, racism made them reluctant to identify as Māori.

**Heather:** Yeah, I grew up thinking that I was a Pākehā – I didn't even know that I was a Māori until you know, it was brought up, it's like, 'Oh – oh, yeah, okay.' [Laughing] You know, I used to think, 'Don't associate me with those Māoris.' [Laughing] You know, that's how I was. That's just the world that I was living in. (Rotorua, 40–44)

In our study, a few Māori described their experiences as fair-skinned Māori. When an individual can 'pass' as Pākehā, the option to identify as Māori is personal and is influenced by the connections they feel toward their Māori ingroups, such as whānau, friends and larger social groupings such as hapū and iwi. Appearing to be Pākehā affords individuals a number of privileges, and they experience less racism. Houkamau and Sibley (2015a) write that when most other factors are accounted for, home ownership is considerably higher for Māori with fair skin than for Māori with racially defined physical features. In a country that can comfortably be characterised as imperialist, white supremacist, capitalist and patriarchal (as described by bell hooks, 2000), being Māori and brown-skinned has serious implications for health and wellbeing. For Heather, it is not surprising that in her child's mind, not identifying as Māori was self-protective.

The path towards learning te reo Māori requires an intentional embrace of te reo Māori, Māori culture, and Māori identity. This is not always easy, given experiences of racism during childhood and adolescence. Those who described experiencing racism during adolescence expressed how these views extended to them not wanting to learn te reo Māori.

> **Ariana:** I do definitely remember Intermediate [school] being a time when anxiety around my language started to come in. And knowing that I had to start pushing against the racism that was coming in. And casual racism, some straight in your face, from teachers, from other students, from friends. Our [. . .] internalised racism that we'd throw between each other as we learnt our own language. So, mispronouncing each other's names or mocking your iwi for something, [. . .] we used them as whanaungatanga, but looking back it definitely was just internalised racism with no other understanding of how to have those conversations. (Te Whanganui-a-Tara, 30–34)

Ariana insightfully points out that rangatahi can use their internalised racism to connect with one another. This insight is echoed by Moewaka Barnes, Taiapa, Borell and McCreanor (2013), who discuss ways in which racist media representations of Māori can contribute to internalised racism. They suggest that the shame that

Māori experience for being Māori indicates internalised racism: 'The influences of racialized assumptions are manifest in feelings of shame, occasional contestation and a general sense of the low value assigned to Māori culture' (68). However, Ariana also expresses the idea that if she and other rangatahi had a literacy and understanding based on anti-racist ways of connecting, they could have expressed whanaungatanga differently. Rangatahi can learn anti-racist ways of connecting if these ways are role-modelled in their environments, including at school.

As we've seen, racism continues to be a prominent feature of our society. As Māori language revitalisationists, we often need safe places to retreat to where we can give our time and energy to positive expressions of our language and culture.

*Visibility of te reo in media and communities*
There was a sense among some participants that attitudes towards te reo Māori, in media and in communities more widely, were becoming more positive. Attempts by media outlets to engage with their audiences using te reo Māori had a positive impact on societal perceptions. Previously, overt and explicit expressions of racism have been readily sanctioned by the media. Today, with younger audiences not consuming much mainstream media, social media has played a substantial role in shifting attitudes towards te reo.

Hond (2013) asserts that language visibility can be supported through 'reinforcing positive and practical prompts to community language use, particularly through broadcasting, signage and print media' (120–121). On television, te reo Māori is still not normalised outside of the designated Māori channels, and this was also perceived as a barrier by learners of te reo. It meant that learners needed access to Māori Television or Te Reo Channel to hear te reo Māori being used consistently.

**Te Reimana:** Another barrier, even on TV, how like, it's always Pākehā. You know, but like [. . .] the reo is slowly getting integrated into, you know, prime time TV, you see it on the news now. (Ōtepoti, 20–24)

With this said, two of our participants who worked in broadcasting commented that considerable shifts were being made in the use of te reo Māori in television. A reporter noted that speaking te reo Māori could give them access to insights and conversations with Māori speakers. Te reo Māori allowed them to ask certain questions, and interviewees knew that they were speaking directly to a Māori-speaking audience who would have a basic understanding of the subject.

The presence of te reo Māori in a community, more broadly, shapes our perceptions of how Māori-language-friendly that community is. When Māori speakers and learners hear or see te reo Māori in public spaces, te reo feels more 'integrated' in our world. We asked participants in the Manawa Ū study to rate their attitudes towards te reo Māori as well as their exposure to te reo Māori in their communities. There was a positive correlation between participants' attitudes towards te reo Māori and the prominence of te reo Māori in their communities ($r = .22$). What these results mean is that people who have positive attitudes towards te reo Māori are also likely to belong to a community that is supportive of te reo Māori in general. Hearing te reo Māori spoken ($r = .62$) and seeing te reo Māori around their community ($r = .42$) strongly correlated with community support of te reo. A full table of findings is available in the technical report.

If we are to extend the use of te reo Māori from homes into communities, we require resources that are dedicated to doing so. At a local level, councils can increase the visibility of te reo Māori, but their resources and efforts vary. Participants in communities where there was no reo Māori in public spaces expressed their frustration and a sense that the absence of te reo devalued it.

Iritana: The reo, for me, I fear that, they [councils] are not promoting it. You know, they are not promoting it at all. They could have all these signs up and everything. (Hokitika, 65–69)

Although some societal attitudes are moving in the right direction, there are long-standing issues that stem from ideologies that are imperialist, white supremacist, capitalist, and patriarchal; these are not addressed by broadcasters speaking te reo Māori in their introductions or at a surface level. Change is needed at a policy level. Change requires deeper thinking about racism and how it has affected Māori and our feelings of rangatiratanga in using te reo Māori.

> **Iritana:** I start getting angry I suppose, and frustrated, because if you are going to use those words then learn what they are. That's my whakaaro, and I voice my opinion when it comes to things like that. (Hokitika, 65–69)

## Using te reo at work

The final theme that came up in our discussions about societal attitudes and values related to te reo Māori in workplaces. We found that reo Māori speakers are highly prized in most employment settings. Te reo Māori job opportunities provided Māori with several benefits: an income, occasions to socialise using te reo, and an environment where their reo Māori skills were affirmed. In workplaces where multiple employees spoke te reo Māori, it was easier to establish Māori language norms. Confident speakers of te reo Māori who also held tertiary qualifications were financially rewarded. Māori businesses and iwi employers were also keen to take on Māori speakers of te reo.

Most individuals aged 40+ who had become fluent speakers of te reo Māori as second language learners had not anticipated the employment benefits that they would subsequently receive. By contrast, highly proficient reo Māori speakers currently involved in tertiary study had strong expectations that businesses would need to cater to the needs of the Māori-speaking community. Fluent speakers in their early 20s indicated that they were preparing for highly skilled employment and would be opting for reo-Māori-speaking roles. It appears there are

generational differences about the beliefs and expectations around
Māori language employment, with younger generations showing more
awareness of the economic opportunities that te reo Māori represents.

The benefits of speaking te reo, not solely financial, were prolific for
fluent speakers, as Heremia notes:

> **Heremia:** The by-product of me on this [Māori language] journey is
> that I've now got a financial gain also. Having picked up te reo Māori,
> [. . .] employment opportunities [. . .] have opened up from this journey
> which is why I always refer to it as a journey because so many different
> doors have opened up from this. And if one single act hadn't happened
> when it did, I may not have been able to access some of these doorways
> that have opened, and some of them have been financial, and others
> have been more gratifying than the financial aspects. So, it definitely
> has impacted me financially. (Ahuriri, 40–44)

Heremia's observations were shared by most individuals who had
Māori-language-based careers.

> **Corban:** Learning te reo has actually opened up a lot of opportunities.
> Nearly every job I've had in my professional career has, you know, te
> reo has been an advantage and I've used it in most of my positions. In
> some cases, it has been a requirement. (Ōtautahi, 25–29)

From our qualitative findings, a total of 326 participants (37.9%)
indicated that te reo Māori was an essential part of their job, meaning
that they relied on their ability to use te reo Māori as part of their work.
In comparison, 382 (39.0%) indicated that te reo Māori was not an
essential part of their job. The remaining 153 (17.8%) indicated that
they were not currently in employment. This was the case for rangatahi
aged 17–20, who made up most of the responses (42.7%). The main
types of role in which te reo Māori was essential included teacher /
lecturer / kaimahi / kaiāwhina reo; roles in the public service; roles

in the health industry; advisory roles; researcher/assistant. The top five fields of employment in which te reo Māori was not essential included management, administration, customer service, hospitality, and the public sector.

We also asked participants whether they experienced discrimination in the workplace. In situations where discrimination in the workplace was present, participants expressed higher levels of language anxiety ($M$ = 3.18) than those who did not experience discrimination in the workplace ($M$ = 2.80; $p$ < .001). From this, we can assert that workplaces have an impact on people's lives and experiences of language learning.

We also asked people whether they would consider relocating to have greater access to te reo Māori. The responses indicated that there were two main conditions for relocation to be a likely reality in the future: a) a person was not currently in employment where te reo Māori was necessary and b) it felt *achievable* to gain employment where te reo Māori was used.

Although our workplaces have changed since COVID 19, including more remote-working options, the reality is that many Māori in employment spend a lot of time working away from home. Workplaces can progress the normalisation of te reo Māori through their support of te reo Māori use, including using strategic HR policies of hiring Māori-language-speaking staff. Those who have needed to retrain due to COVID 19 redundancies or job loss could consider employment options that are more inclusive of te reo Māori in their daily practice. The more time we spend using te reo Māori in our daily lives, the greater the possibility of its normalisation.

In workplaces where te reo Māori is still growing, workmates who are supportive of te reo use, regardless of their own level of proficiency, help to create a supportive Māori language work culture.

**Andrea:** With my work community I think it's become more acceptable, more sort of normalised where colleagues sit very quietly in the room, working quietly but they are listening to speakers using te reo Māori.

Then you'll get little comments like, 'That's really cool,' while they talk amongst themselves. After one of these incidents, one of the staff approached me and said, 'I actually understood a little bit of what you were saying,' which really surprised her. (Waikato, 55–59)

Those who have proficiency in te reo Māori and who speak it at work and elsewhere, particularly when they encourage others to do the same, help to motivate those around them to use te reo Māori. Although we are still contending with some deep-seated negative views in our society, there is also a lot of positive energy towards te reo Māori, which some individuals find helpful in their decisions to extend their language use.

> **Iritana:** I think it is because a lot of the community now, are wanting to know, to learn the reo. It's just amazing. (Hokitika, 65–69)

## Summary

As we've seen, our communities need contexts in which to speak te reo Māori, including employment options that extend beyond education. Specific language communities provide incentives to use and improve our te reo Māori, particularly when we feel that our belongingness to those communities is related to the goal of language normalisation.

When thinking about the necessary conditions for language normalisation, we need tangata whenua who know te reo Māori and *use* te reo Māori. Muller (2016) cautions, 'The reality is that a language not used by its people or the wider population will inevitably become moribund' (42). We have not yet reached a state where the incidental learning of te reo Māori is taking place in most communities. Therefore, we need to prioritise speaking te reo Māori in all interactions where it is possible.

Our participants indicated that they were very aware of racism towards Māori and how this extends to attitudes towards te reo Māori.

Racism towards Māori people, culture and language clearly harms the acquisition and use of te reo Māori. Racism can be explicit, or it can be expressed in subtle, insidious ways. The systems that support this must be disestablished if te reo Māori is to be normalised. One way in which Pākehā can support this process is to take on responsibilities that assist in addressing racism within their own cultural group at interpersonal and structural levels. This means that Māori are not carrying the additional labour that is required to achieve a state of anti-racism. Some participants in our research also shared their experiences of discrimination in the workplace. This had a direct impact on their levels of language anxiety. Language anxiety can interrupt the cognitive processes that are needed when we are learning a language (MacIntyre, 1994). Tangata whenua in workplaces where racism was common expressed that knowing te reo Māori, and tikanga Māori, allowed them to feel a sense of cultural protection.

While it may be hard to quantify the value of seeing and hearing te reo Māori in public places, our research indicated that when tangata whenua see ourselves and our language in public and in the media in positive ways, it reinforces the social value of te reo.

By contrast, when the only accessible narratives about Māori are negative, they tend to become the fallback position whenever individuals are cognitively strained (such as being tired or stressed). Depictions of Māori in mainstream media contribute to implicit biases and discriminatory behaviours toward Māori (Moewaka Barnes, Taiapa, Borell, & McCreanor, 2013; Nairn et al., 2012). We need to ingrain a new set of narratives about what it means to be Māori for our future generations. These narratives need to include the beauty and dynamism of Māori communities.

Te reo Māori revitalisation and normalisation efforts need to include all our people. We need to consider new ways of approaching the same issues that have created the conditions where less and less of us, as tangata whenua, can speak and use te reo Māori. Hond (2013) writes:

To be excluded from access to the world of your heritage is a deeply disempowering experience. To have whole communities excluded is a cataclysmic event few groups are able to fully recover from. (14)

Our role as descendants of our tūpuna is to hold on to our language for our future generations. This can be achieved when it is the collective goal of tangata whenua, for tangata whenua, irrespective of our diverse realities.

*Questions to wānanga*
1. How is te reo Māori used in public spaces?
2. How do you feel about non-Māori use of te reo Māori?
3. What are some parameters around how non-Māori engage with te reo Māori from your perspective?
4. How do you feel that the time pressures associated with Māori language revitalisation impact on your use and acquisition of te reo?
4. How often do you hear or see te reo Māori in your daily environment?
5. How do you feel about your community's language use?
6. Is it possible for you to relocate to increase the amount of Māori language opportunities available to you?
7. If you are considering re-training in another field, what options might include daily use of te reo Māori?
8. How are employers in your organisation supporting te reo Māori?
9. If you are an employer, what could your organisation do to increase the normalised use of te reo Māori within your organisation?

# 9: What does it all mean for tangata whenua who are learning te reo Māori?

For te reo Māori to thrive as a language, we need Māori-speaking communities. This book asks readers to think about what it is that creates the best conditions for these communities, and how we can strengthen our relationships with others through our reo. We need support, encouragement, and opportunities to practise as we grow our confidence in te reo, and community is where we are likely to find these things.

We also need to be resourced and enabled to take ownership of our learning. At the formal language-learning stage, feeling a sense of rangatiratanga allows us to be in control of how we choose to take part in a Māori language classroom, which also helps us to find the right fit as we progress. Being in touch with our bodies and thought processes is part of gaining rangatiratanga in Māori language contexts. Learning how to listen to our body's signs that we are in a state of distress during a Māori language interaction, and how to bring ourselves back to a state of mauri tau, will help us to learn and use the language. Gaining a state of mauri tau requires that we are aware of the types of environments where we feel safe to practise using te reo Māori, with the understanding that we will likely make some errors in our speech. By practising in safe environments, we are more likely to feel mauri tau. In these environments, we can also welcome gentle corrections; our brains can take the correction on board because we are not overly focused on 'presentation', or how competent we might appear to others. Furthermore, developing our skills in the technical aspects of language learning can help us to feel more confident during interdependent learning.

## Māori identities and te reo Māori

The narratives that lead Māori to reo Māori classrooms are largely connected with identity. Our historical narratives contribute to the identities that we occupy and the positions we feel comfortable claiming. Understanding how Māori identities have evolved in a colonial context can be helpful for tangata whenua to navigate the tensions between our identities and our desires to be Māori language speaking. Te reo Māori can act as an entry point for those of us who have had our connections with other ways of being Māori interrupted by the processes of colonisation. Learning te reo Māori gives us opportunities to participate in Māori language contexts, and perhaps become familiar with cultural practices during hui. Feelings of familiarity can be a comfort to learners, especially when reo Māori dominant spaces are relatively new to them.

Fear of failure continues to be an issue for many learners and speakers of te reo Māori. At the base of this fear is that we deeply care for our culture, and our language, and we do not want to be perceived as inadequate in an area that is so deeply significant to us. Not only this, but when our ability to claim a Māori identity seems to be tied to knowledge of te reo, our language errors – which are to be expected when learning a language – can impact how we see our cultural selves and our identity claims. Our study showed that Māori with higher levels of proficiency in te reo are less likely than those with lower levels to agree that te reo Māori is tied to their ingroup membership as Māori. We could interpret this to mean that those proficient in te reo Māori may be participating in other kaupapa Māori that support their cultural identity positions, so they are perhaps less reliant on te reo to make their claims. It also suggests that they are likely to have achieved their level of proficiency with the support of a community. The relationships that we have with members of our community (whānau, hapū, hapori reo Māori), as opposed to the language specifically, could be seen as a foundation for our views surrounding te reo and our Māori identity claims.

## History and te reo Māori

Our historical contexts provide us with the backstory of how we came to be in the spaces and identities that we occupy today. History also provides us with an understanding of the language trauma that we have inherited. When colonial trauma is left unknown or unaddressed, a learner might blame themselves for being unable to speak their ancestral language. As a society, if we remove the guilt and blame that Māori language learners sometimes experience for not already being proficient speakers of te reo, this frees up emotional space, allowing them to focus on the task of language learning.

The trauma our tūpuna went through is not the defining feature of their existence. Our tūpuna were dynamic, entrepreneurial, highly observant, and in tune with their taiao, with many other positive traits. Highlighting historical trauma does not diminish their greatness; it merely helps us to contextualise some of the inherited challenges that present themselves in our lives, all of which can impact our ability to learn and speak our ancestral language. Participants in our study expressed that once they understood structural racism, including state-sanctioned violence towards our tūpuna, some of whom were children at the time, they were better able to understand their learning barriers. Consciously acknowledging and articulating historical trauma does not make the trauma less painful, but it can help us to interpret some of our reactionary behaviours, some of which may be enacted unconsciously, around learning te reo.

## Promoting conditions for reo growth

It is essential that we prepare spaces for our tipu to grow. I acknowledge that perhaps the analogy of a marā is overdone, but it fits within the language-learning context. When a plant does not flourish, we do not focus on its inabilities as a tipu; we change the conditions to ensure that the tipu has the right nutrients, light or shade, and protection from the elements. We focus on ways to encourage growth. When we learn te reo Māori we require the same kinds of attention. Table 8 identifies environmental factors that support the growth of reo Māori speakers, reo Māori-speaking whānau, and reo Māori-speaking communities.

In formal learning environments, classes that embody whanau-ngatanga and manaakitanga produce positive outcomes for learners, helping to reduce the language anxiety that can be crippling to tangata whenua learning our ancestral language. A classroom that fits your preferred learning style is likely to make the experience more enjoyable, so that you associate Māori language learning with positive experiences.

The limited contexts in which tangata whenua can use te reo Māori freely, outside of private spaces such as the home, remains a challenge. What this means for language speakers is that whenever the opportunity arises, we need to prioritise te reo. For me, this means renegotiating relationships with my Māori-speaking friends and whānau, giving ourselves permission to stop a conversation we are having in English and reminding ourselves to speak te reo Māori. Reo Māori interactions are particularly important in the presence of our children, as we are modelling behaviours that we want them to adopt as adults.

The Tūhono model can help us understand why two people might be encouraged to interact in te reo Māori. The model identifies two conditions that increase the likelihood of two Māori/English speakers opting for te reo Māori: similar abilities and a shared preference for te reo. When these conditions are in place, there is a much greater chance of a reo Māori interaction. When we have speakers to practise with who are at the same level as us, it removes some of the barriers to reo Māori use. This is because we prefer to speak with those whom we know have a similar level of competence, and because feeling comfortable in our interactions helps to prevent language anxiety, which can interrupt the flow of language production.

Table 8: Factors that support the growth of te reo Māori

| Individual | Whānau | Community |
|---|---|---|
| A learner of te reo Māori can make language errors and interpret these in non-identity-based ways. | Seeing value in learning and using te reo. | Elimination of racism. Disrupting dominant narratives that are derogatory towards Māori. Breaking down systems that produce and maintain unequal distribution of wealth and outcomes of poverty, such as disproportionate rates of incarceration and health/education disparities. |
| Understanding one's triggers for anxiety or distress, which may become heightened in Māori language speaking environments, and finding ways to bring the body into a state of mauri tau. | Having practical strategies to increase reo use, including appropriate language (vocabulary). | Elimination of factors that create time poverty (unequal distribution or labour, low pay). |
| Finding hoa haere, friends who can help us to navigate the language learning journey and who will actively use te reo Māori with us. | Having critical awareness about te reo use, including the importance of using te reo with both children and adults. | Positive examples of Māori identities throughout media that Māori consume. Elimination of racist and derogatory news media. |
| Creating feelings of personal safety that encourage the self to enter Māori language interactions. | Using te reo Māori as the normal language of communication in the whānau. This may happen incrementally. | An increase in the number of contexts where te reo Māori is both available and used. |

## Whānau language use

The Manawa Ū study confirmed that whānau play a considerable role in the desire to learn te reo Māori, as well as providing contexts where te reo can be spoken. Study participants were more likely to speak te reo Māori with whānau than those in the general Māori population. This is largely due to our sampling methods, including collecting most of our survey data at Te Matatini 2019, a place where te reo Māori, and Māori arts, were more normalised than in most spaces. Even with participants for whom te reo Māori was the main language in the home, there was a notable drop in Māori language use among high-school-aged children, and among adults speaking to adults at home. Normalising te reo Māori in the home continues to be a challenge, which is why additional strategies and resources are required to support kāinga kōrero Māori to retain te reo Māori as the main language of use as children grow up.

Māori who were wanting to learn te reo indicated that being able to speak te reo with whānau was a considerable motivation. Visiting whānau who kōrero Māori has multiple benefits. Firstly, whanaungatanga can have multiple health benefits. When whanaungatanga within a whakapapa relationship is coupled with the use of te reo Māori, the benefits are extended. Qualitative narratives from this study indicated that whānau were supportive of other whānau members who were learning te reo Māori. Those with high levels of proficiency were able to support the use of te reo in their whānau by providing motivation to learn, hear and speak te reo in the whānau, help with grammatical corrections, and offer encouragement more generally.

How and where we use te reo Māori is a central focus of language revitalisation and normalisation. The language we speak with whānau continues to play a role in micro-level goals. Kāinga can be occupied by multiple generations who may participate in and benefit from te reo Māori use. Kāinga kōrero Māori can often offer a space that is sheltered from the racism and discrimination that Māori language speakers experience more broadly in society. With that said, transitioning into creating kāinga kōrero requires a shift in language norms. We often heard from whānau who had recently had children, and who were transitioning towards being kāinga kōrero Māori. One of their challenges was receiving visitors who had only known the whānau as English-speaking prior to the couple having children. Making the change to a Māori-speaking kāinga required the consistent use of te reo Māori in the presence of those who were unfamiliar with te reo being spoken in such homes, which helped to redefine the language norms of that household.

The Kura Whānau Reo study involved over 30 parents who were learning te reo Māori and who had chosen to send their children to Māori-medium education (Te Huia, Muller, & Waapu, 2016). This study indicated that whānau at the beginning of their transition into being kāinga kōrero can benefit from educational environments and kaiako who are supportive of adults learning te reo alongside their tamariki. Educational environments such as Te Ataarangi not only provide places where adults can be upskilled in te reo; they also take into consideration the needs of the whānau, including their reo Māori needs, and allow parents to bring tamariki along to classes. Supporting these findings, the Manawa Ū study indicated that whānau are managing multiple commitments. Those who have children indicated that they were more likely than non-parents to struggle to find time to engage in formal Māori language learning. This further supports the need for strategies that support whānau who are already carrying heavy labour loads.

## Community factors that contribute to te reo Māori use

Participants in our study confirmed that factors that promote te reo Māori in the home interact with te reo Māori outside the home. Hui Māori, where te reo is the main language of use, provide a setting for us to hear and speak the language, using both receptive and productive skills. These quantitative findings complemented qualitative findings in which participants shared that members of their whānau who regularly attended hui Māori tended to have greater exposure to te reo. Our participants also indicated that the benefits of general exposure to te reo Māori were maximised when they had a basic grasp of the language. Exposure to te reo is very helpful in driving our motivation to learn it. But when we have a working knowledge of te reo, the real-world contexts in which we encounter it help bring the language to life.

If te reo Māori is to achieve normalisation in our society, reo Māori speakers need to use te reo Māori for all kinds of reasons, including functional ones. Employment roles that require te reo Māori have two potential benefits: when a workplace incorporates te reo, we can be financially rewarded for the ability to use te reo Māori, alongside our other skills. If we are not the sole Māori-speaking employee in the organisation, we have an additional context in which to use te reo.

It was notable that many participants in our study indicated that they were generally unaware of the financial benefits associated with being Māori-speaking in the professional workforce. Te reo Māori is a language that can shape one's career path, and this needs to be more widely acknowledged, particularly in our education system. By contrast, university students who had been through kura kaupapa Māori and who would soon join the workforce indicated that they expected to find roles in which te reo was the main language of communication. Furthermore, options that relegated Māori speakers to traditional employment, such as teaching, were seen as limiting the possibilities for Māori-speaking rangatahi. Community language growth requires that te reo Māori is available across many contexts, which means that employers need to expand the diversity of their workplaces to incorporate the Māori language requirements of their service users.

The impacts of racism in Aotearoa continue to inhibit the full and free use of te reo Māori. The underlying structures that allow racism towards Māori people and te reo Māori need to be addressed from all angles, from interpersonal interactions that perpetuate violence through to policy. Understanding the underpinnings of racism, and the whakapapa that it has with colonial ideologies, can help us to identify the genesis of patterns that are detrimental to tangata whenua and our language.

Te reo Māori can be transitioned back into a dominant language of use within our homes and communities. Language revitalisation requires a critical mass of speakers who see te reo Māori as relevant and useful, and who have the access and ability to integrate it into their daily lives. Members of our community who are not Māori-language-speaking can also support te reo Māori through their encouragement, even in small ways.

Finally, tangata Tiriti can help us to achieve normalisation of te reo Māori. While it may seem counterintuitive, learning te reo Māori is perhaps not the strongest contribution that tangata Tiriti can make to demonstrate their support for te reo. As Atakohu Middleton (2021) suggests in her opinion piece 'Pākehā allyship needs to extend beyond te reo':

> Te reo revitalisation is political. The work we do to support our reo is inextricable from the work we do to reclaim what has been lost and assert our mana motuhake, our right to control our destiny. We can't divorce our language activisms from the activism (still) required to see improvements in Māori education, health, housing and employment, to tackle disproportionate rates of incarceration, and to challenge racism.

As we know, learning te reo Māori is a highly emotional process for tangata whenua, as it is connected to our personal and collective identities, both of which interact with the colonial violence that continues to impact our lives.

Tangata Tiriti can support te reo Māori by investing in the deconstruction of systems and structures that perpetuate the unequal distribution of power and resources at the expense of tangata whenua. These systems have direct impacts on the uptake and use of te reo Māori in our society. To break down these systems, tangata Tiriti must examine the ideologies that underpin these systems and how they may manifest in their own thoughts and behaviours. This process is emotionally challenging, and tangata Tiriti will need to develop new tools and techniques to help them work through the challenges. However, the outcomes are likely to be positive if they align their intentions and actions towards the realisation of rangatiratanga for tangata whenua.

Tangata Tiriti can also work with Māori language communities to see how they can support us to learn our ancestral language. This may include tangata Tiriti using their privileges to support Māori language use among tangata whenua. These ideas are only the beginning of further conversations that will take place, I'm certain.

What I hope readers have gained from this book is an understanding that Māori language acquisition is achievable. As tangata whenua, we experience the challenges of learning and using our language collectively. When we respond to these challenges together, we are better equipped to overcome them. Our relational bonds are at the core of our collective strength. Citing John Rangihau's conceptual model of Māoritanga, Higgins (2004) notes that 'Rangihau encases his notion of Māoritanga within the concept of aroha (profound love)' (10). From this standpoint, a central defining feature of what it means to be Māori is conceptualised in the notion of aroha. If we can apply that understanding to our Māori language revitalisation challenges, it will be aroha that returns te reo Māori from our tūpuna to their whakatipuranga. If we are to achieve language revitalisation, our aroha for te reo needs to be greater than the struggles that we are faced with. The aroha that we feel towards one another as descendants of tūpuna who crafted te reo Māori is ever-present. Kia kaha tātou!

# Acknowledgements

Kei aku manu taki, kei aku manu tāiko o te reo Māori e hāpai nei i tō tātou reo rangatira hei oranga mō mātou mō ō waihotanga, nei te au o mihi e rere atu ana ki a koutou. Kei te kimi taunga tonu ngā manu o te wao i te hinganga o te tini kua ngaro atu ki te pō. Ko te ngākau marū tēnei e tuhi ana i ngā kupu mei kore ake e rongo te ao wairua. Ki te hunga e ārahi tonu nei i a mātou te hunga e ako reo rua ana, kāore e ārikarika ngā mihi mai i te whatumanawa mō koutou e noho ana hei taituarā mō mātou ngā rangatahi i tēnei ao hurihuri.

This book was written with the support of many. Our participants who spoke to us about their deeply personal experiences cannot be thanked enough. Your views and experiences moved me, and I'm sure others will feel similarly. The participants who took time to complete our surveys also gave considerable time to our study. My calculations equate to 237.6 collective hours contributed. Again, the questions that participants answered were also personal. It is my sincere hope that the collective voices shared in this study are used to empower tangata whenua on the journey towards reclaiming te reo Māori as their normal language of communication. We also give thanks to those who helped arrange interviews with focus group participants, including Koko Hotere, Tutu Kautai, Justyce Maniapoto, Arihia McClutchie, and Tihou Weepu-Messenger. Without your support, our focus group interviews would not have been able to explore the diversity of Māori language experiences.

This week marks 50 years since Te Petihana Reo Māori, the Māori language petition of 1972, signed by over 30,000 (Meredith, 2015), was brought to the steps of Parliament, carried by Hana Te Hemara. Ngā Tamatoa, the Te Reo Māori Society, and Huinga Rangatahi supported this initiative and were crucial in this movement (Ministry for Culture and Heritage, 2021) that subsequently led to Te Wiki o te Reo Māori. The aspirations of these rangatahi to have te reo Māori formally acknowledged and recognised by all of Aotearoa is an aspiration that is still being actualised, as affirmed by Prof Higgins in her speech at Makuru: Ngā Hua o te Petihana Reo Māori. With this said, if it were not for the hard work of tangata whenua over consecutive generations to resist forces of colonialism, we would be in a far different position today from where we are now with respect to language revitalisation. I acknowledge the physical and emotional toll that these acts of resistance have taken on our people to ensure that te reo Māori is retained for future generations.

As I write these acknowledgements, I am flooded with memories. I am overwhelmed with gratitude to those who continue to provide inspiration and support. This book is dedicated to Max Aranui, husband to my cousin Hinekura Maniapoto Aranui, who was instrumental in supporting the reo Māori aspirations of our whānau, including through a series of wānanga. I would think about Max often as I reflected on some of the experiences of our participants. Max passed away during the weeks that I started writing this book. His presence is felt ā-wairua, but is also sincerely missed by each of us who had the privilege of knowing him huri noa i te ao.

When we collected data for Manawa Ū ki te Reo Māori, which makes up the finding of this study, we had experienced severe losses in many reo Māori communities, including the passing of Hema Temara, Te Wharehuia Milroy (CNZM QSO), Wiremu Kaa and Waana Davis (QSO) to name a few. Between completing the Manawa Ū ki te Reo report and writing this book, iwi experienced further losses, including those who were instrumental to Māori language recognition, such as Dr Huirangi Waikerepuru (CNZM). Bereavements such as the loss of Dr Huirangi Waikerepuru introduced new ways of dealing with tangihanga under COVID 19 restrictions. Earlier this year, the loss of Dr Moana Jackson had a devastating impact on many who'd had their experiences as tangata whenua in a colonial context validated by this quietly spoken, intellectual giant. In the same week that Moana passed away, so too did Dame June Jackson (DNZM QSO), leaving her whānau and community in mourning. When people from our communities who are critical knowledge-holders of te reo Māori and mātauranga Māori pass on, these loses are magnified at the collective level. Each of these losses were ever present during the time that this book was written.

At a whānau level, we experienced challenges relating to grief during COVID 19 ourselves, as we also saw the departure of own koro Winston (Te Winitana) Maniapoto, who was a leader in the field of Māori health, our cousin Kirione Maniapoto, Maraea Turnbull, sisters Aunty Celia and Aunty Andrea Marshall, Uncle Wayne Taitoko, and Koro Colin Te Huia. This is an incomplete list of loved ones who passed on, most of whom departed this life prematurely.

With the many deaths that take place alongside us the living, the urgency of cultural and linguistic revitalisation is ever-present within us, particularly from the perspective of intergenerational language transmission. I am grateful for the opportunity to have time to reflect on what all of this means. As time is our most precious commodity, I am grateful to those who care for our babies while we attend to the issues raised in this book. Without naming names, we know who you are, and we are immeasurably appreciative.

To our research team, Tai Ahu, Dr Maureen Muller, thank you for the interviews that you undertook and the care that you put into these kōrero. Ririwai Fox, thank you for your quantitative research contributions, your skills are very much relied upon and appreciated. Alana Haenga O'Brien, Kahu Haimona, Ataria Sharman, thank you all for the many hours of transcription and the thought that you gave to interpreting the long-answer responses, as well as your roles in collecting survey responses at Te Matatini alongside Venise Clarke, Te Tāruna Parangi. Thanks to Melissa Fiu for keeping your administrative role. To Paul Edwards and Rhianan James, your contributions are invaluable to our team at Te Kawa a Māui. Always willing to go beyond what's required.

To Te Matatini and the Aheiha campaign team, including Mere Takoko and others who helped to test the survey prior to it being launched, your feedback made a difference – thank you. Also to Paul Meredith, who supported us with this aspect of data collection.

Immensely grateful to Te Mātāwai (past and present team members), including Mikaia Leach, Ria Tomoana and Jonathan Kilgour for your many contributions and support for this research, and for funding Manawa Ū ki te Reo Māori. To Poia Rewi, I cannot thank you enough for the thought that you put into writing the Foreword, which involved taking considerable time to read this book and synthesise its meaning, amongst the many ways in which you support our communities across Aotearoa.

Thanks to Dr Ruakere Hond, Prof. Richard Benton, Dr Arama Rata and Prof. Chris Sibley for your considered feedback in the design of the Manawa

Ū ki te Reo Māori survey. The feedback had an impact on the results that we gathered and the meaning that we were able to make from the survey responses based on your guidance.

To Ashleigh Young, our editor, thank you hardly seems sufficient! I am grateful for your positive response to my initial request for support to write this book, published by Te Herenga Waka University Press. The way that you've helped reshaped some of my clumsy wording is very much appreciated. Thanks also to Tayi Tibble and your role as the publicist, and to the rest of the THW team, thank you all.

Ngā Pae o te Māramatanga, thank you to the support that you provide to many indigenous academics nationally, and globally. I am grateful to be a recipient of the Ngā Pae o te Māramatanga publication grant that helped me with aspects of this book.

To the team at Te Kawa a Māui, Te Whānau o Te Herenga Waka, Toihuarewa, you are the most consistently supportive colleagues I could ask for, koia ahau e mihi ana. Ngā mihi hoki ki a koe Hollie Smith rāua ko Kelly Keane-Tuala i ā kōrua mahi whakaako, kia wātea ai ahau ki tēnei pukapuka ahakoa ngā pēhitanga ki runga i a kōrua. To our DVC Māori, Prof. Rawinia Higgins, thank you for your leadership in these challenging times and support as a wahine Māori academic more generally. To Maria Bargh and Ocean Mercier, your support as Heads of School over the past few terms was instrumental in allowing this research to take place.

Tāne Morris, thank you immensely for your cover art designs. Also to my cousin Jessica Sanderson, your support with traversing this space was highly valuable.

Grateful for my friends who keep me accountable and uplifted even when I don't know I need it. To my many diverse and unorthodox whānau who accept me and support me, ko tātou tātou. Ki taku tāringi, tē taea te whakakotahi i ngā rau aroha mōu. Thank you for being my darling, pāpā to our babies, and friend and confidant. Finally, ki ā māua tokorua, ko kōrua tō māua ko Pāpā ao. He aroha mutunga kore ki a kōrua.

# References

Archibald, J. (2008). *Indigenous storywork: Educating the heart, mind, body, and spirit.* UBC Press.

Awatere, D. (1984). *Maori Sovereignty.* Broadsheet.

Bauer, W. (2008). Is the health of te reo Māori improving? *Te Reo, 51,* 33–73. search.informit.org/doi/10.3316/informit.586988214570105

Benton, N.B.E & Benton, R.A. (1999). *Revitalizing the Māori language. Consultants' Report to the Māori Development Education Commission.* Māori Development Education Commission.

Brash, D. (2004, Jan. 27). Nationhood: Don Brash speech Orewa Rotary Club. *Scoop New Media.* scoop.co.nz/stories/PA0401/S00220/nationhood-don-brash-speech-orewa-rotary-club.htm

Bright, N., Lawes, E., Keane, B., & McKinley, S. (2018). *He reo ora: Māori language revitalisation activities and resources in homes and communities.* Te Wāhanga – New Zealand Council for Educational Research for Te Mātāwai.

Brittain, E. & Tuffin, K. (2017). Ko tēhea te ara tika? A discourse analysis of Māori experience in the criminal justice system. *New Zealand Journal of Psychology (Online), 46*(2), 99–107.

Brooking, K. [@KajunBrooking]. (2022, July 6). *How Te Reo speaking Maori look at the rest of us Hori's.* [Image attached]. [Tweet]. Twitter. twitter.com/KajunBrooking/status/1544521228354211846?s=20&t=Ba0wMZAdbRZR5r7Rtcx9Xg

Brown, A.M. (2019). *Pleasure activism.* AK Press.

Chrisp, S. (2005). Māori intergenerational language transmission. *International Journal of the Sociology of Language, 172,* 149–181. doi.org/10.1515/ijsl.2005.2005.172.149

Coombes, A. (2006). Memory and history in settler colonialism. In A. Coombes (Ed.), *Rethinking settler colonialism: History and memory in Australia, Canada, Aotearoa New Zealand and South Africa,* 1–12. Manchester University Press.

Cooper, A. (2018). *Filming the colonial past: The New Zealand Wars on screen.* Otago University Press.

Crenshaw, K. (1989). Demarginalizing the intersection of race and sex: A Black feminist critique of antidiscrimination doctrine, feminist theory and antiracist politics. *University of Chicago Legal Forum, 1989*(1), 139–167.

Crocker, T. (2016). Reconciliation and resolution the Office of Treaty Settlements and the Treaty of Waitangi claims process in Aotearoa New Zealand. In P. Adds, B. Bonisch–Brednich, R.S. Hill, & G. Whimp (Eds.), *Reconciliation, representation and indigeneity: 'Biculturalism' in Aotearoa New Zealand*, 81–94. Universitätsverlag Winter.

DiAngelo, R. (2018). White fragility: *Why it's so hard for white people to talk about racism*. Beacon Press.

Duran, E. (2019). *Healing the soul wound: Trauma-informed counseling for Indigenous communities*. Teachers College Press.

Durie, M. (2001). *Mauri ora: The dynamics of Māori health*. Oxford University Press.

Edwards, A.J. (2020). *Blood quantum: A Pūrākau approach to understanding the impact of 'blood quantum' in Māori identity*. [Doctoral thesis, University of Waikato]. Research Commons. hdl.handle.net/10289/13766

Edwards, W., Theodore, R., Ratima, M., & Reddy, R. (2018). Māori positive ageing. *NZ Medical Journal, 131*(1484), 10–12. journal.nzma.org.nz/journal-articles/maori-positive-ageing

Gaertner, S.L., Dovidio, J.F., Nier, J., Hodson, G., & Houlette, M A. (2005). Aversive racism: Bias without intention. In L.B. Nielson & R.L. Nielson (Eds.), *Handbook of employment discrimination research*, 377–393. Springer.

Gloyne, P. (2014). Te Panekiretanga o te reo. In R. Higgins, P. Rewi & V. Olsen-Reeder (Eds.), *The value of the Māori language: Te hua o te reo Māori, 2*, 305–318. Huia.

Godfery, M. (2021, Sept. 14). Give Lorde a break. Non-Māori must speak Māori for it to survive. *The Guardian*. theguardian.com/world/2021/sep/14/give-lorde-a-break-non-maori-must-speak-maori-for-it-to-survive

Gray, J. (2021, Sept. 10) 'Tokenism in full force': My take on Lorde's album. *The Big Idea*. thebigidea.nz/stories/tokenism-in-full-force-my-take-on-lordes-album

Gregory, A., Borell, B., McCreanor, T., Moewaka Barnes, A., Nairn, R., Rankine, J., Abel, S., Taiapa, K., & Kaiwai, H. (2011). Reading news about Māori: Responses from Māori audiences. *Alternative: An International Journal of Indigenous Peoples, 7*(1), 51–64.

Hamley, L., Groot, S., Le Grice, J., Gillon, A., Greaves, L., Manchi, M., & Clark, T. (2021). 'You're the one that was on Uncle's wall!': Identity, whanaungatanga and connection for takatāpui (LGBTQ+ Māori). *Genealogy, 5*(2), 54. doi.org/10.3390/genealogy5020054

Haque, E. & Patrick, D. (2015). Indigenous languages and the racial hierarchisation of language policy in Canada. *Journal of Multilingual and Multicultural Development, 36*(1), 27–41.

Harris, V. (2017). The case for language learner strategies and how it responds to modern foreign languages. In V. Harris, *Language learner strategies: Contexts, issues and applications in second language learning and teaching*, 9–26. Bloomsbury Academic.

Hartmann, W.E & Gone, J.P. (2014). American Indian historical trauma: Community perspectives from two Great Plains medicine men. *American Journal of Community Psychology, 54*(3–4): 274–88. doi.org/10.1007/s10464-014-9671-1

Hayden, L. (2020, 2 Dec.). Inside the *Stuff* apology to Māori. *The Spinoff.* thespinoff. co.nz/atea/02-12-2020/inside-the-stuff-apology

Higgins, R. (2016). Ki wīwī, ki wāwā: Normalising the Māori language. In P. Adds, B. Bonisch-Brednich, R.S. Hill, & G. Whimp (Eds.), *Reconciliation, representation and indigeneity: 'Biculturalism' in Aotearoa New Zealand*, 25–38. Universitätsverlag Winter.

Higgins, R. & Rewi, P. (2014). ZePA-Right-shifting: Reorientation towards normalisation. In R. Higgins, P. Rewi, & V. Olsen-Reeder (Eds), *The value of the Māori language: Te hua o te reo Māori*, 2, 7–32. Huia.

Higgins, R., Rewi, P. & Olsen-Reeder, V. (2014). *The value of the Maori language: Te hua o te reo Māori, 2*. Huia.

Higgins, R.R. (2004). *He tānga ngutu, he tuhoetanga te mana motuhake o te tā moko wahine*. [Doctoral dissertation, University of Otago]. OUR Archive. hdl.handle. net/10523/157

Higgins, T.R. (2014). Kia ora tonu mō ake tonu e! In R. Higgins, P. Rewi, & V. Olsen-Reeder (Eds), *The value of the Māori language: Te hua o te reo Māori, 2*, 269–90. Huia.

Hinton, L. (2001). Language revitalization: An overview. In L. Hinton & K. Hale (Eds)., *The green book of language revitalization in practice*, 1–18. Brill.

Hofstede, G. (2011). Dimensionalizing cultures: The Hofstede model in context. *Online readings in psychology and culture, 2*(1), 2307–0919.1014. doi.org/10.9707/2307-0919.1014

Hogan, F. (2021, June 5). Colonisation a good thing for Māori 'on balance' – National MP Paul Goldsmith. *Newshub.* newshub.co.nz/home/politics/2021/06/ colonisation-a-good-thing-for-m-ori-on-balance-national-mp-paul-goldsmith. html

Hond, R. (2013). *Matua te reo, matua te tangata: Speaker community: Visions, approaches, outcomes*. [Doctoral thesis, Massey University]. Theses and Dissertations. hdl.handle.net/10179/5439

Hooks, B. (2000). *Feminism is for everybody: Passionate politics*. Pluto Press.

Houkamau, C.A. (2010). Identity construction and reconstruction: The role of socio-historical contexts in shaping Māori women's identity. *Social Identities, 16*, 179–196. doi.org/10.1080/13504631003688872.

Houkamau, C.A. & Sibley, C.G. (2015a). Looking Māori predicts decreased rates of home ownership: Institutional racism in housing based on perceived appearance. *PLoS ONE 10*(3), e0118540. doi.org/10.1371/journal.pone.0118540

Houkamau, C.A. & Sibley, C.G. (2015b). The revised multidimensional model of Māori identity and cultural engagement (Mmm-Ice2). *Social indicators research, 122*(1), 279–96. jstor.org/stable/24721417

Hunia, T. M. (2016). *He kōpara e kō nei i te ata/Māori language socialisation and acquisition by two bilingual children: A case-study approach*. [Doctoral thesis, Victoria University of Wellington]. Doctoral Theses. hdl.handle.net/10063/5045

Jackson, M. (2020). Where to next? Decolonisation and the stories in the land. In *Imagining decolonisation*, 55–64. Bridget Williams Books.

Jackson, M. (2011). Hui reflections: Research and the consolations of bravery. In *Kei Tua o Te Pae hui proceedings: The challenges of kaupapa Māori research in the 21st century, Pipitea Marae, Wellington, 5–6 May 2011*, 71–78. New Zealand Council for Educational Research.

Jackson, M. (1987). *The Māori and the criminal justice system: A new perspective: He whaipaanga hou*. Policy and Research Division, Department of Justice.

Jolley, R.S. (2021, Sept. 17). It has nothing to do with Lorde. *The Spinoff*. thespinoff. co.nz/atea/17-09-2021/it-has-nothing-to-do-with-lorde

Jones, A. (2001). Cross-cultural pedagogy and the passion for ignorance. *Feminism & Psychology, 11*(3), 279–92.

JustSpeak (2020). *A justice system for everyone*. JustSpeak. justspeak.org.nz/ourwork/ justspeak-idi-research-a-justice-system-for-everyone

Ka'ai-Mahuta, R. (2011). The impact of colonisation on te reo: A critical review of the State education system. *Te Kaharoa, 4*(1). doi.org/10.24135/tekaharoa.v4i1.117

Kāretu, T. (1993). Tōku reo, tōku mana. In W. Ihimaera (Ed.), *Te ao mārama 2: Regaining Aotearoa: Māori writers speak out*, 222–29. Reed.

Kendi, Ibram X. (2019). *How to be an antiracist*. One World.

Kirmayer, L.J., Gone, J.P., & Moses, J. (2014). Rethinking historical trauma. *Transcultural Psychiatry, 51*(3), 299–319. doi.org/10.1177/1363461514536358

Lawson-Te Aho, K. (2014). The healing is in the pain: Revisiting and re-narrating trauma histories as a starting point for healing. *Psychology and Developing Societies, 26*(2), 181–212. doi.org/10.1177/0971333614549139

MacIntyre, P.D. (1995). How does anxiety affect second language learning? A reply to Sparks and Ganschow. *The Modern Language Journal, 7*(1), 90–99. doi.org/10.2307/329395

MacIntyre, P.D. & Gardner, R.C. (1994). The subtle effects of language anxiety on cognitive processing in the second language. *Language Learning, 44*(2), 283–305. doi.org/10.1111/j.1467-1770.1994.tb01103.x

McGhee, H. (2021). *The sum of us: What racism costs everyone and how we can prosper together*. One World.

Mcilraith, B. (2022, 19 Aug.). Whittaker's Miraka Kirīmi block shows how passionate Kiwis are about brands. *Stuff*. stuff.co.nz/business/industries/129598237/ whittakers-miraka-kirmi-block-shows-how-passionate-kiwis-are-about-brands

McIntosh, T. (2005). Māori identities: Fixed, fluid, forced. In J.H. Liu, T. McCreanor, T. McIntosh, & T. Teaiwa (Eds.), *New Zealand identities: Departures and destinations*, 38–51. Victoria University Press.

Mead, H.M. (2003). *Tikanga Māori: Living by Māori values*. Huia.

Mead, S.M. (1997). *Landmarks, bridges and visions: Aspects of Maori culture: Essays*. Victoria University Press.

Menakem, R. (2021). *My grandmother's hands: Racialized trauma and the pathway to mending our hearts and bodies.* Penguin.

Meredith, P. (2005). *Urban Māori – Urban networks.* Te Ara– the Encyclopedia of New Zealand. TeAra.govt.nz/en/document/3584/maori-language-petition-memo

Middleton, A. (2021, Oct. 3). HE WHAKAARO | OPINION: Pākehā allyship needs to extend beyond te reo. *Waatea News.* waateanews.com/2021/10/03/he-whakaaro-opinion-pakeha-allyship-needs-to-extend-beyond-te-reo/

Mikaere, A. (2010, Dec. 10). *Māori critic and conscience in a colonising context – Law and leadership as a case study* [Paper presentation]. 27th Annual Conference of the Law and Society Association of Australia and New Zealand, Victoria University of Wellington.

Milroy, J.T.W. (2014). Matua rautia ngā tamariki o te kōhanga reo. In R. Higgins, P. Rewi, & V. Olsen-Reeder (Eds.), *The value of the Māori language: Te hua o te reo Māori, 2,* 197–204. Huia.

Ministry for Culture and Heritage. (2021, Oct. 21). *Māori language petition, 1972.* NZHistory. nzhistory.govt.nz/media/photo/maori-language-petition-1972

Ministry of Justice (2022). *New Zealand crime and victims survey. Cycle 4 survey findings. Descriptive statistics. June 2022. Results drawn from Cycle 4 (2020/21) of the New Zealand Crime and Victims Survey.* Ministry of Justice. justice.govt.nz/justice-sector-policy/research-data/nzcvs/resources-and-results/

Moeke-Pickering, T.M. (1996). Māori identity within whānau: A review of literature. [Dissertation, University of Waikato]. Research Commons. hdl.handle.net/10289/464

Moewaka Barnes, A., Taiapa, K., Borell, B., & McCreanor, T. (2013). Maori experiences and responses to racism in Aotearoa New Zealand. *Mai Journal, 2*(2), 63–77. journal.mai.ac.nz/content/m%C4%81ori-experiences-and-responses-racism-aotearoa-new-zealand

Morrison, S. & Morrison, S. (2017). *Māori at home: An everyday guide to learning the Māori language.* Penguin Random House.

Muller, M. (2016). *Whakatipu te pā harakeke: What are the success factors that normalise the use of Māori language within the whānau?* [Doctoral thesis, Victoria University of Wellington]. Doctoral Theses. hdl.handle.net/10063/5076

Nairn, R., Moewaka Barnes, A., Rankine, J., Borell, B., Abel, S., McCreanor, T. (2011). Mass media in Aotearoa: An obstacle to cultural competence. *New Zealand Journal of Psychology (Online), 40*(3), 2011, 168–175. proquest.com/scholarly-journals/mass-media-aotearoa-obstacle-cultural-competence/docview/1025744861/se-2

Nairn, R.G. & McCreanor, T.N. (1991). Race talk and common sense: Patterns in Pakeha discourse on Maori/Pakeha relations in New Zealand. *Journal of Language and Social Psychology, 10*(1), 245–62. doi.org/10.1177/0261927X91104002

Nairn, R. & McCreanor, T. (2021). 'Time for a troll'; The standard story propping up the colonial state. *Kōtuitui: New Zealand Journal of Social Sciences Online, 17*(2), 153–164. doi.org/10.1080/1177083X.2021.1953084

Nairn, R., Moewaka Barnes, A., Borell, B., Rankine, J., Gregory, A., & McCreanor, T. (2012). Māori news is bad news: That's certainly so on television. *MAI Journal, 1*(1), 38–49.

Nesdale, D., Rooney, R., & Smith, L. (1997). Migrant ethnic identity and psychological distress. *Journal of Cross-Cultural Psychology, 28*(5), 569–588. doi.org/10.1177/0022022197285004

Ngapo, K. (2014). Te nekunekutanga o ngā reo taketake. In R. Higgins, P. Rewi & V. Olsen-Reeder (Eds.), *The value of the Māori language: Te hua o te reo Māori, 2*, 181–96. Huia.

Ngata, T., Rata, A., & Santos, D. (2021). Race-based hate crime in Aotearoa. *MAI Journal, 10*(2), 207–15. journal.mai.ac.nz/content/race-based-hate-crime-aotearoa

Oliver, H. (2017, Sept. 30). 'We're marginalising all kinds of people': A few beers with Dave Dobbyn. *The Spinoff.* thespinoff.co.nz/garage-project/30-09-2017/were-marginalising-all-kinds-of-people-through-no-fault-of-their-own-a-few-beers-with-dave-dobbyn

Oliver, V., Flicker, S., Danforth, J., Konsmo, E., Wilson, C., Jackson, R., Restoule, J.-P., et al. (2015). 'Women are supposed to be the leaders': Intersections of gender, race and colonisation in HIV prevention with Indigenous young people. *Culture, Health & Sexuality, 17*(7), 906–19. doi.org/10.1080/13691058.2015.1009170

Olsen-Reeder, V. (2021, Sept. 26) Privilege and language trauma. *E-Tangata.* e-tangata.co.nz/reo/privilege-and-language-trauma/

Olsen-Reeder, V.I.R.C. (2017). *Kia tomokia te kākahu o te reo Māori: He whakamahere i ngā kōwhiri reo a te reo rua Māori.* [Doctoral thesis, Victoria University of Wellington]. Open Access Te Herenga Waka—Victoria University of Wellington. doi.org/10.26686/wgtn.17058083.v1

Palmer, F. & Masters, T. (2010). Māori feminism and sport leadership: Exploring Māori women's experiences. *Sport Management Review, 13*(4), 331–344 doi.org/10.1016/j.smr.2010.06.001.

Penetito, W.T. (2011). Kaupapa Māori education: Research as the exposed edge. [Paper presentation]. Kei Tua o te Pae Hui Proceedings: The Challenges of Kaupapa Māori Research in the 21st Century, Pipitea Marae.

Pihama, L., Cameron, N., & Te Nana, R. (2019). Historical trauma and whānau violence. *Issues Paper, 15*. New Zealand Family Violence Clearinghouse, University of Auckland. nzfvc.org.nz/issues-paper-15-historical-trauma

Poata-Smith, E.S. (2005). Aotearoa-New Zealand. In D. Vinding (Ed.), *The Indigenous World*, 228–232. IWGIA (International Work Group for Indigenous Affairs).

Pohatu, T.W. (2008). Takepū: Principled approaches to healthy relationships. [Paper presentation]. Proceedings of the Traditional Knowledge Conference 2008, Te Tatau Pounamu: The Greenstone Door.

Rata, A. (2015). The Māori identity migration model. *MAI Review, 4*(1): 3–14. journal.mai.ac.nz/content/m%C4%81ori-identity-migration-model

Rata, A. (2012). *Te pītau o te tuakiri: Affirming Māori identities and promoting wellbeing in state secondary schools.* [Doctoral thesis, Victoria University of Wellington]. Doctoral Theses. hdl.handle.net/10063/2550

Rātima, M.T. & Papesch, T.R. (2013). Te Rita Papesch: Case study of an exemplary learner of Māori as an additional language. *International Journal of Bilingual Education and Bilingualism, 17*(4), 379–93. doi.org/10.1080/13670050.2013.806431

Reid, P. (2011). Good governance: The case of health equity. In V.M.H. Tawhai & K. Gray-Sharp (Eds.), *'Always speaking': The Treaty of Waitangi and public policy,* 35–48. Huia.

Rewi, P. (2010). Culture: Compromise or perish. In B. Hokowhitu, N. Kermoal, C. Andersen, A. Petersen, M. Reilly, I. Altamirano-Jiménez, & P. Rewi (Eds.), *Indigenous identity and resistance: Researching the diversity of knowledge,* 55–74. Otago University Press.

Sheehan, M. (2010). The place of 'New Zealand' in the New Zealand history curriculum. *Journal of Curriculum Studies, 42*(5), 671–91. doi.org/10.1080/002 20272.2010.485247

Smith, C., Tinirau, R., Rattray-Te Mana, H., Tawaroa, M., Moewaka Barnes, H., Cormack, D. & Fitzgerald, E. (2021). *Whakatika: A survey of Māori experiences of racism.* Te Atawhai o Te Ao Charitable Trust. teatawhai.maori.nz/wp-content/uploads/2021/03/Whakatika-Report-March-2021.pdf

Spivak, G. (1988). Can the subaltern speak? In C. Nelson & L. Grossberg (Eds.), *Marxism and Interpretation of Culture,* 271–313. University of Illinois.

Statistics New Zealand (2014). *Te Kupenga 2013 (English) – corrected.* cbg.co.nz/site/cbg/files/TeKupenga13HOTP.pdf

Statistics New Zealand (2013). *2013 Census quickstats about Māori.* stats.govt.nz/assets/Uploads/Retirement-of-archive-website-project-files/Reports/2013-Census-QuickStats-about-Maori/qs-maori.pdf

Statistics New Zealand (2002). 2001 survey on the health of the Māori language. *Key Statistics,* 9–13. stats.govt.nz/reports/2001-survey-on-the-health-of-the-maori-language

Sutherland, I.L.G. & Buck, P.H. (1940). Review of the Māori people today. *The Journal of the Polynesian Society, 49*(4), 608–13. jstor.org/stable/20702849.

Tawhiwhirangi, I. (2014). Kua tū tāngata e! Moving a critical mass. In R. Higgins, P. Rewi, & V. Olsen-Reeder (Eds.), *The value of the Māori language: Te hua o te reo Māori, 2,* 33–52. Huia.

Te Huia, A. (2016). Pākehā learners of Māori language responding to racism directed toward Māori. *Journal of Cross-Cultural Psychology, 47*(5), 734–50. doi.org/10.1177/0022022116645663

Te Huia, A.T. (2013). *Whāia te iti kahurangi, ki te tuohu koe me he maunga teitei: Establishing psychological foundations for higher levels of Māori language proficiency.* [Doctoral thesis, Victoria University of Wellington]. Doctoral Theses. hdl.handle.net/10063/3459

Te Huia, A., Ahu, T., Muller, M., & Fox, R. (2019). *Manawa ū ki te reo Māori: A study of language motivations to enhance the use and acquisition of te reo Māori.* Victoria University of Wellington for Te Mātāwai. tematawai.maori.nz/en/research-and-evaluation/our-research/manawa-u-ki-te-reo-maori/

Te Huia, A.T. & Liu, J.H. (2012). Māori culture as a psychological asset for New Zealanders' acculturation experiences abroad. *International Journal of Intercultural Relations, 36*(1), 140–50. doi.org/10.1016/j.ijintrel.2011.03.003

Te Huia, A., Maniapoto-Ngaia, M., & Fox, R. (2022). *Ko te awa kia rere, ko te iwi kia ora: A study of the cultural and social impacts of Pūniu River care.* Victoria University of Wellington.

Te Huia, A., Muller, M., & Waapu, A. (2016). *Evaluation of Te Kura Whānau Reo.* Ministry of Education.

Te Taura Whiri i te Reo Māori. [@reomaori]. (2022, Aug. 8). *What people think being fluent in te reo Māori is like vs what it's actually like.* [Image attached]. [Tweet]. Twitter. twitter.com/reomaori/status/1556527314137018369

Te Taura Whiri i te Reo Māori. (2008). *He pātaka kupu: Te kai a te rangatira.* Penguin.

Te Uepū Hāpai i te Ora (Borrows, C., McIntosh, T., Young, W., Jones, C., Gilbert, J., Whaipooti, J., Money, R., Nair, S., & Hix, Q.) (2019). *He waka roimata: Transforming our criminal justice system.* Department of Justice. justice.govt.nz/assets/Documents/Publications/he-waka-roimata.pdf

Ting-Toomey, S. (2005). Identity negotiation theory: Cross cultural boundaries. In W.B. Gudykunst (Ed.), *Theorizing about intercultural communication*, 211–233. Sage Publications.

van der Kolk, B.A. (1996). The body keeps score: Approaches to the psychobiology of posttraumatic stress disorder. In B.A. van der Kolk, A.C. McFarlane, & L. Weisaeth (Eds.), *Traumatic stress: The effects of overwhelming experience on mind, body, and society*, 214–241. Guilford Press.

Vogel, S. & García, O. (2017). Translanguaging. In G. Noblit & L. Moll (Eds.), *Oxford Research Encyclopedia of Education*, 32–56. Oxford University Press.

Wa Thiong'o, N. (1992). *Decolonising the mind: The politics of language in African literature.* East African Publishers.

Waitangi Tribunal. (1986). *Report of the Waitangi Tribunal on the te reo Māori claim (Wai 11).* Waitangi Tribunal, Department of Justice.

Walker, R. (1989). Māori identity. In D. Novitz & B. Willmott (Eds.), *Culture and identity in New Zealand.* Government Printing Office.

Winiata, P. (2014). Whāia te ara o tō tupuna a tāwhaki: Whakatupuranga rua mano; he mahere whakapakari i te iwi. In R. Higgins, P. Rewi, & V. Olsen-Reeder (Eds.), *The value of the Māori language: Te hua o te reo Māori, 2*, 151–68. Huia.